PSYCHOLOGIES,

SOCIETAL

PRACTICE,

AND

POLITICAL

LIFE

POSTMODERN

PSYCHOLOGIES,

SOCIETAL

PRACTICE,

AND

POLITICAL

LIFE

EDITED BY

LOIS HOLZMAN

AND

JOHN MORSS

ROUTLEDGE

NEW YORK
and
LONDON

Published in 2000 by
Routledge
29 West 35th Street
New York, New York 10001

Published in Great Britain by
Routledge
11 New Fetter Lane
London EC4P 4EE

*Routledge is an imprint of the
Taylor & Francis Group.*

Library of Congress Cataloging-in-Publication Data

Postmodern psychologies, societal practice, and political
life / Lois Holzman and John R. Morss, editors.
    p. cm.
    Includes bibliographical references and index.
    ISBN 0–415–92555–x— ISBN 0–415–92556–8
    (pbk.)
        1. Psychology—Philosophy—Congresses.
        2. Postmodernism—Congresses.   I. Holzman,
Lois, 1946–   II. Morss, John R.
    BF38.P66 2000
    150'.1—dc21   00–56035

Contents

III
EXTENDING THE DIALOGUE 177

Contributors

HARLENE ANDERSON is a founding member of the Houston Galveston Institute, the Taos Institute, and Collaborative Consultations and has worked for many years as a clinician, educator, and consultant. As a scholar, Harlene has authored *Conversation, Language, and Possibilities: A Postmodern Approach to Therapy* and has coauthored numbers of professional papers. She is a member of the editorial review boards of several journals, including *Family Process; Journal of Marital and Family Therapy; The American Journal of Family Therapy; Families, Systems and Health;* and *Zeitschrift fur Systemische Therapie.*

ERICA BURMAN teaches psychology and women's studies at Manchester Metropolitan University. Her work is in the areas of feminist critiques of developmental psychology, subjectivity, and discourse. Erica's most recent books include *Challenging Women: Psychology's Exclusions, Feminist Possibilities* (coauthor, 1996); *Psychology Discourse Practice: From Regulation to Resistance* (coauthor, Taylor and Francis, 1996); and *Deconstructing Feminist Psychology* (editor, 1998).

LENORA FULANI is a developmental psychologist and political leader of the independent political movement in the U.S. She is coproducer of the All Stars Talent Show Network and codirector of the Developmental School for Youth, two projects that utilize the performatory social therapeutic approach developed by the East Side Institute for Short Term Psychotherapy, where Lenora is on the faculty. She is the author of *The Making of a Fringe Candidate 1992* (1992) and editor of *The Psychopathology of Everyday Racism and Sexism* (1988).

KENNETH J. GERGEN is Mustin Professor of Psychology, Swarthmore College and a cofounder of the Taos Institute. He is an associate editor of *Theory & Psychology* and *American Psychologist*. Ken's recent books include *Realities and Relationships: Soundings in Social Constructionism* (1994); *The Saturated Self* (1991); and *An Invitation to Social Construction* (1999).

MARY GERGEN is Associate Professor of Psychology and Women's Studies at Pennsylvania State University (Delaware County Campus). Among her books are *Feminist Thought and the Structure of Knowledge* (1988) and *Toward a New Psychology of Gender: A Reader* (Routledge, 1997).

LOIS HOLZMAN is Director of Educational Programs at the East Side Institute for Short Term Psychotherapy in New York City and Director of its Center for Developmental Learning. A developmental psychologist, she has worked to bring postmodern practices to child development and schooling as well as the mental health field. She is editor of *Performing Psychology: A Postmodern Psychology of the Mind* (Routledge, 1999) and author of *Schools for Growth: Radical Alternatives to Current Educational Models* (1997). Lois is also coauthor, with Fred Newman, of *Lev Vygotsky: Revolutionary Scientist* (Routledge, 1994); *Unscientific Psychology: A Cultural-Performatory Approach to Understanding Human Life* (1996); and *The End of Knowing: A New Developmental Way of Learning* (Routledge, 1997).

SHEILA MCNAMEE is Professor of Communication at the University of New Hampshire and a founding member of the Taos Institute. She is coeditor of *Therapy as Social Construction* (1992) and coauthor of *Relational Responsibility: Resources for Sustainable Dialogue* (1999), both with Kenneth J. Gergen. In addition to these books, she has authored numerous chapters and articles on social constructionist theory and practice, particularly in the realms of therapy and organization development. Sheila lectures to and consults internationally for organizations and mental health professionals.

JOHN MORSS was until recently Senior Lecturer in Education at the University of Otago, New Zealand. He is currently Visiting Research Fellow at the Centre for Cultural Risk Research, Charles Stuart University, New South Wales. He is the author of *The Biologising of Childhood: Developmental Psychology and the Darwinian Myth* (1990); *Growing Critical: Alternatives to Developmental Psychology* (Routledge, 1996); and coeditor (with T. Linzey) of *Growing Up: The Politics of Human Learning* (1991). John serves as cochair of the International Society for Theoretical Psychology.

ROBERT A. NEIMEYER is a Professor of Psychology at the University of Memphis in Memphis, TN, where he also maintains an active private practice. Most of his research and writing has centered on constructivist approaches in psychotherapy, with a recent focus on their relevance to the experience of loss and grief. Bob is coeditor of the *Journal of Constructivist Psychology* and serves on the editorial boards of a number of other journals. Among his many publications are *Constructions of Disorder: Meaning Making Frameworks in Psychotherapy* (2000) written with Jon Raskin; *Constructivism in Psychotherapy* (1995) written with Michael J. Mahoney; and *Advances in Personal Construct Theory*, Volumes 1–4 (1990, 1992, 1995, 1997).

FRED NEWMAN is Director of Training at the East Side Institute for Short Term Psychotherapy and Artistic Director of the Castillo Theatre, both in New York City. His work as psychotherapist and playwright is greatly influenced by his training in the philosophy of science and language and his years as a political and community organizer. Fred's recent writings focus on methodology in psychology and psychotherapy, including *Lev Vygotsky: Revolutionary Scientist* (Routledge, 1994); *Unscientific Psychology: A Cultural-Performatory Approach to Understanding Human Life* (1996); and *The End of Knowing: A New Developmental Way of Learning* (Routledge, 1997), all coauthored with Lois Holzman. In addition, he is the author of "self-help" books on the social therapeutic approach—*Let's Develop: A Guide to Continuous Personal Growth* (1994); and *Performance of a Lifetime: A Practical-Philosophical Guide to the Joyous Life* (1996).

VESNA OGNJENOVIĆ's work as a psychologist is dedicated to protecting and promoting human development in areas ravaged by war. She is a key initiator of Zdravo da Ste, an extended group of psychologists and non-psychologists working together with refugees in the former Yugoslavia in an effort to build a new social community. Vesna has presented the work of this community at international psychology and education congresses.

IAN PARKER is Professor of Psychology at Manchester Metropolitan University. Themes of his recent work include a critical exploration of therapeutic practices (*Deconstructing Psychotherapy*, 1999, editor); the intersection of Marxism and psychology (*Psychology and Society: Radical Theory and Practice*, coedited with Russell Spears, 1996); and the production and circulation of psychoanalytic explanation (*Psychoanalytic Culture: Psychoanalytic Discourse in Western Society*, 1997). Ian is editor of the *Annual Review of Critical Psychology* and a member of Psychology Politics Resistance.

JOHN SHOTTER is Professor of Communication at the University of New Hampshire. Among his recent books are *Cultural Politics of Everyday Life: Social Constructionism, Rhetoric and Knowing of the Third Kind* (1993); and *Conversational Realities* (1993).

INTRODUCTION

A Decade of Postmodern Psychology

Lois Holzman

and John Morss

Armageddon: Comet hurtles toward earth; Bruce Willis, as (partnerless) father, represents the parent generation in sacrificing itself, manually inserting the fatal device into the body of the alien object, so that the children may live and (more importantly) procreate in appropriate pairings (i.e., attractive male with attractive female).

Independence Day: Invasion by aliens as newly widowed President-father leads defense facilitated by cunning plan inspired by Jeff Goldblum's father; another father sacrifices himself to insert the fatal explosive device into the body of the alien object; the White House is rebuilt.

Deep Impact: Perhaps the less said, the better, but it's pretty oedipal stuff also.

POSTMODERNISM SEEMS VERY MUCH OF THE 1990S. In some ways, very *fin de siècle*. Will it survive the millennium? What impact will we say that it has had? Will it be *Armageddon* or *Independence Day*, or will it be *Deep Impact*? Comet, alien invasion, tidal wave, or mere entertainment? And afterwards, will normal service be resumed?

Postmodernism did in many ways seem to arrive from outer space some time in the 1980s (for psychologists, that is; architects detected it as early as the 1960s). There were discussions in the early 1980s (e.g., Toulmin, 1982) of the significance of postmodernism for scientific thinking and, perhaps by implication, for social science; and Lyotard's milestone *The Postmodern Condition* was published in French in 1979 and in English in 1984. But then, and perhaps still, postmodernism was confused with an array of intellectual-*isms*: structuralist and poststructuralist movements coming out of the Paris of 1968; textual methods such as deconstruction; analytic philosophy of language; social-context psychology of development, to name a few.

Quite soon, postmodernism began to cast its shadow back through the twentieth century: Ludwig Wittgenstein was one of the more plausible protopostmodernists identified by eager acolytes. Retrospective postmodernism reached back and joined hands with turn-of-the-century antiscientism and the intuitionism of Henri Bergson, jumped back more centuries like some time-traveling computer virus and merged with Romanticism, and extended forward into all our perceptions of the future. The network was complete; the signal was synchronized between all the stations: "Checkmate," as Goldblum's *Independence Day* cliché put it. Goldblum, strolling effortlessly from Jurassic theme park to space opera, carrying his screen-bound expertise with him as lightly as his muscle-enhanced torso. Postmodernism sweeps all before it, defines everything interesting as being itself, displaces all other worldviews. "Checkmate." Is that it?

As we write this, it has been ten years since the advent of postmodernism in psychology was "announced" at a 1989 conference in Aarhus, Denmark. There, a small group of psychologists held a symposium at which they discussed the implications of a postmodern culture for their discipline. In 1992 Steiner Kvale, a Danish psychologist and one of the hosts of the conference, edited *Psychology and Postmodernism*, which contained the symposium presentations as well as essays written expressly for the volume (Kvale, 1992a). With a decade of hindsight—and growing popularity of postmodern ideas in psychology—it is worth revisiting how postmodernism and psychology were conceived "back then."

In his introduction, Kvale describes the postmodern age and postmodern thought in ways that have become familiar to scholars: the loss of the Enlightenment belief that knowledge, particularly scientific knowledge, would bring progress and emancipation; the blurring of the boundary between reality and fantasy; the breakdown of many of the dichotomies of the modern age—among the most relevant for psychology are objective reality and subjective interpretation, self and other, and cognition and emotion. As for the state of psychology at the beginning of the 1990s, Kvale noted two indications that its scientific foundations were beginning to disintegrate: among the general population a boredom with psychological knowledge due to the growing recognition that psychologists have less and less to say about the human condition; and the increasing tensions between academic psychology and professional psychological practice (Kvale, 1992b, pp. 1–16).

Over the decade, psychology seems to have dug itself a deeper hole by clinging to (what many say are) ill-conceived and clearly outmoded scientific foundations in the face of a decreasing consumer base (at least in the U.S.). This is the case for academic psychology, which has seen a decline in university courses and positions in the last ten years, and for psychological practice, which is fast being whittled away (and some fear it's only a matter of time before its total demise) by HMOs, psychotropic drugs, and the self-help movement.

At the same time—perhaps adding to mainstream psychology's troubles, perhaps providing a way out of the hole—postmodernism has become more widely known among psychologists. Initially introduced by theoretically- and philosophically-minded social psychologists eager to explore the implications of *postmodern culture* on their discipline, postmodern concerns are today expressed by voices in nearly every subdiscipline of psychology. Most of these concerns stem from how psychology views human beings and, very closely related, how psychologists try to study and help human beings—that is, psychology's model, paradigm, and method. More and more psychologists, most of whom accept the utility and effectiveness of the natural science model for the physical and biological sciences, are finding this model unsuitable and ineffective when it comes to human-social phenomena. This is especially the case when subjectivity, consciousness, and intergroup relations are involved, as in psychological research and practice in cognition and learning, education, development, language and communication, counseling, psychotherapy, and group/organizational dynamics. In addition, the postmodern perspective adds a foundational (philosophical) dimension to social/political dissatisfaction with the way the mainstream paradigm approaches gender, ethnicity and culture, sexuality, religion and spirituality, and many other contemporary topics.

Postmodern critics of psychology point out that the dominant psychological model of human beings (and how to study and help them) distorts not only the complexity of human life but also its unique self-reflexivity and sociality. Further, the modern science model brings with it the philosophical-methodological bias of modern epistemology; that is, that truth, reality, objectivity, causality, and duality are necessary premises of understanding. This bias, postmodernists contend, locks psychology into methods that systematically prohibit pursuing avenues of inquiry that might prove extremely fruitful. Finally, the model does not take into account what many psychologists take to be the human need and capacity for positive and qualitative growth or what others see as the essential relationality of human life as lived.

The proliferation of new interdisciplinary journals and Web sites devoted to postmodern psychology and therapy, narrative and narrative therapies, social constructionism, philosophy and psychology, and so on, suggests that a postmodern sensibility has arrived on the psychological scene. After over a decade of theoretical writings on its potentials and pitfalls, it has not only spawned research and counseling, therapeutic and educational practices, but has also begun to recognize and relook at existing alternative practices with a postmodern eye. At this historical juncture, it seems possible and timely to evaluate the impact of postmodernism in psychology on the discipline and on the broader culture—to survey it, interrogate its impact on practice, and outline possible contours of its future influence.

Hence this book, which brings together a group of highly respected contributors to the postmodernism conversation within psychology. Their chapters reflect on the achievements and limitations of attempts to develop postmodern approaches in psychology in general and within specific areas of research and practice. The authors have among them authored or edited nearly forty books on social, developmental, educational, and clinical psychology, the most recent of which focus on postmodern concerns. They represent different points of view, from the cautious attitude of Marxist and feminist psychologies (which remain suspicious of what is perceived as postmodernism's playfulness and relativism) to the more celebratory attitude of social constructionism, and beyond—to the anarchism of the deconstructionists and the antiparadigmism of the radical activity theorists/social therapy practitioners. For the most part, the authors are conversing with their respective traditions and occasionally with each other. We have not asked them to do a lot of work contextualizing their discussions because we wanted to preserve (and show) the conversations they are currently engaged in. Our task as editors is to help them converse with you, and we hope that this introductory chapter and our running commentary throughout this volume invite you to come in, in whatever manner you choose.

Even more to this point (and something that gives us great pleasure) are the voices of response that dialogue with and address the issues and concerns set forth by the contributing authors. These guest commentators have varying levels of familiarity with the postmodernist movement, but none are *ideologically* committed to postmodernism. Their comments are meant to add a degree of accountability and self-reflection.

Postmodern Psychologies, Societal Practice, and Political Life addresses contemporary issues of controversy for psychology, among them multiculturalism, culture, and psychological functioning; the "reality" of psychological phenomena; identity and identity formation; language, communication, and discourse; the potential and dynamics of human development; and the role and status of psychological research in today's world. Specific chapters provoke readers to think anew about the objects of study and methods psychology has been invoking and employing for decades. Concepts such as performed activity, developmental performance, relational responsibility, dialogically structured understanding, and social epistemology are introduced as new possibilities for social-psychological practice. In this way, the book provides an up-to-date, rigorous assessment of postmodernism in psychology and, at the same time, offers resources for further exploration of alternative ways to engage in the psychological study of human life as lived.

In June 1997, the East Side Institute for Short Term Psychotherapy, a research and training center "for human development and community" based in New York City, hosted a conference/retreat entitled "Unscientific Psychology: Conversations with Other Voices." The idea was to gather a small and diverse group of interested people—practitioners, scholars, and nonprofessionals—to talk together about whether and how postscientific and postmodern psychology can impact on the social and political issues facing the world's people. The 140 people in attendance were a diverse group in several ways. They were academics, practitioners, faculty, students, and people with no other credentials than a feeling that the topic was interesting and of some importance. They came from 17 countries—from the U.S., with its well over 100,000 psychologists, to Azerbaijan, which has a mere handful. Among the practitioners were those who work with inner-city young people from Brooklyn, Harlem, and the Bronx, war-ravaged refugees in the former Yugoslavia, children and families in a South Africa being reconstructed, poor communities in the cities of Venezuela, women and men who have been psychiatrically institutionalized, people in drug treatment programs, and others who seek help (or are said by authorities to need it). Researchers and students came from universities and institutes all over the U.S. and Canada, as well as Buenos Aires, Cape Town, Sydney, Leipzig, Vienna, Caracas, Manchester, Glasgow, and cities from New Zealand to Scandinavia. Most participants identified with one or another progressive and/or nonmainstream tradition, among them postmodernism, social constructionism, deconstructionism, Marxism, feminism, radical psychology, narrative therapy, social therapy, cultural-historical psychology, activity theory, and critical theory (in spite of a collective aversion to labels!).

The events of the two-day gathering focused on how to address postmodern and postscientific psychology and the related question of how to create "conversations with other voices." In other words, the "how" referred equally and inseparably to addressing the topic of postmodern psychology and its relationship to societal practice *and* to creating environments in which this topic could be addressed. Could we *create* conversation, instead of *having* the same familiar ones we've all had before? Could we utilize new ways of presenting the work we do—our beliefs, theories, findings, questions, doubts, hopes? Could we create a *cultural* event out of the conference on psychology that brought us together? How were we to perform together?

To heighten the collective exploration of these questions, the conference/retreat mixed the usual academic fare with experimental experiential/performatory activities. There were eight formal presentations, a performance workshop at which participants created and performed an improvised play based on their lives (led by Fred Newman and based on his "Performance of a Lifetime"™ interactive growth theatre project), and three simultaneous conversations on topics participants decided they wanted to pursue, followed by performances created out of these conversations that were shared with the conference body. Only the formal presentations have made their way in any recognizable form into this volume; they appear (in widely varying degrees of revision) as essays by Erica Burman, Lenora Fulani, Kenneth J. Gergen, Mary Gergen, Lois Holzman, John Morss, Ian Parker and John Shotter. (Fred Newman's contribution was written expressly for this volume, as were all the commentaries of Part III Extending the Dialogue.)

Somewhere near the end of the process of completing this book, it occurred to us to ask each other why we were its editors. Was it merely a coincidence that we are both developmental psychologists? Developmental psychology, after all, has not exactly embraced postmodernism. On the contrary, one could make out a reasonable case that developmental psychology is the last holdout for the modernist psychological paradigm. This could, of course, be thought of as "resistance" if it is to be maintained that the field of human development is especially challenged by postmodern ideas. Certainly, it has been—by developmentalists already working in critical ways who, to varying degrees, have tried to take postmodern ideas on board (e.g., Erica Burman, Rex and Wendy Stainton Rogers, Valerie Walkerdine, and ourselves). But challenging and transforming are very different things, and in spite of mounting criticism of the ideological and methodological biases of the orthodox notion of developmental change and of the damaging practices done in its name, psychology has thus far been successful in defending the grandest of its grand narratives. As developmental psychologists with a postmodern sensibility, we feel it incumbent upon ourselves to carry the questions of postmodernism to the conservative heart of contemporary, firmly modernist psychology.

We also wondered whether our chosen title was misleading. For the implication to be drawn from the juxtaposition of "postmodern psychologies," "societal practice," and "political life" is that postmodern psychologies have, or should have, something to say about societal practices and political life. But can they? Prior to postmodernism, the built-in dualism of theory/analysis and what it was "about" was taken for granted, but postmodernism is, if nothing else, a challenge to that dualism—in a socially constructed, relationally responsible, dialogically structured world of human performance, the distinction between subjective and objective loses its theoretical (and perhaps practical) force. As a challenge to grand narratives—statements that come to be taken as facts (truths) about how the world is (e.g., the grand narratives of progress, modern science, evolutionary theory)—postmodernism questions whether there is anything for them to be "about." Shouldn't it wonder the same about itself? In other words, if postmodernism is to guard against becoming yet another grand narrative, can there be anything for postmodern thought—in psychology and elsewhere—to be about? This is a fascinating question—raised, but ultimately (and fortunately, we feel) unanswered in this volume.

Nevertheless, some specific societal practices are addressed by our authors. Not surprisingly, it is scholarship itself that gets the most attention; after all, it is the societal practice they know best. Yet all venture out—deeply concerned with political life, psychological and educational practices, and practices that foster or hinder multiculturalism/diversity/equality. They introduce new tools and new kinds of tools of practical (some say practical-critical, or revolutionary) understanding, including *conversation, performance, spectacle,* and *story.* They offer us ways to move forward without knowing where we're going—as John Shotter puts it, to "not become entangled in our own rules" and to be "more 'at home' in the complicated 'landscape' of human phenomena without the continual need to consult and puzzle over maps" (Shotter, p. 125).

In the last few years, accounts of the postmodern in psychology have become fragmented. Many different orientations now coexist. There are still the enthusiastic celebrants—not always the same people as before, but people newly discovering the sometimes heady excitements of postmodern talk. There are attempts to redefine postmodernism in more detailed and often more narrow ways that perhaps tap its power or, alternatively, accommodate it to the vicissitudes of the psychological establishment. There are attempts to retrospectively identify long-dead writers (e.g., Bakhtin, Vico, Vygotsky) as postmodernists (or protopostmodernists) and thus make connections with movements that do not self-identify as postmodern. There are decisions by earlier adherents or fellow travelers to distance themselves from postmodernism because it is either proving inadequate or proving too successful in its popularity. There are serious attempts to rehabilitate approaches that postmodernism seems to have outflanked, such as critique or neo-Marxism. And, as always, there remains the stubborn refusal in some quarters ever to take the idea or its proponents seriously.

It may be appropriate for the landscape of psychological postmodernism to be confused, noisy, and full of unpredictable movements and repositionings (at least, one might say, it demonstrates our mature distance from the bored stability of modernism, with its order and its calmly rational facade); but this is not of much help to the student or to the psychologist keen to learn about the relevance of these issues. Confusion and fragmentation might even at times seem to constitute a deliberate smoke screen, protecting those whose thinking is characterized more by vigor than by rigor. So what sense can and should one make of the contemporary scene and the place of postmodernism in it? Does postmodernism make a difference? These are some of the questions that, in different but often complementary ways, the authors attempt to answer in the chapters that follow.

Whether any of this matters to how ordinary people the world over live their lives is the real subject of this book. The issue that drew the contributors to this volume and so many others to the 1997 conference "Unscientific Psychology: Conversations with Other Voices" continues to be in the forefront:

> If social policy is to undergo a humanistic and democratic transformation, it is more important than ever that we examine the subjective constraints limiting our collective ability not only to make these changes, but to move forward as a world—and, of course, the relationship between these and objective constraints. We want to address whether and how the new psychologies—which some call postmodern or postscientific—can impact on the pressing social problems of the day. (Holzman, Invitation to "Unscientific Psychology" conference/retreat)

REFERENCES

Kvale, S. (Ed.) (1992a). *Psychology and postmodernism*. London: Sage.

Kvale, S. (1992b) Introduction: "From the archaeology of the psyche to the architecture of cultural landscapes." In S. Kvale (ed.), *Psychology and postmodernism*. London: Sage, pp. 1–16.

Lyotard, J.-F. (1984). *The postmodern condition: A report on knowledge*. Manchester, U. K.: Manchester University Press.

Toulmin, S. (1982). *The return to cosmology: Postmodern science and the theology of nature*. Berkeley, CA: University of California Press.

I

POSTMODERNISM

AND

PSYCHOLOGY:

OASIS

OR

BLUR?

The title we have given to Part I reflects (or instantiates) the dilemma of "being postmodern" in a still-modernist world. In particular, it shows the trap language so often gets us into—for we (the editors) really do not mean that we, or you, must *choose between* "oasis" and "blur." Most likely, postmodernism is currently both—or neither. Moreover, we do not wish to implicate the authors in this section in some version of modernist predictive social-scientific analysis, stating what they fear or cheer will become of psychology and of postmodern thought and practice.

It is because such an either/or dichotomy is familiar, comfortable, and seemingly understandable that we chose it. For we mean to highlight that "either/or" is comprehensible only within a particular discourse, within modernism's grand narrative, so concisely summed up nearly 450 years ago by Bishop Butler: "We are what we are and not another thing." Physicists rejected this truism many, many years ago, but psychology still clings to it. Among the many grand narratives that comprise the discipline of psychology, the story it tells of static, stable things and objects (especially people) that fall neatly into dichotomous categories—an instance or identity of this or that (invariably some come to be accepted as "normal," "good," or "right" and others as "abnormal," "bad," or "wrong")—is one that postmodern psychology is attempting both to expose and transform. Continuous process, interconnectedness, meaning-making, relationality, and activity are just a few of the concepts that seem to make a better fit with life-as-lived than the terms employed in the discourse of mainstream psychology (or at least, they tell a more compelling story). That the authors presented in Part I all share this view is important to keep in mind as you read their essays, for it is from this jointly accepted perspective that their divergent views become meaningful in relation to societal practice and political life. At issue is how to create new human practices—given how hidden and/or distorted are the historicalness, the politicalness, and the interconnectedness between us by the seemingly objective scientific model of physical objects, particulars, and discrete ahistorical individuals. Can there really be postmodern method? If so, can we make it matter to the people of the world?

> Two Cheers
>
> for Postmodernism:
>
> Living
>
> the Paradox
>
> John Morss

FACT OR CONCEIT?

The millennium is all around us. It seems so massive as to have been literally unavoidable. What option did any of us have, on midnight of
December 31, 1999, other than to be swept into it? (And should it not
seem odd that I could have written that sentence in May of 1999?). Yet
the most substantial issues arising from the arrival of the year 2000 are
very clearly constructed directly by human technical activity, especially
by the way we designed computer calendar mechanisms in the 1980s.
Those very real and very socially constructed issues have overshadowed
the "factual" question of whether a new millennium should be celebrated at the start of 2000 or twelve months later.

We are in postmodernism whether we like it or not, at least in the
sense that it is all around us. Its ubiquity in our talk—every psychologist has surely at least "heard" about it—gives rise to a kind of
gravitational pull even on those activities in psychology that seem most
remote from its field of operations. What is the appropriate way for psychology to respond to this disturbing phenomenon? My suggestion is
that, like the new millennium which it only slightly predated, postmodernism in psychology is to be celebrated with enthusiasm but also with
caution. Like the millennium, postmodernism in psychology brings a
lot of hype with it; it creates an advance wave of scare stories; it seems
to open up a new sense of possibility; and we may be celebrating it at
the wrong time. Yet it is something that we ourselves have made. Surely
the "fact" that we have made it now, and made it the way that we have,

must tell us something about ourselves now.[1] Postmodernism is a condition that we find ourselves in.

The cultural movement in the humanities and the social sciences of the late twentieth century that we call postmodernism contains multitudes. Postmodernism has been around long enough for a variety of reactions to set in, and these responses are now just as much part of the complexity that is postmodernism as is any "original" sense. What Lyotard (1984) or Baudrillard (1988) said of postmodernism is now of little other than historical interest. Lyotard's own descriptions are at the same time too scientistic and too vague, Baudrillard's too off-the-wall, too self-indulgent. Lyotard's cold postmodernism and Baudrillard's hot postmodernism are now little more than the retro component of a contemporary remix, a dance party of celebration, rejection, and assimilation. The classic texts now jostle for status with popularizations and with positions such as that of British sociologist Anthony Giddens, for whom postmodernism is actually a late or high form of modernism; with the conservative-intellectual response of those who argue that this has all been done before within modernism (by Dada, surrealism, the stream-of-consciousness novel, Lewis Carroll, Laurence Sterne); with the well-rehearsed arguments about postmodernism as a conspiracy of late capitalism and of the admen; with the rejection of postmodernism on the populist grounds of obscurantism in its presentation or vainglory in its advocates; and with as great a range of positive responses, from the delirious to the pragmatic to the mealymouthed. How can psychology (both in its practices and in its articulations) respond to such a diffuse stimulus?

In some rough-and-ready fashion, I think we have to try (collectively) to identify what aspects of the postmodern mood or style we want to keep and which let slip. We have to position postmodernism within psychology. But doing this is fraught with paradox—for example, the paradox that *postmodernism has been a modernist phenomenon.* This suggestion is a double-edged one. What I mean is that postmodernism as a cultural event has had a form that postmodernism itself treats as characteristic of modernism—a modernism that it (postmodernism) most emphatically rejects. Postmodernism has been an "it's new, it's the latest thing, don't you know about it yet?" kind of event. Further, the reception of postmodernism—its real effect, taking place over a number of years, constituted through the responses of many interlocking communities—has been such as to prompt questions about "What's next? What will follow it?" These questions usually connote a rather literal reading of the postmodern as a chronologically sequential period in some series such as classical to modern to postmodern, thus employing a form of stage theory of history that is, most emphatically—according to postmodernism—a modernist analysis.

To this account of the postmodern as modern might be added remarks about the grand-narrative status of "postmodernism" itself (Lyotard is useful at times), and perhaps remarks about the arguably modernist style (enlightening, consciousness-raising) of the emancipatory objectives expressed by some ("affirmative") postmodernists.[2]

My suggestions for the appropriation of postmodernism are made in light of this paradoxical context. We should, I think, *retain*:

- postmodernism's celebration of *diversity* (although we struggle to articulate nonliberal accounts of difference)[3];
- its sense of *irony*: not so much "seize the day" as "seize the afternoon" (although this irony may be found just as well in Günter Grass or Milan Kundera);
- its undermining of the *grand narrative* (although no one might agree as to what a grand narrative actually looks like);
- the *interruption* of text by text, of center by margin, of margin by margin, of academic earnestness by bad jokes (margin through Georgia) and vice versa, of adults by children and vice versa, of performance by rehearsal, of on-stage by off-stage, of life by death and vice versa, of bullet points by essays [4];
- the awareness of the ambivalence of critique: the *critique of critique*. For what we have learned about the limits of critique is among the most disturbing cognitive consequences of postmodernism and related movements.

CRITIQUE AND BEYOND

Critique—whose best exemplar has always been Marxist critique—has been our strongest intellectual weapon for over a century. In particular, critique has defended us from mere *analysis*. Analysis seeks to comprehend the world in terms of large systems, to theorize. Critique has, on our behalf, attempted not merely to interpret the world, but to change it. But in many ways critique is too good a weapon, too sharp for our wit. It is like the laser-guided bombs of modern smart warfare and like the official statements that go with such high-technology destruction. "We have hit him hard . . ."[5]. Critique is designed to hit the enemy hard *and then move on* to the next target.

Critique involves an appeal to some framework of expertise or authority in the analysis of some cultural text or process. Critique is always related, in a *defensive* manner, to a standpoint (such as Marxism or feminism, or perhaps even, in principle, political conservatism— "family values" and so on). Its tone tends to the moralistic, the admonishing, issuing dire warnings about arguments it considers threatening. Something important should be noted. Critique tends to appeal to the consensual view of some community: "You want these things to happen, don't you? You don't want these (other) things to happen, do you?" The fervor and the rhetoric can become almost patriotic in style as well as content. Strangely, then, direct appeal is made to the communally agreed (and avowed) values of a community. This is strange because critique tends to be associated with a realist ontology—appealing to certain nonnegotiable facts[6]— rather than with a relativist approach, with its appeal to communal conversation. The social-constructionist appeal made by realist-critical authors is a strange postmodern paradox. By and large, social constructionism is hostile to critique, as are postmodernism and deconstruction. It points to communalities between critic and critiqued. If only through its relativistic temper, social constructionism disarms the critic.

We have now therefore learned, very painfully, that critique is potentially oppressive, silencing other voices and so on; that critique is always in service of a system, however nascent; that critique, if nothing else, sets up an institution, a body of knowledge (such as "critical psychology," perhaps)—books, careers, key ideas, conferences, "annual reviews"—that may mirror the larger institutions that it criticizes. Critique has tried, but failed, to assimilate Foucault's arguments about the power dimension of knowledge. Critique claims to reveal truth, metaphorically at least by simply showing us that truth, demystifying us, enlightening us ("Look, this is what is going on"). Any serious attempt to position postmodernism within psychology must decide where it stands on critique.

Clearly, I agree with those who urge that we go "beyond critique" (Gergen, 1994a)—just as critique can itself claim to have gone "beyond analysis." But I question whether we can simply "put critique behind us" as if somehow all the critiquing has been done, all the flaws of the present institutions identified, and that now we can dust ourselves down, take a deep breath, and commence the honest toil in a cleansed landscape, as if we believed the hollow rhetoric of that tiresome cliché, "deconstructing and reconstructing" (much found in narrative therapy discourse as well as theoretical psychology discourse): a phrase that is as journalistically trite as "from Bauhaus to our house." "Going beyond critique" is going to require continual engagement with it; like the poor, critique will always be with us. Every critique (even if it masquerades as "deconstruction") must be met with a critique of critique. In a sense, we must keep on critiquing in order to go beyond it.[7] For to hit critique hard (even in a rather gentle manner) and then move on to something constructive would be to indulge in a kind of critique: another postmodern paradox.

Going "beyond critique" will not be easy, therefore. Returning to a more classical, theory-based *analysis* as an alternative to critique will not help. What can we do? What we perhaps are painfully learning is the protean and self-protective nature of our enemies. Hierarchy, totality, and authority are even better survivors than capital itself. A thoroughgoing and indefatigable social constructionism is required— one that is rigorous enough to avoid such pitfalls as humanism and naturalism. We must, I think, acknowledge the thorough constructedness of the human and of the natural[8], including both the values and the brute facts so defended by advocates of critique. After Foucault we have to be suspicious of the self-serving, romantic functions of the repression hypothesis (according to which some natural impulses are seen to have been repressed by "power"). We can no longer place our faith for salvation in the liberated natural impulses of "man." We need to find ways of recognizing diversity, multiplicity (that is, resisting totality), while keeping hierarchy at bay. We must be prepared to take risks. For, historically, psychology's (the social sciences') way of recognizing diversity has been to establish levels or stages, that is, to establish hierarchies.[9] Hierarchy involves the establishment and the protection of privilege and status. What tools or methods do we have against it? In the remainder of this essay I want to examine briefly three quite probably inconsistent possibilities: critical psychology, deconstruction, and anarchism. All three are given new twists by the postmodern condition that we find ourselves in.

CRITICAL PSYCHOLOGY AS TRUTH-TELLING: A POSTMODERN METHOD?

As suggested above, critical forms of psychology may achieve little more than the institutionalization of critique. Certainly most presently known versions of critical psychology are based on critique of some stripe or another. Marxist critique, feminist critique, postcolonial critique have all yielded critical psychologies. Although sometimes denied, I think it generally accurate to assert, as I do above, that critique claims to reveal the truth. Influenced by postmodernism and poststructuralism, and sometimes even by psychoanalysis, critical psychology may describe its claims as only one of many interpretations or stories. But this relativistic humility is rarely more than skin-deep. Contemporary critical psychology, by and large, believes itself to be illuminating social truths as it progressively strips off the veils of illusion or ideology. Is this very modernist approach to truth-finding a necessary component of critical psychology, or could its relation to truth be reworked?

Some possibilities are suggested by the role of power in truth-finding. Edward Said's (1994) description of the intellectual as one who needs to be prepared "to speak the truth to power" is an important clue here. It would be a mistake I think, and one that would undermine Said's point, to imagine "truth" in this context to refer to something transcendental. The Old Testament prophet is not a helpful image here. A relativistic account of truth is required I think, but a rigorous one. For it is possible that truth exists *only* in such contexts of resistance to power. Truth might be reactive. If Galileo mutters, under threat by the Inquisition, that the earth really does move around the sun, that statement seems to me to have some higher status than its production by a teacher in a contemporary junior classroom. What I am suggesting is that truth cannot be spoken *by* power but only against it. (Perhaps what children say to adults cannot but be the truth.) What is suggested here is a significant rethinking of the important but flawed idea of the social construction of truth. It seems inadequate simply to equate truth with consensus, so that whatever some group of people agree becomes the truth. In particular, this account seems to neglect the macrodimensions of power and truth, such as geopolitical factors, and to reduce truth and its defense to the level of a social psychology experiment.

Given the above, critical psychology might be able to rescue itself from the dead end of critique and from the sterility of analysis. The postmodern climate might encourage us to allow a radical relativism into our worldview. Critical psychology needs shaking up just as much and as often as does the mainstream (shaken *and* stirred). Perhaps this is just what we mean by "deconstruction."

DECONSTRUCTION: MODERN OR POSTMODERN?

Deconstruction does not need another definition, but it does need to be separated from other processes. As implied above, I most strongly wish to differentiate it from critique but I also wish, if possible, to clarify its relationship with the postmodern, since the phrase "postmodern deconstruction" has become ubiquitous.

In contrast to critique, with its hit-and-run attitude, deconstruction seems to me to be much more prepared (sometimes even obsessed) with staying around, staying in touch, identifying with its "target"—refusing, sometimes, just to go away and forget.[10] And the reflexive sense of deconstruction should not be overlooked: the "deconstructs itself" of the French *se deconstruire*. Rather than being done by an agent to an object, deconstruction is done by an object to itself, with some assistance from outside. On some occasions it is almost as if a mirror were held up so that the object has no choice but to activate its lines of fragmentation. (The making-public of some corrupt system, the "whistle-blowing" through the media, seems sometimes to have a similar effect). Deconstruction is thereby just a reminder, a *memento mori*, or even a painstaking *mending* of a text or an object—a mending so detailed and articulated that it paralyzes the object. Deconstructing is sometimes a loving to death.

If these characteristics are consistent with a postmodern environment, then that is well and good. Indeed, it would be well worth emphasizing. The scrupulous avoidance of interpretation in both postmodernism and deconstruction would suggest some communalities. However, given the laxity with which the term postmodern is applied, "postmodern deconstruction" seems a hostage to fortune, threatening the special kind of precision that the word "deconstruction" sometimes tries to invoke. Do those who use the double-barreled term "postmodern deconstruction" intend to convey that there are nonpostmodern senses of deconstruction (there probably are, but is this what they mean?). That double-barreled descriptor somehow seems to trivialize the endeavor, to reduce someone's project, with whatever special features it has, to some generic brand of (at least quasi-) critique. There is too pervasive a sense of preaching to the converted when the double term is used (some fellow thinker has performed a postmodern ["hurrah!"] deconstruction ["hurrah again!"] of . . .—and then moved on to the next target . . .).

I think my concern is that what is understood by "postmodern deconstruction" is in fact an uneasy combination of analysis and critique, avoiding each in turn (as being "modern") only by retreating to the other. Something needs to save us from the paralysis of that two-party system: perhaps an approach that has actually worked through the serious consequences of that glib phrase "anything goes."

ANARCHISM

There is arguably only one *political* position that resolutely rejects hierarchies and totalities, and that is anarchism. Anarchism, of course, is not one position but a cluster of positions. In its classic formulations, it tended to the voluntaristic and the individualistic (born free but everywhere in chains): if the artificial constraints of state and government (either representative or dictatorial) were to be removed, the naturally cooperative and inherently rational impulses of every human individual would be released. In some respects then, classical anarchism might be seen as foreshadowing a social constructionist universe of a certain (1970s?) variety.[11]

Anarchism as a politics has, I think, immense strengths and very great moral suasion. However, its classic forms are unacceptably romantic, individualist, rationalist, even evolutionist in cast, and certainly humanist. If some form of anarchistic psychology is to be advocated now, it will have to accommodate somehow to the probably irreversible "post" status of all these characteristics.

Anarchism would have to transcend romanticism—to establish a rather hardheaded recognition of the constructedness of the supposedly natural impulses to cooperation and so on. That is I suppose a recognition of the constructedness of human goodness. It may be that Marxism and its descendant traditions cannot do this. They are forced, willingly or unwillingly, to set a ring fence around some core values, which neither the harsh corrosive of traditional critique nor the "sweet poison" of postmodernism will be allowed to disturb. This realism, in this kind of sense, is, I believe, a profoundly sentimental attitude. Any uncritical attachment to a set of values is sentimental, but more than this, sentimentality refuses to accept responsibility for values and for intervention based on those values. This sentimentality involves the refusal of Vico's discovery that we can only (collectively) understand what we have (collectively) made, and of the related ethical imperative actually to work on that process of understanding.

In many versions of social construction, the kind of anarchism I am thinking about would entail enormous responsibility for human agents[12], for the devices by which we habitually protect ourselves from responsibility would be largely swept away. Something of the moral/ethical flavor of existentialism might emerge here, but stripped of its subjectivism and its humanism. Such issues have been explored by Shotter (1993) and by Gergen (1994b). Shotter, appropriating Bakhtin, discusses the micropolitics of conversation through which any and every response has the choice of colluding with or challenging hegemonic practices.[13] Every word and spoken form has a "taste" or flavor, whether of the slaughterhouse or of the boudoir, sites of the struggle for the control of meaning. The user is incriminated in a chain of production, just like the wearer of a fur coat or the player of the ivory keys of a parlor piano. Despite its verbal fluency—its apparent tendency for verbal diarrhea, following the constipation of a modernist structuralism—postmodern talk is bitterly aware of the costs of that fluency ("loose lips sink ships"). Yet another paradox: a stutter, a stumble, a drunkard's hopeless insistence on precision.

How might these new responsibilities become manifest? For example, an anarchistic rejection of developmental theory would entail that we could no longer justify our treatment of children on the basis of supposed developmental needs (by which I mean needs different from the needs we may recognize in adults). A huge raft of professional people whose livelihoods depend on servicing these children's supposed needs— teachers for example, and those parasitical on them such as college and university lecturers—would be challenged to justify their actions on more solid grounds (which is to say, grounds that do not pretend to be solid). Most of the activities of parents would be called into question. The world would indeed be a different place.[14]

Conclusions

In terms of academic practice, an anarchistic psychology would capture much of the skeptical ground of postmodernism, or perhaps would share occupancy with it. It might be able to harness the techniques of deconstructive argument. It would certainly challenge any realist advocate to justify to an audience his or her decisions about precisely what is going to be held to be real and nonnegotiable. Claims about realism are not infrequently made with the high moral tone of warning—with, as it were, the voice of the parent. Who has the right to take such a tone? With Bakunin (1882/1977, p. 312), I refuse to be *told* what is real and what is not, what is negotiable and what is not. Above all, perhaps, I resist being told that our intellectual devices may be directed only at certain targets, while other targets are sacrosanct; that even though sophisticated people such as ourselves could of course find ways of undermining these certainties, and that the weapons we have devised to attack our enemies' positions would also be just as effective if directed against our own conceptual/value foundations, *we must not do so*. The vulnerability of these commitments of ours to our own weapons is not, apparently, to be considered an indication of limitations in those commitments. Those commitments have a privileged status: they are *ours*.

This is surely a form of patriotism. Rather than subjecting our commitments (our ego investments?) to fresh scrutiny, our attention is redirected (projected?) outward to the enemy—a defense mechanism indeed. Critique turns out to be paranoia. In comparison, the analytic approach is a narcissism admiring a finely articulated body, defining and delineating its organs and its locomotions from an appropriate distance, in complete ignorance that it is looking at itself. The harsh light of day— a light far more fierce than that of the "Enlightenment" as we know it so far—needs to be turned on psychology's critics as well as its "willing executioners." We do not know who will be burnt by that sun. But Y2K is as good a time as any to find out.

Acknowledgments

I have benefited considerably from discussions with Robert Johnston on postmodernism and psychology.

Notes

1. Even Marx would agree: if postmodernism is a means of production (of information perhaps), then it is in postmodernism that we find our epoch defined. But for a subtle alternative, see Beck, 1992.

2. *cf* Pauline Rosenau's 1992 distinction between "affirmative" and "skeptical" postmodernisms.

3. Liberal accounts buy diversity, or plurality, at the cost of a conceptual totalization. Differences become alternative aspects of a universal type. Perhaps the task might be reformulated (in a phrase that recalls Sampson, 1999) as *connecting with difference*.

4. Ten years ago I would have been tempted to write something like "interruption" to register the violence of the transgression.

5. I am not being precise here in relation to types of critique; *cf* Simons's and Billig's 1994 book, which tries to look at possibilities of ideology critique after postmodernism—with rather limited success I feel, after a couple of very useful early chapters.

6. But this (one would think) central core of any realist account—a list or sketch of what it holds to be real, and what negotiable—sometimes turns out to be something of a blank check drawn to the order of some expert position from which instances of nonnegotiable reality will be identified at some future time. . . . To deny the human constructedness and hence the inherent negotiability even of such notions as racism or sexual abuse (Stainton Rogers and Stainton Rogers, 1992), seems to me to deny the possibility of the malicious distortion of those notions or of their cynical appropriation by the state, or of their potential exploitation in populist contexts, or of sheer secular change in the uses of words. I therefore say: "I refute it thus." Not as did Dr. Johnson, "refuting" Berkeley's so-called idealism by kicking at a stone, but as a social-constructionist refuting realism by *saying* "I refute it thus," a series of noises that make sense only in a community with shared understandings.

7. As Ken Gergen has observed, the abandonment of critique would itself be a totalizing move (Gergen, 1994a, p. 70).

8. See Beck, 1992, and Macnaghten and Urry, 1998, for accounts of the radical constructedness of nature.

9. Hierarchization in developmental theory is exhaustively discussed in my *The Biologising of Childhood* (Morss, 1990).

10. And certainly having difficulties over "forgiving" also (Derrida, 1999).

11. I may appear disrespectful about early social constructionism in *Growing Critical* (Morss, 1996) especially when attempting to write my chapter on Marxism in a Marxist style, but the differences between early and contemporary writings in that tradition are striking. The relativism perhaps latent in the early position is now explicit, with the implications being thoroughly scrutinized. Social constructionism, first emerging as a perhaps rather detached analysis of social experience, has proved capable of engaging with the textuality, the surprisingness and the ethical weightiness of that experience in ways that critique has not thus far.

12. Humberto Maturana says:"[T]he stabilization of human conduct always entails a restriction of creativity through a restriction of the possible interactions of the individual human beings outside those prescribed by the society that they integrate. The extreme case of this, of course, takes place in a totalitarian society of any kind. Or, in other words, the spontaneous course of the historical transformation of a human society *as a unity* is towards totalitarianism; this is so because the relations that undergo historical stabilization are those that have to do with the stability of the society as a unity in a given medium, and not with the well-being of its component human beings that may operate as observers. *Any other course requires an ethical choice; it would not be spontaneous, it would be a work of art, a product of human aesthetic design*. . . . Such a [nonspontaneous] society is necessarily a nonhierarchical society for which all relations of order are constitutively transitory and circumstantial to the creation of relations that continuously negate the institutionalization of human abuse. Such a society is in its essence an anarchistic society. . . (Maturana, 1980, p. xxviii, emphasis added). See also Holzman, 1999.

13. The monological is not by any means the product of one person's voice as such—any one person may be capable of expressing many voices—but of a system acting as a totality, a notion that approaches Gramsci's notion of hegemony (Shotter, 1993). The conversation of several people may be jointly monologic, for example, a therapeutic conversation between therapist and client may co-collude with a larger discourse (e.g., a discourse about patriarchy), or a large group of people may co-collude with the discourse of "polite academic discus-

sion." "Political correctness," to the (limited) extent to which it represents a genuine constraint in conversation, amounts to a monologic.

14. David Oldman, 1994, in a fascinating analysis of childhood as a class, proposes that every aspect of "normal" development will be found to serve the direct or indirect interests of the (adult) "childworker" (a childworker is one who makes a living by exploiting children's "needs"). These considerations and others raise serious questions about what we might understand by "children's rights."

REFERENCES

Baudrillard, J. (1988). *Selected writings*. Stanford, CA: Stanford University Press.

Beck, U. (1992). *Risk society: Towards a new modernity*. London: Sage.

Bakunin, M. (1882/1977). In G.Woodcock (Ed.), *The anarchist reader*. Glasgow: Fontana/Collins.

Derrida, J. (1999). The future of the university. Conference keynote address. Auckland, NZ, August.

Gergen, K. (1994a). The limits of pure critique. In H. Simons and M. Billig (Eds.), *After postmodernism*. London: Sage

Gergen, K. (1994b). *Realities and relationships*. Cambridge, MA: Harvard University Press.

Holzman, L. (Ed.). (1999). *Performing psychology: A postmodern culture of the mind*. New York: Routledge.

Lyotard, J.-F. (1984). *The postmodern condition: A report on knowledge*. Manchester, UK: Manchester University Press.

Maturana, H. (1980). Introduction. In H. Maturana and F. Varela, *Audopoiesis and cognition*. Dordrecht, Holland: Reidel, pp xxviii–xxx.

Macnaghten, P., and Urry, J. (1998). *Contested natures*. London: Sage.

Morss, J. R. (1990). *The biologising of childhood*. Hillsdale, NJ: L. Erlbaum.

Morss, J. R. (1996). *Growing critical*. London: Routledge.

Newman, F., and Holzman, L. (1996). *Unscientific psychology: A cultural-performatory approach to understanding human life*. Westport ,CT: Praeger.

Oldman, D. (1994) Childhood as a mode of production. In B. Mayall (Ed.), *Children's Childhoods: Observed and experienced*. London: Falmer Press, pp 153–166.

Rosenau, P. (1992). *Postmodernism and the social sciences*. Princeton, NJ: Princeton University Press.

Said, E. (1994). *Representations of the intellectual*. London: Vintage.

Sampson, E. (1999). Opening address. Millennium Conference in Critical Psychology. Nepean, Sydney, April.

Shotter, J. (1993) *Cultural politics of everyday life*. Buckingham, UK: Open University Press.

Simons, H. and Billig, M. (Eds.). (1994). *After postmodernism*. London: Sage

Stainton Rogers, R., and Stainton Rogers, W. (1992). *Stories of childhood: Shifting agendas of child concern*. Hemel Hempstead, UK: Harvester/Wheatsheaf.

Four

Story-Theories

about and against

Postmodernism

in Psychology

Ian Parker

THIS CHAPTER TAKES UP ARGUMENTS within contemporary critical psychology about the nature of scientific paradigms, culture, reality, and experience. I will use four "story-theories" to frame these issues: first, an exploration of how postmodern ideas have given shape to the way some critical psychologists have attempted to move the "paradigm shifts" in psychology forward; second, an attempt to connect these ideas with a broader view of the state of psychology in capitalist society; third, a review of the implications of the postmodern turn in psychology and in other disciplines for our understanding of the real world; and fourth, a reflection on the way postmodern psychologists might be tempted to dissolve critical psychology into therapy. The line running through the discussion of postmodern psychology in these story-theories, and summarized in the concluding section of the essay, is that critical psychologists skeptical about postmodernism should use it, but *tactically*, to keep struggling against the still-dominant modern psychology, for it is modern psychology that keeps the postmoderns in its grip and it defines most of the theoretical parameters of those who think they have escaped the discipline.

Why four "story-theories"? In February 1997 the front page of a liberal-left British daily newspaper, *The Guardian*, presented four different explanations of confusion over whether the lead singer with the Manchester band Oasis, Liam Gallagher, was actually going to marry his girlfriend, Patsy Kensit, or not. The press, mainstream and tabloid, had been obsessed with rumors of the wedding for over a week, and now it was time to ask: "What's the story?" The first explanation canvassed in the article was "The postmodern story-theory." This posits that Liam and Patsy are locked into a postironic symbiosis with an increasingly marketized media, where there is a continuum between truth and untruth and between the exploiter and exploited. Under this theory, there never was going to be a wedding, but it suited both band and media to play along with the construct (*The Guardian*, February 11, 1997).

The other possibilities reviewed were "The naked commercialism story-theory" (to distract attention from a new album release by Oasis archrivals, the Essex-based band Blur), "The extremely unlikely story-theory" (that the wedding had been called off because of media attention), and "The 'Don't know what the story is, but we've all been had again' theory" (as a replay of music press hype over a possible band split between Liam and Noel, his brother, the previous September).

There is a double movement going on here between form and content, between the *structure* of the narrative that is used to tell us four stories about the wedding and the *topic* which is reframed four times over. At the same time as this structural fragmentation occurs, something happens to the topic such that we fail to learn anything more about it. Here the post-modern story-theory wins out overall. All that we can know is that we can know many different things. So, something *serious* is happening to our mode of understanding, our structuring of the phenomenon, at the very moment that the process *trivializes* what we are trying to understand— the topic. Because this example is only about Oasis, trivializing the topic more than it has been already doesn't really matter much, but when we turn to the discipline of psychology, it really does matter *how* we trivial-ize it, *why* we do it, and *when* we move into a serious reflection on what we are doing. I will trace my way through these issues using headings from those media speculations about Liam and Patsy, so we start with the postmodern story-theory.

THE POSTMODERN STORY-THEORY

The last thirty years have seen an increasing interest in "social-constructionist" perspectives in psychology in general (Gergen, 1985), and in approaches that locate the stuff of psychology in discourse in particular (Burr, 1995). This movement represents a critical reflexive shift away from the search for mental paraphernalia inside each individual's head and toward a socially mediated and historically situated study of action and experience. This is an endeavor postmodernism both encourages and sabotages.

The "new-paradigm" turn to language in the 1970s encouraged a challenge to traditional laboratory-experimental psychology (Harré and Secord, 1972). Criticisms of laboratory experimentation in psychology at the end of the 1960s were fired by anger at the deceptive and demeaning practices that underpinned the discipline, and humanist arguments were often more important then than "scientific" ones. There were attempts to balance humanism and science, for example, in the slogan "for scientific purposes treat people as if they were human beings" (Harré and Secord, 1972, p. 84). Despite this clear bid to be a new scientific paradigm for psychology, scientific rhetoric soon dropped into the background, and it was as a *relativizing* (if not yet fully relativist) current of work that the new-paradigm arguments quickly spread from social psychology (Harré, 1979) to studies of the self (Harré, 1983; Shotter, 1984), emotion (Harré, 1986), and cognitive psychology (Edwards, 1997; Harré and Gillett, 1994). Social constructionist and discourse-analytic approaches made it possible to conceptualize human psychology as something culturally located and historically specific, and they have even served as a warrant for renewed discussion of Marxist accounts of the individual subject as an "ensemble of social relations" (Parker and Spears, 1996).

"Postmodern psychology" is the latest rubric, then, for the critical and then "deconstructive" line of work which spread from social psychology to other areas of the discipline from the 1970s through to the end of the 1980s (Kvale, 1992). But as it turned postmodern, it started to pose problems for those critical psychologists who were trying to combat "modern" psychology without being trapped into something which served as its equally apolitical mirror image. Although a collection of critical essays in social psychology published in 1974 was entitled *Reconstructing Social Psychology* (Armistead, 1974) and a follow-up some fifteen years later was called *Deconstructing Social Psychology* (Parker and Shotter, 1990), little of substance in the complaints and political impulse had changed. Concerns about the political passivity of a politics of "deconstruction" for feminists were included in the latter book (Burman, 1990), but this has not hindered the application of "deconstruction" to other topics in psychology (e.g., Burman, 1994; Parker, Georgaca, Harper, Stowell-Smith, and McLaughlin, 1995).

Postmodernism and Power

Some of the dangers of full-blown relativism that mar much recent postmodern psychology can already be seen in the rhetoric of the earlier days of the new paradigm. It will be clearer what the consequences of this rhetoric are if we consider social-constructionist accounts of power. One of the influential alternative theoretical "new-paradigm" traditions in psychology during the 1970s was "ethogenic" social psychology, in which close observation of the roles people adopted in different situations and the rules they followed was combined with gathering "accounts" from people about those roles and rules (Harré and Secord, 1972; Marsh, Rosser, and Harré, 1974). Notwithstanding Harré's (1986) own sustained argument for realism in the sciences, he then argued that power is "an ontological illusion, real only as an accounting resource" (Harré, 1979, p. 233). This claim would not necessarily be problematic if it were supplemented by an analysis of the way "accounting resources" are structured so as to distribute power and perform it in the exercise of knowledge, for example, but Harré is insistent that social systems that appear to be structured around power are "nothing above the multiplication of personal power" (Ibid.). Any "account" we may want to give of power in society or the state, then, is leveled down to one of many "accounts" that any of the other players may be offering. This example is so telling precisely because it comes from someone who is a realist, who then makes use of social constructionism, and then, perhaps, regrets its effects (Harré, 1992, 1995).

Postmodern psychology and "deconstruction" in psychology have included writers who want to understand and challenge power, but, bit by bit, psychologists who should know better have succumbed to the apolitical impulse of postmodernism. The emergence of a version of "discourse analysis" in social psychology towards the end of the 1980s (Potter and Wetherell, 1987) was given the tag quote (from Ken Gergen) in publishers' publicity of being a "postmodern psychology." This hope for something entirely new has set the scene for a discourse of critique that has continued apace ever since. The fragmentation of what we know about Liam and

Patsy into the four different versions works rather like a discourse analysis, and in that respect it makes sense to view discourse analysis in psychology as a postmodern story. However, we can get a better sense of why new-paradigm and then postmodern hopes in psychology sold us short with respect to issues of power only if we turn to the wider societal context. To do this, we need the naked commercialism story-theory.

THE NAKED COMMERCIALISM STORY-THEORY

The variety of critical movements relativizing alienating and oppressive psychological knowledge about people have usually been characterized by an insistence that the "individual" and the "social" were so interrelated that a strict distinction between the two sides of the equation was seriously mistaken. The argument that psychology *is* social (e.g., Armistead, 1974) was an influential theme in early critical perspectives, and it continues today (e.g., Gergen, 1994). Critics also often pointed out that attempts in "social" psychology to specify *how* the individual and the social were connected reproduced the selfsame dualist problematic (Buss, 1975; Henriques, Holloway, Urwin, Venn, and Walkerdine, 1984). This is where descriptions of "dialectical" relationships started to appear, particularly in developmental psychology, where dialectics was employed as part of an account of the way in which an "individual" child emerged out of the relationship between infant and mother (e.g., Riegel, 1976). Psychology, like other bourgeois disciplines, however, has been adept at absorbing and neutralizing Marxist concepts. And just as "alienation" has been redefined as an individual feeling of worthlessness rather than an account of the real separation of people from their labor (e.g., Seeman, 1971), so the term "dialectics" is often used in psychology simply to describe the balance between the individual and the social, between inside and outside, or between objectivity and subjectivity.

The latest "postmodern" version of this domestication of dialectics in psychology can be seen in "deconstruction." Just as modern psychology succeeded in destroying what was genuinely radical about dialectics, now postmodern psychology is doing the same job for the discipline on deconstruction. The argument that deconstruction in psychology ought to emphasize undecidability, and that the moral of Derrida's work is that we should perpetually defer judgment about what may or may not be the case or what may or may not be right or wrong (e.g., Hepburn, 1999) is of a piece with the rhetorical balancing so beloved of bourgeois culture. This version of deconstruction, which is deliberately counterposed to approaches in psychology that attend to the power and politics of the psy-complex (e.g., Burman, 1994; Parker et al., 1995), is closer to the U.S. liberal-pluralist readings of Derrida's work than the progressive uses of deconstruction in literary theory in Europe (Norris, 1996). While this rhetorical balancing strategy presents itself as being the most open inclusive defense of conversation about how the world may be, then, it is actually very selective about which theoretical traditions are included and about which readings of theories will be allowed.

Against this postmodern relativism, we should be sympathetic to those "critical relativists" who refuse to brook *any* attempt to resort to science in psychology, whether to improve or challenge it. For the radical textualists in the discipline who analyze the way "development" and "emotions" are "storied" into being (e.g., Curt, 1994; Stainton Rogers, Stenner, Gleeson, and Stainton Rogers, 1995), an embrace of old modern "realist" psychology is also a dangerous invitation to critical psychologists to be seduced back into the discipline and to join in the enterprise of demarcating the "mere" story from the "real" psychology (and so to carry on with all-the-more arrogance than before). The "critical-relativist" position, then, entails "a social constructionism whereby people are viewed as readers and writers (written upon and read) within the textuality of culture. People (and this includes people who are psychologists/social scientists) actively construct (and are actively constructed by) versions of the 'way things are,' versions which are always-already enmeshed with the moral, political and ideological concerns of Being" (Stenner and Eccleston, 1994, p. 96).

Postmodernism and Ideology

Postmodernism appears in psychology in at least *three* different versions, in which it sells itself to those jaded with the old paradigm as living in the story worlds of "Opportunity," "Progress," and "Reflection" (Parker, 1998a). Lyotard (1979-1984), one of the key theoreticians of the "postmodern condition," can be recruited to each of these market segments and he can even seem compatible with the reflexive "critical-relativist" argument. What Lyotard does, however, is to try to strip the modern and the postmodern of their insistent movement forward, of the anticipatory dynamic of modernism. The futurism of modern experimental art, for example, is overshadowed by a reflection on narrative as something that is only in the present and from which there is no escape, backward or forward: "What seems to be moving in such moments is less 'history' than that which is unleashed by its rupture and suspension; and the typically modernist images of the vortex and the abyss, 'vertical' inruptions into temporality within which forces swirl restlessly in an eclipse of linear time, represent this ambivalent consciousness" (Eagleton, 1985, p. 67).

Postmodernism in the story-world of Reflection is part of a world that values that restlessness and sees it as an always-already-present quality of modern experience. This vision of the postmodern condition as consisting of "games of perfect information at any given moment" leads Lyotard to hope that it would furnish "a politics that would respect both the desire for justice and the desire for the unknown" (1979-1984, p. 67). It is a moot point as to whether postmodern ideas generally offer anything to those in the real world. What is for sure is that when psychologists get hold of postmodernism, they tend to turn it into an ideology that celebrates the way things are instead of providing any way out.

Postmodernism, Psychology, and Capitalism

Psychology has always traded in ideological representations of mind and behavior, so it is hardly surprising that postmodern psychologists should carry on that tradition. But the relationship between modernity and ideology, and between postmodernism and psychology, is complex and contradictory. Postmodern psychology encourages individuals to subvert and surpass the rules of the game laid down by the discipline. But even as we should give credit to these critical writers, we need to be careful not to overestimate what they can achieve, for two reasons.

First, psychology has continually failed to fix behavior and mental mechanisms as it would wish, and it has been repeatedly challenged by writers who have explicitly wanted to improve it and turn it around to the cause of resistance and liberation. The psy-complex, as a dense network of theories and practices inside and outside the academe and the clinic, is a dangerous and pernicious regulative apparatus, but it still fails. Its subjects look for holistic alternatives that will respect their experience and acknowledge diversity, and the reductive and reified models it peddles are often, quite rightly, treated with contempt. Some people are impressed by psychology, and those who are training to be psychologists and hoping for a share of the power are most susceptible, but fortunately many people are suspicious of psy-complex apparatchiks and are mocking of those who speak its language. They have not needed postmodernism so far to help them resist psychology. Postmodern writing does draw attention to the way "modern" psychology caricatures notions of historical progress and represses self-understanding, but it then itself paralyzes and ironizes our grasp of history and agency in return. It is, then, a liability for those who have always already struggled against the discipline with an eye to history and agency.

Second, postmodernism is itself, of course, a kind of conceptual commodity in a world still defined by parameters of progress, reflection, and opportunity. It has to be marketed to audiences who weigh up whether it will help them to move forward and whether it will facilitate self-understanding. However, although critical psychologists are sickened by the way psychology fails them—the way it takes the hope of historical progress and makes a caricature of it in the steady accumulation of facts from discrete controlled variables, and systematically represses self-understanding because it threatens to introduce a spiral of subjectivity into its supposedly objective studies—some of them are still reluctant to buy postmodernism (e.g., Roiser, 1997). They are right. As we have already seen, postmodernism relativizes our accounts of the world to such an extent that we cannot then produce a critical understanding of the social and economic conditions that produce the kind of oppressive practices and ideas psychology routinely trades in. We can see how extremely unlikely and pernicious the postmodern story is if we look at how it corrodes realist accounts outside psychology.

THE EXTREMELY UNLIKELY STORY-THEORY

Postmodern relativism provokes irrational conspiratorial views of the world, mystifies our understanding of state power, and undermines historical narrative. To say the story postmodernism tells is "extremely unlikely" is the least of it. Conspiracy theory and mystification in the place of social analysis and reasoned argument abound in "postmodern" sectors of contemporary culture. One trivial example is discussions on the Internet recently about the connections in the narrative of the film

The Wizard of Oz and the Pink Floyd album *Dark Side of the Moon*—in which, for example, the Tin Man in the film reveals that he doesn't have a heart at exactly the same point in the album where the heartbeat appears. Another serious example is Baudrillard's claim that the Gulf War in Iraq did not *really* happen. Such a claim plays a profoundly ideological role. Postmodern celebration of irrationality and mystification also has disastrous consequences for the past and the present, and historical revisionists are all to ready to jump on the postmodern bandwagon to erase the past (*cf* Norris, 1996). Remember Walter Benjamin's warning: "Only that historian will have the gift of fanning the spark of hope in the past who is firmly convinced that *even the dead* will not be safe from the enemy if he wins" (1939, p. 247). The theoretical resources that relativist researchers draw upon are part of a wider discursive turn in the human sciences that carry conservative as well as progressive prescriptions for social activity (Callinicos, 1995; Eagleton, 1991; Geras, 1995; Norris, 1996). Critical psychologists—relativist and realist—have expressed concern about this, but attempts to address the issue have tended to illustrate and explore the problem rather than clarify and resolve it (e.g., Parker, 1998b). There is, however, always room for hope, for, notwithstanding the naïve or malign excesses of the Baudrillards and the historical revisionists, relativist arguments are untenable. They break down because we, and those who make such arguments, do still live in the real world.

Postmodernism and the Real World

We all, at times, make realist assumptions about the world, and it would not be possible for us to discuss alternative accounts if we did not: "conversation as between separate intelligences itself presupposes a structured and differentiated segment of public 'matter' between them, independently of their jointly finding or deciding or agreeing that it is so structured and differentiated" (Geras, 1995, p. 118). Even those in the relativist camp will display due caution about denying the existence of a world, and they are eventually compelled to take back most of their untenable antirealist claims. This is why a little textual analysis will reveal a rhetorical balance between extravagance and caution in the very same arguments advanced by "postmodern" writers such as Rorty (e.g., 1989, 1992). There is always a rhetorical balancing act in the arguments of "relativists" in which they take back many of the extreme claims they make, almost in the same breath. A close examination of Rorty's writing, for example, reveals that theoretical claims about pragmatism are always balanced by a recognition that it could not really be defended if it were taken to the limit (Geras, 1995).

While Rorty's writing is characterized by an extravagant relativism, this is always moderated by assurances that "of course" this or that shared knowledge that we have about the world can be taken for granted and will *not* be subjected to scrutiny; this is because: "He cannot cope with explaining how, if there is not something which is what it is apart from any description, there could be something which preexisted all description; as to the best of our knowledge there is" (Geras, 1995, p. 132). There must be a "real" social world that we share in order to be able to make sense of Rorty's argument, and so: "Like most people, Rorty needs some terms for the brute facticity of things, if he cannot have this coherently, then incoherently it must be. For without it he cannot cope. He cannot cope with the overwhelming paradox and absurdity which will follow upon losing the world" (Geras, 1995, p. 132).

Often, however, what stems this relativism, and grounds the claims in something we can recognize as "real," are different rhetorical devices that assure the reader that they live in the same world as Rorty. In the process, these devices draw the reader into the text so that the world they inhabit with him while they read it is suffused with ideology. One grounding device, for example, is the appeal to the audience as members of a common culture, a covert nationalist rhetoric that, in Rorty's writing, makes the United States appear in the text as the home of liberal democracy (Billig, 1993).

Rorty is one of the postmoderns who resort to the argument that they are not so much antirealist as "antirepresentationalists": "Like Berkeley and Kant . . . contemporary antirepresentationalists insist that they do not deny the prior and independent reality of the referents of many beliefs" (Rorty, 1992, p. 41). In a riposte to Eagleton's (1991) discussion of ideology, Rorty agrees with the attempt to discover alternative accounts of a situation that a Marxist may see as "oppressive," in this case in an analysis of the interests of a galley slave who may realize later that the life he was leading was buttressed by forms of discourse which misrepresented his true interests: "Antirepresentationalists can happily agree with Eagleton that when the galley slave thought he was a justly lashed worm, he was wrong, and that he is now right in thinking that his interests consist in escaping the galleys" (Rorty, 1992, p. 41). However, ideology as such is dissolved as a category, and there is no way that the analysis of the slave's situation could be construed as *actually really* oppressive. For Rorty, what the slave does when he starts to talk about his situation differently is to talk about his situation differently; so the anti-representationalist "will also construe this claim as saying: if the slave tries the discourse of emancipation he will come out with better results than those he achieved with the discourse in which he viewed himself as a worm" (Rorty, 1992, p. 41).

Postmodernism and Modern Psychology

How does this play itself out with respect to *psychology*? Here we have to be very careful, for realism as such may not be so much an antidote to postmodernism as something that leads back to modern psychology. Realism in psychology has rested on the argument that human beings should be respected as structured entities that engage in "second-order monitoring" (Harré and Secord, 1972). This reflexive power of human beings means that a watertight "closed system" that (nearly) obtains in the natural sciences could not apply in psychology, save by the most brutal suppression of reflexivity and so the destruction of human psychology itself. Psychology was seen by Harré and Secord (1972) as one level in an open system of structures that was embedded in biological structures and social structures. They argued that psychological matters are of moral-political concern, as with other sciences, but in this discipline all the more so because the forms of knowledge that psychology produces are deployed by its very objects of study. Psychology cannot accurately "represent" psychological functioning because, as a shared system of knowledge, it is part of it. However, patterns can be identified to model already existing but mutable structures that permit and constrain behavior and the accounts people may give of it.

While these arguments cut against "old-paradigm" psychology, they do not in themselves serve as a critical counterweight to the dangerous aspects of postmodern psychology. Postmodern psychology refuses to take seriously accounts of the real world—the world in which the discipline of psychology causes so much harm—so why should it take seriously realism (or "critical realism") in psychology when it claims to study "real" psychological processes? This refusal by the postmoderns is actually a mixed blessing for critical psychologists, for many of us have been trying to refuse the reification of things psychologists think they have "discovered" as real things for years. For critical psychologists who do want to develop their work in the context of an understanding of ideology and power in the real world, the realist ratification of psychology is dangerous. Postmodernism is sometimes attractive to critical psychologists precisely because critical realists outside psychology do often threaten to buttress *modern* psychology. Postmodernism then seems the only way out. Collier (1994), for example, argues that while he does not hope for a "critical-realist psychology" (quite rightly), he then lets existing theories in psychology (such as Chomsky's) off the hook by suggesting that already established theories might be challenged or refined by critical realists (Collier, 1994, p. 207). This is why some critical psychologists sometimes play with postmodern and relativist ideas *inside* the discipline of psychology while using realist (and necessarily antipostmodern) ideas to contextualize what the discipline does on the *outside* (Parker, 1999a). Critical psychologists are trying to avoid being duped into assumptions about human beings made by psychologists, *modern or postmodern.* They insist that they don't know what the story is about fixed human nature, thinking, or behavior, and they don't want to be had again by any theory which lures them into thinking they should know (*cf* Newman and Holzman, 1997).

THE "DON'T KNOW WHAT THE STORY IS, BUT WE'VE ALL BEEN HAD AGAIN" THEORY

Postmodernism is very appealing to critical psychologists because it manifests itself as a "psychological" phenomenon, appearing in everyday experience as an expression of present-day uncertainties about identity and meaning, and because it is marked self-consciously and self-referentially in contemporary culture. We can see the experiential aspect of postmodernism in the following two dreams reported by colleagues a few years back. One of the dreamers is a woman, a teacher and psychotherapist. The second dreamer is a man, a clinical psychologist.

The first dream. She is wending her way up and around the contours of a mountain range. She is passing hedges and hillocks and stones as she makes her way up to the top. She reaches the top of one of the higher hills, and realizes that it is in the shape of a letter. As she looks across the pattern of hills below her she realizes, and she feels anxious as she realizes, that it is one of a series of letters that together spell out the word "postmodernism." She wakes up.

The second dream. He discovers that one of his legs is made of metal. It is a false leg. He knows, as he looks down at his flesh-and-blood leg on one side and at his metal leg on the other, that one of his legs is modern and the other is postmodern. He knows which is which, but he also knows, when he awakes, that others may not know. When he does wake up, he describes the dream to friends, and asks each of them if they know which leg is which.

These dreams display an attempt, in the first dream, to find meaning in nature and, in the second dream, to determine the meaning of bits of the body. There is a concern in both with individual identity and with how it might be located. To see the word "postmodernism" written over nature is at least to be aware of culture as a construction, and to puzzle over real and false bits of the body is at least to ask what is what. Such themes in contemporary culture also, of course, serve as an invitation to therapy. Therapy operates as a domain in which critical reflection all too often turns into decontextualized "reflexivity," and this reflexivity is then often viewed as equivalent to a postmodern psychology.

Postmodernism and Reflexivity

One of the symptoms of therapeutic discourse in psychology is that there is often a simple appeal to "reflexivity" to solve problems of politics and power in the discipline. Some writers in the tradition of discourse analysis also appeal to reflexivity even though they are otherwise extremely suspicious of anything that looks therapeutic, to the extent that talk of subjectivity of any sort is accused by them of slipping into simple humanism (Parker, 1999b). Reflexivity is often felt to be a kind of space that we can escape into as if we could then look upon the discipline from a distance; or reflexivity is sometimes even thought to be a solvent in which the abusive aspects of psychology can be dissolved. The activity of thinking back and thinking around an issue, and situating oneself, which is a valuable and necessary part of therapeutic work, is thought to illuminate all problems *and*, in that very process, to solve them.

This is caricaturing a bit, of course, but it is important to draw attention to the mistake sometimes made by radicals in the discipline when they imagine that simply to turn around and reflect on what we are doing, as researchers or practitioners, is enough. This is not to impugn critical reflection on our practices, and I want to draw a contrast between reflexivity as such and *critical reflection*. While reflexivity is something that proceeds from within the interior of the self, and participates in all of the agonizing confessional work that Foucault (1976) so brilliantly describes, critical reflection traces the subjective investments we make in our everyday practice, and traces them to the networks of institutional power that contain us.

While reflexivity can be a passive contemplative enterprise that all too often succeeds in paralyzing the individual as he or she takes responsibility for the pain and troubles of a painful and troubling set of circumstances, critical reflection is an active rebellious practice that drives the individual into action as he or she identifies the exercise of power that pins him or her into place and the fault lines for the production of spaces of resistance. Although postmodernist writers often suggest that "reflexivity" can serve as a solution to conceptual and social problems, at the very same time there is a sliding from term to term that sabotages the possibility of a critical vantage point being constructed from which to reflect critically on what is happening around the writer and why (Parker, 1992).

Postmodernism and Therapy

Family therapists and social workers who have been working through different systemic traditions are now arriving at an approach to presenting "problems" as being located in discourses and narratives that structure families as well as identified patients within them, and quite a few of these have been persuaded that they are "postmodern" (McNamee and Gergen, 1992). The "story metaphor" is seen as central to "the philosophy of postmodernism" that brings these approaches together (McKenzie and Monk, 1997, p. 85). In some cases there is a hope that postmodernism will lead to a state of "co-construction" in which "psychotherapy practice as manipulation disappears" (Fruggeri, 1992, p. 45), or that it will afford clients "a free conversational space" (Anderson and Goolishian, 1992, p. 29). Postmodernism here is being treated as if it were equivalent to Rortyesque liberal pragmatism in which all the problems disappear when we have conceptually "deconstructed" them, and there is a debate now within this field of deconstructive therapy over the role of real problems and relatively enduring patterns of power (e.g., Parker, 1999c).

Postmodern Sectors of Capitalist Culture

We can view the appearance and transformations of elements of modern *and* postmodern culture within the broader frame of contemporary capitalist culture—a culture underpinned for good and ill by the philosophers of the Western Enlightenment—and in this way we can understand the way in which issues of autonomy and collectivism, scientism and fundamentalism operate through "dialectical reversals" (Parker, 1998a). This theoretical stance avoids falling back into modern psychology in fright as an alternative to postmodern psychology. There is some understandable unease—for example, among narrative therapists who have enthusiastically taken a "postmodern" turn because it seemed to invite a more ethical relationship to clients—that it may actually lead to something more akin to fundamentalism. Now we see concerns from those who have been advocating the postmodern turn in narrative therapy that this kind of "narrative fundamentalism" (Amundson, 1994) will carry with it worrying moral-political assumptions:

> Though the postmodern emphasis on stories or narratives (as opposed to theory or truth) is intended as a statement of modesty, there can be an easy slippage into the reification of Narrative as a foundational form of knowledge. This can in turn lead to implicit assumptions about "better" and more "appropriate" narratives for clients and to a notion of therapy as a form of story assessment and repair. In such a case, the appeal of postmodern plurality has been diverted into modern singularity. (Lowe, 1999, p. 82)

With respect to narrative therapies that now often characterize themselves as "postmodern," it has been pointed out that these approaches, which seem so thoroughly social, still routinely appeal to the individual "self" as a source of meaning and as the place to which all the reflexive capacities to engage in discursive activity will be traced (Newman and Holzman, 1996). For Kendall and Michael (1997, p. 12) this relationship is turned on its head, with "a dialectical view of psychology and the objects of psychological knowledge" blamed for the way postmodern (social) psychology slides into the idea that it might be possible to release individuality. Gergen, their object of scorn here, may indeed be guilty of appealing to some notion of the free individual who makes choices in the postmodern land of opportunity, but his celebration of autonomy in the midst of relationality needs to be understood as a part of a dialectical process *within* capitalist culture rather than a deliberate leitmotif of postmodern thought. Lowe's (1999) comment about "postmodern multiplicity" threatening to give way to "modern singularity" is pertinent. The issue here is that the "modern singularity" being referred to is an organic motif of purification that has always carried with it particular dangers in capitalist culture.

What counts as "self" is always defined in relation to an Other, while othering proceeds through the constitution and unmaking of self. Therapeutic reflection can help us to follow this through, but it needs to break from modern psychology and postmodern psychology in order to do this adequately. "What if there were no truth and no self?" postmodernists might ask, and they may ask that because they want to deconstruct and disperse truth and self. What we must ask *before* we make that voluntarist leap to ridding ourselves of those relationships is *how* those relationships are sustained. It really does matter *how* we dissolve those relationships, *why* we do it, and *when* we move into a serious reflection on what we are doing.

CONCLUSION

Cultural phenomena are not static; they are characterized by certain distinctive features that mark them as coming from particular economic and political settings and as having emerged within certain intellectual and institutional contexts. By intellectual contexts, here I mean the contradictory sites of reflection and resistance where organic intellectuals of many kinds crystallize and mobilize communities, and not only academic communities (Gramsci, 1971); and by institutional contexts, I mean the various organizational settings where knowledge is formalized and sedimented and where people are encouraged and inhibited from thinking by practical-discursive formal communities, including academic ones (Kendall and Michael, 1997). One of my concerns about postmodernism in psychology is how we can maintain a dialectical tension between structure and topic and between seriousness and triviality—which brings us back to the trivial example we opened the essay with.

As well as the four possible theories about the story of Liam's and Patsy's lost wedding, *The Guardian* floated another late alternative contender, that they had really got married after all. Sometimes it seems as though it is too late, and we must either be with the radical postmoderns or with bad old reactionary psychology. This is not to say that advocates of postmodernism in psychology are unaware of the dilemma. In a presentation that challenged the form and content of traditional academic work, Mary Gergen explored some of the tensions between feminism and postmodernism, asking whether the relationship between the two would really work, whether it would be, as she put it, "deadlock or wedlock" (Gergen and Gergen, 1995). Liam and Patsy did eventually get married, and they then separated after acrimonious public disputes.

We have to understand what the parameters of the choice might be, and to be careful now not simply to jump from the postmodern back to the modern. The problem is not so much that postmodern psychologists have jumped too far out of psychology, but that they are still held in thrall by that still very powerful, very modern discipline. The old paradigms are still in place, the cultural and economic societal conditions that made psychology possible still reign, realism is still used by psychology when it suits it and disregarded when it offers an account that conflicts with it, and psychology increasingly seduces people into psychology through therapeutic discourse. Critical psychologists now have the double task of combating postmodern psychology's inability to move beyond the parameters of the discipline (as its either loyal friend or bewitched helpless mirror image) and combating, as ever, old modern psychology.

REFERENCES

Amundson, J. (1994). Whither narrative? The danger of getting it right. *Journal of Marital and Family Therapy, 20 (1)*, 83–87.

Anderson, H., and Goolishian, H. (1992). The client is the expert: A not-knowing approach to therapy. In S. McNamee and K. J. Gergen (Eds.), *Therapy as social construction*. London: Sage.

Armistead, N. (Ed.). (1974). *Reconstructing social psychology*. Harmondsworth, UK: Penguin.

Benjamin, W. (1939). Theses on the philosophy of history. In W. Benjamin (1973), *Illuminations*. London: Fontana.

Billig, M. (1993). Nationalism and Richard Rorty: The text as a flag for *Pax Americana*. *New Left Review*, *202*, 69–83.

Burman, E. (1990). Differing with deconstruction: A feminist critique. In I. Parker and J. Shotter (Eds.), *Deconstructing social psychology*. London: Routledge.

Burman, E. (1994). *Deconstructing developmental psychology*. London: Routledge.

Burr, V. (1995). *An introduction to social constructionism*. London: Routledge.

Buss, A. R. (1975). The emerging field of the sociology of psychological knowledge. *American Psychologist*, *30*, 988–1002.

Callinicos, A. (1995). *Theories and narratives: Reflections on the philosophy of History*. Cambridge, UK: Polity Press.

Collier, A. (1994). *Critical realism: An introduction to Roy Bhaskar's Philosophy*. London: Verso.

Curt, B. (1994). *Textuality and tectonics: Troubling social and psychological science*. Buckingham, UK: Open University Press.

Eagleton, T. (1985). Capitalism, modernism and postmodernism. *New Left Review*, *152*, 60–73.

Eagleton, T. (1991). *Ideology: An introduction*. London: Verso.

Edwards, D. (1997). *Discourse and cognition*. London: Sage.

Foucault, M. (1976). *Discipline and punish*. London: Allen Lane.

Fruggeri, L. (1992). Therapeutic process as the social construction of change. In S. McNamee and K. J. Gergen (Eds.), *Therapy as social construction*. London: Sage.

Geras, N. (1995). Language, truth and justice. *New Left Review*, *209*, 110–135.

Gergen, K. J. (1985). The social constructionist movement in modern psychology. *American Psychologist*, *40(3)* , 266–275.

Gergen, K. J. (1994). *Realities and relationships*. Cambridge, MA: Harvard University Press.

Gergen, K. J., and Gergen, M. M. (1995). Relationalia: a hyperlogue. Paper delivered at the Understanding the Social World conference, Huddersfield, UK, September.

Gramsci, A. (1971). *Selections from the prison notebooks*. London: Lawrence and Wishart.

Harré, R. (1979). *Social being: A theory for social psychology*. Oxford, UK: Blackwell.

Harré, R. (1983). *Personal being: A theory for individual psychology*. Oxford, UK: Blackwell.

Harré, R. (1986). *Varieties of realism: A rationale for the natural sciences.* Oxford, UK: Blackwell.

Harré, R. (1992). What is real in psychology? A plea for persons. *Theory and Psychology, 2(2)* , 153–158.

Harré, R. (1995). Review of M. Douglas and D. Hull, *How classification works. Common Knowledge, 4(3)*, 157–159.

Harré, R., and Gillett, G. (1994). *The discursive mind.* London: Sage.

Harré, R., and Secord, P. F. (1972). *The explanation of social behavior.* Oxford, UK: Blackwell.

Henriques, J., Hollway, W., Urwin, C., Venn, C., and Walkerdine, V. (1984). *Changing the subject: Psychology, social regulation and subjectivity.* London: Methuen.

Hepburn, A. (1999). Ab/uses of deconstruction in psychology. *Theory and Psychology, 9(5)* , 639–665.

Kendall, G., and Michael, M. (1997). Politicizing the politics of postmodern social psychology. *Theory and Psychology, 7(1)* , 7–29.

Kvale, S. (Ed.). (1992). *Psychology and postmodernism.* London: Sage.

Lowe, R. (1999). Between the "no longer" and the "not yet": Postmodernism as a context for critical therapeutic work. In I. Parker (Ed.), *Deconstructing psychotherapy.* London: Sage.

Lyotard, J.-F. (1979/1984). *The postmodern condition: A report on knowledge.* Manchester, UK: Manchester University Press.

McKenzie, W., and Monk, G. (1997). Learning and teaching narrative ideas. In G. Monk, J. Winslade, K. Crocket, and D. Epston (Eds.), *Narrative therapy in practice: The archaeology of hope.* San Francisco: Jossey-Bass Publishers.

McNamee, S., and Gergen, K. J. (Eds.) (1992). *Therapy as social construction.* London: Sage.

Marsh, P., Rosser, E., and Harré, R. (1974). *The rules of disorder.* London: Routledge and Kegan Paul.

Newman, F., and Holzman, L. (1996). *Unscientific psychology: A cultural-performatory approach to understanding human life.* Westport, CT: Praeger.

Newman, F., and Holzman, L. (1997). *The end of knowing (and a new developmental way of learning).* London: Routledge.

Norris, C. (1996). *Reclaiming truth: Contribution to a critique of cultural relativism.* London: Lawrence and Wishart.

Parker, I. (1992). *Discourse dynamics: Critical analysis for social and individual psychology.* London: Routledge.

Parker, I. (1998a). Against postmodernism: psychology in cultural context. *Theory and Psychology, 8(5)*, 621–647.

Parker, I. (Ed.). (1998b). *Social constructionism: Discourse and realism*. London: Sage.

Parker, I. (1999a). Against relativism in psychology: On balance. *History of the Human Sciences, 12(4)*, 61–78.

Parker, I. (1999b). Critical reflexive humanism and critical constructionist psychology. In D. J. Nightingale and J. Cromby (Eds.), *Social constructionist psychology: A critical analysis*. Buckingham, UK: Open University Press.

Parker, I. (Ed.). (1999c). *Deconstructing psychotherapy*. London: Sage.

Parker, I., Georgaca, E., Harper, D., Stowell-Smith, M., and McLaughlin, T. (1995). *Deconstructing psychopathology*. London: Sage.

Parker, I., and Shotter, J. (Eds.). (1990). *Deconstructing social psychology*. London: Routledge.

Parker, I., and Spears, R. (Eds.). (1996). *Psychology and society: Radical theory and practice*. London: Pluto Press.

Potter, J., and Wetherell, M. (1987). *Discourse and social psychology: Beyond attitudes and behavior*. London: Sage.

Riegel, K. F. (1976). The dialectics of human development. *American Psychologist, 31*, 689–700.

Roiser, M. (1997). Postmodernism, postmodernity and social psychology. In T. Ibanez and L. Iniguez (Eds.), *Critical social psychology*. London: Sage.

Rorty, R. (1989). *Contingency, irony and solidarity*. Cambridge, UK: Cambridge University Press.

Rorty, R. (1992). We anti-representationalists. *Radical Philosophy, 60*, 40–42.

Seeman, M. (1971). The urban alienations: Some dubious themes from Marx to Marcuse. *Journal of Personality and Social Psychology, 19(2)*, 63–84.

Shotter, J. (1984). *Social accountability and selfhood*. Oxford, UK: Blackwell.

Stainton Rogers, R., Stenner, P., Gleeson, K., and Stainton Rogers, W. (1995). *Social psychology: A critical agenda*. Cambridge, UK: Polity Press.

Stenner, P., and Eccleston, C. (1994). On the textuality of being: Towards an invigorated social constructionism. *Theory and Psychology, 4(1)*, 85–103.

Method,

Measurement,

and Madness

Erica Burman

IT IS NOW COMMONPLACE in critical psychology circles to regard the rational unitary subject of psychology as rigid, incoherent, and shot through with racist, sexist, and heterosexist assumptions. With the current "turn to the text" prompted by "post" perspectives and the resurgence of humanist critiques of experimental psychology (in the form of "qualitative psychology"), we have also come to understand better the reciprocal relations between how psychology conducts its research and the representations of subjectivity it claims to have discovered. We have even started to situate the material of the psyche as socially and historically produced, not least through the contribution of psychology to the proliferating technologies of subjectivity that structure how we talk and think about our "selves," our "identities," and our "relationships."

Equipped with these tools promoting a healthy mistrust for psychology's self-serving and reactionary truths, we can start to ask more interesting and relevant questions about what we can and should do as "unscientific"—politically committed and scientifically skeptical—psychologists and psychotherapists. That is, I want to move the discussion on from "unscientific psychology" as a topic or arena, perhaps even a body of knowledge, to consider what we, as embodied and acting ("unscientific") psychologists, *do.* Beyond denouncing the purveyors of psychology's pernicious pseudoscience and elaborating and justifying an alternative basis for knowing (or not knowing), how do these ideas enter into or, indeed, reflect (if we believe that thought follows from action) our *practice?*

Later in this essay I will take examples from recent work I have been involved with (primarily as an academic supervisor) on the relations between racialized and gendered identities. I am particularly interested in elaborating how acknowledging and addressing the role of racialized and gendered identifications in therapy connect with researcher-researched, as well as therapist-client, relationships. From the outset I should emphasize the dialectical relationship between the framework of ideas with which I approached the interpretation of the research—informed by current debates in women's studies and postcolonial studies—and the research students' own perspectives and accounts of research processes. The ideas here are very much a joint production, and are based on research and therapeutic practice in which I was not a central protagonist but, rather, the supervisor/spectator.[1]

Far from simply reiterating long-standing dualisms between clear, "hard" (masculine), scientific psychology and messy, "soft" (feminine) psychotherapy, I take specific examples of practice to help us elaborate our theories. In particular, I want to argue that these examples highlight how departing from the logic of identities need not plunge us into a relativist melting pot that blurs all boundaries or obscures lived differences and inequalities. Rather, this can offer us alternative ways of conceptualizing and negotiating structural relationships, such as those organized around racialized, gendered, and professional identities, and that can inform and strengthen feminist and antiracist work in psychology.

PSYCHOLOGY MAKES US MAD

But first, something on how psychology makes us mad, in the sense of pathologizing irrationality as well as individualizing political resistance into personal distress. We know these slogans well, but it is easy to underestimate the myriad and insidious ways in which psychology, as the science of the singular, disembodied mind, confirms the power of the dominant groups by placing them at its center, as the norm. It is then a short but crucial political step from the statistically patterned norm (of "what is") to the moral-political (and clinical) evaluation of normal (i.e., "what should be"). Foucault's analyses highlight how dispensers of the "psy-complex" police the threshold between acceptable and reprehensible parental, sexual, or legal acts. Further, through the production of the docile, self-regulating subject, they govern even thoughts, especially now through contemporary U.S. practices—but ever-expanding elsewhere—that tie services through legal or financial constraints to reporting of any disclosures deemed prosecutable. It is also clear how these policing practices impact on oppressed and disadvantaged individuals and groups—working class people, black people, women, gay men and lesbians, and so on—to further marginalize and stigmatize them.

We could turn all this around to show how scientific psychology operates within a closed (rigid and authoritarian) framework, exhibiting a pathological manic defense against perturbation of its core tenets. In making its theories and models in its own (white, male, middle-class, heterosexist) image and disallowing dissent, connection, or relationship between these isolated, asocial subjects, its practices of self-management turn out to be not only self-centered (centered on itself) but also self-censored. Perhaps this goes some way to explaining why psychologists (among the range of professions involved) are among the most fervent believers in, as well as dissenters from, the "psy-complex": after all, either way, our stakes our high.

But the explicit expulsion of passion and unreason from the well-guarded islands and castles of academic and (as I will argue) clinical psychology does more than displace these qualities onto devalued groups. In the effort to mask (or "whitewash") the invested and contested character of its research and therapeutic practices, and in the name of detachment and measurement, scientific psychology excises precisely that material that expresses, analytically and bodily, resistance to or difference from, its own body of theory. Like the psychopath, whose mythological diagnostic profile parodies the image of the white, controlled and controlling, hyperrational masculinity leading to profoundly irrational conclusions (Stowell-Smith, 1995), we could say that the madness psychology legislates upon in others is really its own.

But what do such critiques of traditional psychology mean for how we conduct our therapy or our research—or our daily lives, for that matter? Psychology currently admits only dead description of our actions and interactions, inert records of products not processes, and products constructed according to its own warped—or at best partial—imaginings. Only that which matches its categories can be recognized, and even then only in terms of equivalence or deficiency. The static character of its acts of judgment abstracts and reifies precisely that which should be our political and analytical focus. Resistance is always relational: resistance is to something. Without denying or romanticizing distress, we might want to claim, as Joel Kovel has done (Kovel, 1990), that to be distressed in an unjust and oppressive society is a more politically healthy condition than to be happy. An unscientific psychology should offer us alternative models and paint us new possibilities of how the power of psychology can be dismantled and how our work as psychologists can be reconfigured towards the work of personal and political emancipation and liberation.

METHOD AS A DISCIPLINARY PRACTICE OF POWER

I have already talked about the intimate relation between psychology's models and its methodological practices. Methods are the fetish of the psychologist, our only claim to disciplinary distinctiveness—such is the explicit claim to expertise that differentiates psychology from "mere" counselors, nurses, and social workers. Even claiming this was a struggle, as highlighted by Rose's (1990) account of how psychologists battled with doctors to win the franchise of expertise on testing. Tests of ability and adjustment drive home the power of psychology as a method-as-theory to define and categorize individuals and populations. An unscientific or progressive psychology clearly takes issue with the acts of privilege and exclusion psychology performs, by challenging the very foundations of method on which they are based—repudiating notions of generalizability, standardization, replicability, and so on that permit the abstraction and decontextualization of human action into disembodied response or outcome.

These arguments may be well rehearsed and uncontroversial to those committed to challenging psychology's complicity in oppressive practices. Or are they? The recent careers and relations between discourse and qualitative research in (at least British) psychology provides food for thought. After the emergence in the 1970s of the "new paradigm" in psychology (e.g., Reason and Rowan, 1981), qualitative approaches seemed to have acquired some (moral if not intellectual) respectability, with discourse work as a late successor moving the grounds of debate in the 1980s and 1990s from offering more complete or less distorted descriptions of the contents of people's minds to accounts of the textual structuring of subjectivity. With its antihumanist commitments and anti-individualism, discourse work challenged much qualitative psychology which was (and continues to be) deeply humanist and often individualist in character. As such, qualitative work tends to reproduce static categories of identities construed as separate and inherent (and putatively essential, but these days often only "strategically" so). These presumed separate identities could thus be related to each other only in additive terms, a combining rather than a more mutually molding and constitutive relation, reflecting the broader contemporary discourse of identity politics.

On the other hand, the destabilizing features of discourse work are often read by novice qualitative researchers as ironizing the material under analysis and, as such, as disrespectful to research participants (and this is a political choice that does, and should, guide selection of methodological approach). All this became more complicated during a brief moment in British psychology in the early 1990s when discourse work was considered synonymous with feminist psychology—by both proponents and opponents alike. Needless to say, this assumption needed to be dispelled not only because it was inaccurate but also because, where true, it was gaslighting (or marginalizing) explicitly feminist work. Further, it unhelpfully perpetuated the stereotypical gendering of research methods. This tendency to reinvent the method-theory opposition through an essentializing of feminist research as qualitative has increasingly been a site of feminist commentary (Pugh, 1990).

Whatever the differences, discourse and qualitative researchers have typically been united in their opposition to positivist psychology— although there are now signs that some varities of discourse work are starting to shed their critical qualities and be assimilated into traditional psychology through traditional claims to rigor and technique. Perhaps this is one reason why discourse research has seemed to be outflanked from the left by the qualitative research that it had presumed to have surpassed, and why qualitative work currently holds the radical edge, in British and European psychology at least, with a vast proliferation of new books on interviewing and other qualitative methods.

QUALITATIVE METHODS AND THE PSYCHOLOGICAL POLITICS OF "RACE" AND GENDER

Given psychology's disciplinary powers of persuasion to contain and deradicalize critique, I have recently been struck by how the transformative potential of research interventions, especially as conducted by students embarking on psychological training, lies primarily in the political commitment of the researcher rather than being ensured by any technical or methodological device (Burman, 1997). This is because the denial of the politics of method underscores the intimate relation between psychology's models and its methodological practices.

Nevertheless the quantitative legacies of normalization and pathologization have also informed the well-known patterns of overrepresentation, or alternatively absence, of cultural minorities and women in health and mental health services (Cochrane, 1977; Fernando, 1991; Ratna and Wheeler, 1995; Sashidaran and Francis, 1993). Qualitative research has been seen by researchers subscribing to a variety of theoretical orientations (health research, action research, feminist research) as a means of exploring how these statistical patterns arise, the stories of individual lives that lie behind them, as well as identifying practices that help to counter them. Thus a recent British book entitled *Researching Cultural Differences in Health* (Kelleher and Hillier, 1996) reports work that is almost entirely qualitative, with those few studies that use quantitative analyses combining this with qualitative approaches.

Similarly, students now approach me to conduct research elaborating the meanings behind the numbers—or at least to explore *accounts* of those meanings. I am going to draw on three small-scale pieces of research I have supervised that address intersections of "race," gender, and professional power relations. I aim to indicate how taking identifications as a topic within the research, rather than presuming them, can work to support feminist and antiracist mental health practice.

HELPING SILENCES SPEAK

But before I do that, I want to situate this work within the broader political project of attempting to identify and rectify those topics and sets of experiences that are marginalized or silenced within dominant culture. But, as much feminist and other critical work is now pointing out, the ushering into discourse of subordinated knowledges also creates its own difficulties. While the project of "giving voice" often inspires qualitative research into minority positions, it threatens to reproduce the very paternalistic relations it claims to dismantle, this by virtue of presuming the power to afford that "giving" of voice. Here the critiques of multiculturalism formulated from the mid 1980s (e.g., Sivanandan, 1985; Anthias and Yuval-Davis with Cain, 1993) as abstracting and essentializing "culture" remain relevant. They highlight how "culture" becomes transformed into a self-contained, politically docile training or educational package. What (in debates about British education) disparagingly has been called the "sari, samosa, and steel band" variety of cultural pluralism suffers from three major problems. First, it elides culture with religion; second, it equates culture with national identity; and third, and above all, this often state-sanctioned approach refuses to admit newly emerging and unstable cultural identities that connect with and transcend existing national and cultural categories.

In terms of research strategy, the alternative to claiming to "give voice" is that of documenting exclusions. This, too, is not without difficulties. It can work to fix those fields of activity and lived experiences, thus reiterating their status as other and excluded. Still worse is the problem of seeming to "speak for" the marginalized person or group, thus presuming their incapacity to speak for themselves, or even inadvertently appropriating those accounts to the researcher's agenda and ignoring projects and perspectives that diverge from it (Opie, 1992; Reay, 1996). There is also the risk of imposing some kind of representative status upon one's participants (albeit covertly) by claiming the general relevance of the accounts generated. Indeed this problem is overdetermined by the very term "voice," with its humanist invitation to bolster individualism or to reproduce the individual-society divide by reading off social categories from individual accounts. Correlatively, the incitement to discourse can itself be disempowering for already marginalized persons, for whom maintaining silence may well have proven a vital strategy of resistance (e.g., Bhavnani, 1990). In a similar vein, the current enthusiasm for participatory approaches in development work has been criticized as working to make visible power structures and informal networks of isolated and marginal communities in ways that render them more vulnerable to state manipulation and regulation (Parpart, 1995).

Overall, whether we want to position ourselves as helpful humanists or grim Foucauldians, we cannot afford to forget how each silence, as it is spoken, nevertheless initiates new silences and creates its own discursive occlusions. Just as the very silences that need to be spoken are themselves legacies of the institutionalization of identity politics, especially through state-sponsored varieties of multiculturalism, so each counterdiscourse to the dominant discourse runs a dual risk: first, of perpetuating that which it counters in the very act of its challenge; and so, second, thereby producing its own exclusions through its claims to authority.

Such are the set of problems that have preoccupied feminist researchers of late—framed, for example, within the problematic of "representing the other" (Wilkinson and Kitzinger, 1996). These have generated calls to attend to the *process* of "othering," that is, of producing or positioning some accounts as "other" (than ourselves). This move includes as a key part the theorizing of the participation and investments of the researcher who designated those accounts as "other." However, while the current focus on research as autobiography is valuable, it can also be viewed as the analogue of postmodern solipsism, threatening to reinvent bourgeois individualism in another name and to disallow any claims or efforts to intervene on behalf of "others." Rather than getting paralyzed by the theoretical conundra or terrorized into political inaction, I think we can use these critiques to inform, rather than proscribe, a critical and reflexive research practice. In particular, we cannot avoid consideration of the institutional positions we occupy as moderately privileged researchers that afford us the means to get certain accounts into circulation. The issue then becomes how to use the power that we can access in responsible and enabling ways, and to specify the means by which we can be held accountable for forms and relations of our interventions.

All this may sound more methodological, or even political, than theoretical. Yet as feminists, among others, have pointed out, these features are inextricably linked (Harding, 1993; Haraway, 1991). The project to explicate and articulate the covert cultural assumptions that underlie psychological and therapeutic models remains a relevant and useful critical research enterprise, and one that invites the application of interpretive approaches in psychology (see also Henwood and Phoenix, 1996).

COMMON THREADS: WOMEN'S STUDIES AND INTERCULTURAL PSYCHOTHERAPY

I now want to move on to discuss convergences of theory and practice between women's studies and intercultural therapy. This work of reading each alongside the other works to enrich both, especially as, so far as I can tell, these literatures have largely developed separately—albeit in relation to a common set of political-practical problems. In women's studies, discussions about racialized identities have recently turned to focus on the dominant, drawing on black critiques and deconstructionist approaches to elaborate how "whiteness" is the unmarked dominant term in relation to which blackness functions as the explicit token of "race." The interrogation of whiteness as a political category (e.g., Frankenberg, 1993), while not without its problems (Bonnett, 1997), has been advocated as a strategy to "color the non" ((charles), 1992), that is, to shift the burden of racialization away from those who typically carry it to those structurally positioned as its beneficiaries, i.e., white people.

Alongside this, another important set of theoretical initiatives has critiqued both the implicit whiteness and Anglo-Eurocentricity of second-wave feminism and the covert masculinity of the representation of "blackness." This has taken the form of historical studies that highlight the interweaving of European colonialism with feminism, such that missionizing or "doing good works" in India or Africa could be promoted as a "feminist" enterprise (in maintaining women's financial independence from men) (e.g., Ware, 1992), or of the complexities and contradictions of white women's relationships with black women (as in studies of mistress-servant relations). Three points have been drummed home (so to speak) from these studies. First, that racialized and gendered positions and identifications are not separate or fixed but are constructed in relation to each other. Thus, rather than portraying the cultural-political project in terms of the double (or triple) oppression experienced by (working-class) black women (or quadruple if we "add in" being lesbian, for example), the focus is now on exploring the *intersections* between "raced" and gendered identifications in terms of "race"-specific gender identities and gender-specific "raced" identities: that is, we can begin to address the gendering of racialization.

Second, these studies of specific historically and geographically situated contexts highlight how the gendered and racialized positions elaborated are produced and performed within particular situations, rather than somehow immanent to (thereby essentialized) categories of identity. This is useful because it can afford analysis of how particular formations of identity can fluctuate and be transformed, rather than be only sedimented (Mama, 1995; Bhavnani and Phoenix, 1994).

Third, further work has usefully elaborated this "cartography of the politics of intersectionality" (Brah, 1996: p. 16) to highlight how definitions of racialized and gendered identities are always also structured around relations of class and sexuality. Each of these dimensions has its own autonomy—so class relations fracture as well as converge with cultural identities, as highlighted, for example, by Adelman's (1995) work on Jewish women in domestic service within Jewish households in sixteenth- and seventeenth-century (what he calls "early modern") Italy. In Europe, North America, and—perhaps most obviously—in the new South Africa, class differences are highly racialized, while sexuality has long been a potent ingredient in racism and colonialism (McClintock, 1995). Similarly, Yuval-Davis and others have clarified how configurations of national identity presume particular sets of gendered and sexual arrangements (Yuval-Davis, 1997). More conceptually, the ways in which racism and sexism can be regarded as analogous or as asymmetrical has become a recent site of analysis (Zack, 1996).

These conceptual, often historical, debates in women's studies may seem a far cry from critical psychology or psychotherapy. Yet I believe they offer useful insights to and parallels with discussions of psychotherapy. Psychotherapy research has for too long retained a commitment to positivist methodologies, as if warranting its subscription to inappropriate approaches as a bizarre form of methodological triangulation. Quantitative measurement of salient factors in the success of psychotherapeutic models or relationships has, by definition, fixed the gender, class, racialized, and even sexual dynamics that form the very material under scrutiny within psychotherapy (Tharp, 1991; Tyler, Susswell, and Williams-McCoy, 1985). The acknowledgment of specific issues faced by black people in mental health services has often reified and racialized class and cultural issues, to produce fixed and homogeneous representations of black identities—as separate from gender, sexuality, and class (Sue and Zane, 1987; Thomas, 1995).

Thus the methods of research are themselves inscribed by and perpetuate such representations. In an equally self-confirming manner, the institutional response advocated is that of "matching" client with "like" therapist: so, black with black; woman with woman, and so on. But a moment's reflection illuminates the stupidity and impossibility of such measures. Just as identity-politics feminism enjoined women to stack up their proliferating sets of identities (conceived of as separate and additive), so the list of possible factors by which therapist and client could be "matched" lengthens to absurd proportions. Clearly there are practical limits which in daily practice govern the extent to which such "matches" will be made (and certainly in the U.K. the current shortage of black therapists alone makes a mockery of such proposals). But beyond this, it is important to clarify the political and conceptual problems obscured but maintained by this approach. I will mention four such problems here.

First, categories of identification are essentialized, that is, treated as ahistorical constants. Second, the "blackness" or other factor according to which therapist and client are "matched" is presumed as a transparent, common characteristic that itself does cultural violence to both participants. Hence, as Noreen Sheikh (1996) discusses, in current state-of-the-art so-called "ethnosensitive" mental health services in Britain, client and therapist may be presumed "matched" by virtue of the latter having some (but by no means necessarily fluent) facility in a minority community language, irrespective of generational differences, status as first- or second-generation immigrant, gender, or religious or cultural identification. Third, not only are we seeing here the reification of culture (often elided with religion), but also the ghettoization of black people in mental health services as a "minority" concern. Once again black people are stereotyped as responsible for "their own" communities—irrespective of personal affiliation, and reiterating the incoherent and reactionary representation of communities as separate. Moreover, all this ignores not only newly emerging categories of cultural identification (e.g., of British Asian or Black British) but also the impact of modern industrialization in globalizing forms of subjectivity and corresponding dis-eases of subjectivity (e.g., Littlewood, 1995). Finally, the attribution of cultural congruity always threatens to efface power tensions and inequalities *within* communities. So a young, black, woman therapist might be deemed inappropriate to work with an older man, or may not be taken seriously as a professional because her family is known to the client. Nor can the upholding of cultural specificity take place without the risk of reproducing broader relations of cultural dominance—as where a client may feel he or she is not being offered the best or proper therapy when faced with a black practitioner (Kareem and Littlewood, 1992; Sheikh, 1996; Gowrisunkur, personal communication, 1996).

Let me make clear that I fully support the development of autonomous black or culturally specific services. However, their current organization and resourcing are such that all too often they function tokenistically: both in terms of the delivery of their own services and, where funded from within the statutory sector, because they function to provide a useful rhetorical "blackwash" of an otherwise predominantly white service, both conceptually and staff-wise.

There are deeper conceptual problems that tend to be obscured or presumed resolved by the device of matching. This is because cultural matching as an intervention focuses on changing the mode of delivery of services rather than the process or content of what is being delivered. It is thus subject to the same sets of limitations as early varieties of transcultural psychiatry and counseling which focused more on questions of access to services (by, for example, working with interpreters or conducting therapy in a minority language), rather than engaging in a broader, more conceptual reevaluation of the cultural relevance and adequacy of what was on offer (e.g., Mercer, 1987). (Nor can it be presumed that notions of "relevance" or "adequacy" are either self-evident or politically innocent; Dawes, 1986). Either way, the models underlying therapy tend to remain presumed as transcending cultural particularity. The question of the universality of therapeutic models—along with other grand narratives of (white, masculinist) development is now an explicit topic of debate (e.g., Kurtz, 1992; Littlewood, 1992).

It is in this context that intercultural counseling and therapy has developed, mobilizing many of the same arguments as those elaborated in women's studies but specifically in relation to therapeutic models and practices. It is beyond the scope of this essay to outline and evaluate the tenets of approaches to intercultural therapy (but see Kareem and Littlewood, 1992). My more limited concerns here are with the convergences of the two conceptual frameworks, and the practical benefits of combining the two for feminist research in psychotherapy. In particular, feminist and intercultural approaches share a commitment to a notion of culture that does not treat only minoritized peoples as bearing ethnicity. Nor is intercultural therapy something that is an alternative to black-on-black (or white-on-white) therapy, although it is often seen in this way. Rather, intercultural therapy highlights the negotiation of cultural identifications as they inevitably arise within and throughout a therapeutic relationship (Kareem, 1992).

It is important to note that this is not some new brand or model of therapy. In this sense, intercultural therapy does not suffer from the problems that attend claims for, for example, black psychology—which, in the act of elaborating a separate form of psychology, always threatens either to reinvent features of the dominant Anglo-U.S. psychology under another name, particularly by uncritical subscription to its methods (Mama, 1995), or to ignore how, simply by virtue of its oppositional status, it is informed by the structure of that which it seeks to counter. As I understand them, intercultural approaches do not claim to have invented new conceptual models, but rather offer critical and additional "takes" on the existing repertoire of therapeutic approaches, although perhaps for pragmatic issues of accessibility and as primarily practiced in the voluntary sector in Britain, they seem to lean towards brief analytic work. While (with some notable exceptions, e.g., Holland, 1995) this work can be criticized for failing to take gender sufficiently seriously as a structural dimension of racialization, it does seem that there are possibilities of putting the two sets of ideas—from women's studies and intercultural therapy—to work together.

MORE ON THE POLITICS OF (RE)REPRESENTATION

At the beginning of this essay I indicated that I would be connecting my discussion of the politics of method as relating to debates in both women's studies and intercultural therapy with comments about some research projects. Yet the project of telling you about these studies produces precisely the same set of interpretive and political problems—around culture and power—that I have just outlined. Let me focus these problems around two sets of questions.

A first difficulty is one of suddenly seeming to talk traditional psychology: of case studies and procedures. How can I discuss these research projects without subscribing to a positivist narrative of numbers and classifications—precisely those that in other contexts I want to challenge? Yet I would argue that what is under contest here is not the existence of numbers and classifications but the broader frameworks within which they are situated: their reification and abstraction into the samples, factors, and conditions of scientific psychology.

The second—more serious—problem is this. How can I presume to represent the work of these students to you without appropriating either their work or their "voices?" Am I not vulnerable to the charge of exploitation, of taking advantage of my position as their supervisor to speak for them and to benefit from their labor? Is there anything I can say which would do more than "protest too much" and avoid taking responsibility for the structural inequalities of the supervisory relationship?

More specifically, how can I describe these students' work (even as their "work" rather than their "findings") without reproducing traditional power relations that map onto the (capitalist and patriarchal) mental-manual division of labor (their labor, my ideas)? Even this account positions me as omniscient supervisor legislating upon the "experience" of my supervisees—a position that, first, ignores or downgrades the reciprocal character of the supervisory relationship, through which I learnt as much as my supervisees as we worked together on their projects; second, this apparent appropriation of experience/labor is made all the more invidious by the convergence within two of the three studies with dominant power relations configured around "race," as also reproduced by the use of black women's writings in (white?) women's studies.

One response would be to say that I was an active co-constructor of the accounts produced in these studies (a position we adopt in Aitken and Burman, 1999) in the sense that the analyses were a joint production. While the register of scientific psychology would interpret this as an undermining of the students' individual achievements (and thus I would not mobilize this account in another setting), here I want to point out how to do otherwise would be to deny the sociohistorical process of the joint (but not equal) production of the research.

Clearly, being an involved party does not give me the right to own or speak for this work (especially as its supervisor, given the long and lamentable tradition in psychology of supervisors stealing their students research). Another way of addressing this would be to claim that this is my story: my story of their story. In doing this, as ever, pluralism threatens to obscure the maintenance of prevailing power relations. The proliferation of stories invited here also threatens to reproduce individualism (the individualism of psychology, reiterated within psychology's representation of the researcher as singular and without "race" or gender): you have your story; I have mine.

But this disallows a shared story. Instead, without sidestepping the inequalities of power and our different positions and perspectives on this research, I want to claim that this *is* a shared story; but it is not the only story. Clearly the students and I each have a plethora of diverging stories of the research—not least that I was the supervisor and they were the students, although my impression is that these were not always the paramount issues at play in the relationship. This is an agreed account, drafted by me and accepted by them, to be told to you (but see Aitken and Burman, 1999, and Sangha, Burman, and Gowrisunkur, 1996, for accounts authored primarily by the researchers themselves). Once again we are in the business of partial narratives, contested but intersecting identities, and alliances forged rather than presumed.

I can only wish that Noreen, Kuljeet, and Gill were able to talk to you themselves. But risky as it is (and it does feel—politically rather than only personally—risky), I want to talk about this work because I believe it is so important, and because it needs to be talked about. Local and situated as these studies are (for topologies of "race" are surely a key barometer of political histories and geographies), I want to argue that, paradoxically, in their specificity, they have a general relevance for unscientific psychologists. I want to use the privilege of my position here to talk about these studies, and the interpretive and political issues of representation and accountability this imports are not only no greater than those undertaken by the students themselves in their research reporting practices, but are also no excuse for not doing the political work. The current vogue for autobiography in feminist research misses the point: the point is that feminist research aims for more than (rather than, as with traditional psychology, denying) autobiography.

Departing from scientific psychology may have robbed our representations of ourselves and others of their simplicity, but these simplifications (into quantifiable variables) were cruel. Having said all this, how—practically—can I describe these projects? There can be no innocent, transparent linear account, as in the predictable journal article format—design, sample, procedure, and so on. But narratives—even little stories—do have temporality, so here's a first description, and others will follow. (I am reminded here of another researcher's—Jane Marshall's—analysis of the different accounts of her study produced for different audiences and at different stages of development of the project, Marshall, 1995).

The three projects I draw on were all conducted under my supervision as part of postgraduate degrees. I encouraged the researchers to meet with each other, and I like to think that this mutual knowledge also acted to support each of them in their individual work, highlighting here too the value of working towards similar goals across differences and challenging the isolation and individualism of research. (Clearly there is also an equivalent tale of working across differences of professional and radicalized power differences that could be told about the process of supervision.)

The first project, conducted for her MSc by Kuljeet Sangha, a British-born South Asian woman, was based on the analysis of the accounts of two women of South Asian background who were referred to a local National Health Service (NHS) psychotherapy service, and juxtaposed their perspectives with those of three providers of therapy working in different institutional settings: NHS, private, and voluntary sector (Sangha, 1996; Sangha et al., 1996).

The second project, conducted by Noreen Sheikh as part of her MSc in Psychology and Counseling, involved interviews between herself and eight other self-identified black women, mental health professionals within one health authority of the NHS, focusing on the ways they represented the relationship between their gendered and radicalized identifications within their accounts of their practice (Sheikh, 1996).

The third project was conducted by Gill Aitken, a white woman who already possessed a doctorate and who had given up an academic post to do clinical psychology training. As a feminist antiracist activist, she wanted to devote her clinical doctorate to researching black women's access to and experiences of clinical psychological services in the area (having already conducted a statistical audit of who used the psychological services, Aitken, 1996c, 1996d). Owing to the paucity of black women referrals to services (which made the issue of documenting absences a crucial topic, as is ever the case in researching black perspectives within mainstream institutions, Ullah, 1995; Wheeler, 1994), her study focused primarily on a single case study of the accounts of a client, her referrer, and the therapist of the process of the therapy. In this essay I will draw particularly on the therapist's and client's accounts (but see Aitken, 1996a, 1996b; Aitken and Burman, 1999).

FROM BINARY IDENTITIES TO INTERSECTING (AND SHIFTING) IDENTIFICATIONS

Having introduced the projects, I will now explore how theoretical debates and commitments around gender and intercultural issues entered into their conduct. Beyond those issues of (self) representation I have already discussed, I want to explore three further issues that exemplify in this crucial practical arena the relevance of conceptualizing identities as relational and intersecting for professional practice in mental health.

The study that forms my main focus here was conducted by Aitken, a white woman clinical psychologist in training, who was studying black women's referrals to and engagement with clinical psychological services. Here I focus on the relationships set up between a (self-defined) black woman client, her white woman therapist, and the researcher, as she documented and participated in the process of the therapy by interviewing therapist and client four times before, during, and after the eleven-month therapy. This is not only a very unusual research design, but one which is also fraught with ethical problems around the containing of confidential information and maintenance of therapeutic boundaries, alongside a commitment to challenge and change oppressive professional practices (see Aitken, 1996b; Aitken and Burman, 1999). Yet these "problems" also gave rise to political and therapeutic resources and opportunities. I will move between account of the research and commentary upon it, to tease out three theoreticopolitical points at issue, and, where appropriate, will juxtapose this with aspects of the two other projects.

Shifts around "Race"

First, Gill Aitken's project was explicitly presented as an exploration around the role of radicalized and gendered identities in therapy; with the researcher presenting herself as white, she nevertheless found herself unstably racially positioned. An important focus of the researcher's discussions with the client was not only her own preparedness to adopt an explicitly antiracist stance (and covertly to support the client's ability to ask questions of her therapist concerning this and the therapeutic model in use), but also to take responsibility for raising the issue of "race" and racism as a feature of their own relationship.

The value of not presuming the facticity and stability of radicalized identities—by methodological design or conceptual framework—emerged when the researcher noted that the client's comments about "white people" seemed sometimes to include and sometimes to exclude the researcher. She started to wonder whether this was out of fear of offending her by implicating her directly with racism, or out of some sense of commonality forged through their previous, lengthy interviews. When, to illustrate her own account of her experience of cultural marginalization and perspective on the interrelations of gendered and national identities, she disclosed that she held joint German-British nationality, the client's comment was "I thought you weren't English," and thereafter—also after the researcher further disclosed having a Jewish background—the client noticeably did not include her within the category white. The researcher then discovered that the client subscribed to U.S.-influenced perspectives that position people of Jewish origins as nonwhite (or as people "of color"), thus paving the way for further discussion of the varieties and ambiguities of radicalized positions (see Aitken, 1996b).

This raises two issues relevant to my concerns here. First, the instabilities of racial categorization within the process of the interview were never entirely resolved and were always under negotiation. Second, this episode highlights the importance of avoiding attributions that fix or define the meanings and categories of black/white. This is not a call to avoid or deny differences—especially as structural power relationships—but to attend to how these are played out within and through the complex of prevailing but intersecting power dynamics.

All this highlights how radicalized identifications can be explored as a topic while not presuming them to be constant in their definition or meaning. Similar issues around shifts and ambiguities of (self- and other-defined) classifications also arose in this study in interviews with another woman client who identified as "mixed race" (but declined service involvement after being outraged to discover she had been differently racially classified), where the politics of different identifications in terms of community participation, involvement with family, and choice of partner figured prominently (Aitken, 1996b).

Further, such negotiations are not peculiar to research relations conducted across socially acknowledged differences of radicalized identifications. They also happen to self-identified black researchers for whom the issue of claiming commonality with other black women in exploring women's experiences of racism—in this case in mental health services—cannot be presumed. Here, too, the socially marked "differences" of color entered into the research as well as into professional-client relationships (Sheikh, 1996). This work echoes Lewis's (1996) interviews with black women social workers that highlighted the variability and relative salience of radicalized and gendered positionings in their accounts.

In the case of Kuljeet Sangha's study of clients' and providers' perspectives of psychotherapeutic services, the fact of the apparent convergence of gender and radicalized positions between the researcher and the clients facilitated the fluctuating of the point of commonality in focus: so sometimes gendered identifications were more prominent than radicalized ones. Further and significantly, within this context of researching from a position of radicalized similarity (although there were major differences of religious and cultural background), racism in the provision of therapy at no time surfaced as an explicit topic. In fact, class figured as much more of an issue, underscoring how all too often class is neglected in favor of the more "visible" difference of "race," and their intersections ignored. Of even more interest (and relevance to current debates about "matching"), clients did not express a particular interest in or desire for being in therapy with another black woman, and reported receiving great support from the white woman practitioners they had seen. Rather, the issue of theoretical model (humanist versus psychoanalytic) emerged as more salient to the women's experience of therapy. Thus, as providers, we cannot presume to know how our clients define themselves or define us, or what their self-definitions mean for the kind of service they want or need. No amount of factor analysis or "matching" of variables can replace consulting with the clients themselves, nor can we expect "consistency" in the perceived or reported salience of the radicalized and gendered dynamics of therapy.

Researcher as Activist

Research always does more than research. Such is the non-sense of the discourse of contamination or confounding of variables of so-called scientific psychology. I move now to consider how the range of positions spanned by the researchers in these projects acted as interventions to change the mental health services provided.

In the case of the project with black mental health workers, this worked to consolidate emerging support networks of black women professionals in this area. The project concerned with both provider and client accounts contributed to cross-professional initiatives already under way to highlight the cultural and gender issues within mental health services, and appeared to engender further sensitization to these issues—not only for the participants concerned but also, with more general reverberations, throughout the institutions from which they were drawn.

In terms of the project primarily "tracking through" client and therapist perspectives, the researcher was also intervening in at least three other ways. In relation to the client, the process of the interviews worked first, to model and rehearse for the client ways of asking her therapist about the theoretical orientation of the service she was receiving, and second, to initiate discussion about issues of race/culture, both in terms of the avowed position of the therapist and the presuppositions of her model. Third, the researcher also highlighted issues of gender and sexuality as well as racialization in ways that the client, by the "official" end of the research (for the project still continues in other ways), claimed not to have thought through before.

In relation to the therapist, this project acted as a support for her commitment to changing practice and as an instigator of change. She reported finding the interviews a useful space to reflect and talk issues through, and saw the transcripts as providing a form of internal supervision. Indeed, the research itself clarified for her how she lacked supervisory support to take the issues of addressing cultural specificities forward, and as a result she helped set up a professional forum for this purpose.

Clearly, a project that followed the process of a therapy in the form of interviewing both parties to it also impacted on that therapy. Here some of the most delicate ethical and methodological issues arise. From the accounts, the researcher could hear how issues explored in one dyad were taken up in another; indeed it could be argued that the research became an integral part of, as well as adjunct to, the therapy. This, of course, is a far cry from the traditional role of researcher as detached observer. So, in her interviews with the researcher, the therapist recounted how the client would comment on how she (the client) interacted differently when with the researcher. Further, the therapist attributed the client becoming more challenging about professional and cultural assumptions to the client having "had another session with" the researcher (Aitken and Burman, 1999).

Correlatively, the fact that this was a therapeutic as well as a research project also entered into the forms and accounts of the project—so that the client has chosen not to write about the experience of being part of this research with the therapist in case she returns to the service and works with her therapeutically again. Most important, it seemed that the research helped to provide a basis for therapist and client to explore cultural limitations of existing (cognitive analytic) models and to start elaboration of ways of reconceptualizing these in more appropriate ways. So here we have an example of collaborative practice initiating reflection upon and transformation of psychological models (Aitken and Other, in preparation). Finally, more broadly, the setting up of the study drew attention to the sad but largely predictable absence of black women being referred to clinical psychology services (irrespective of the racial-ethnic composition of the areas served by referrers or, indeed, the racial background of the referrers themselves). As a result of this work, the professionals involved have reported changing their practice through their involvement in the study, the client participants have continued to meet with each other and with the researcher, and all participants are planning further writing and research projects together.

Researcher as Co/Nonprofessional

The fact of conducting a research project cannot be isolated from other identities or professional positions the researcher assumes or occupies. It was my impression that as both a South Asian woman and a (moderately) independent researcher outside the providing services, Kuljeet Sangha was spontaneously more explicitly challenging to the therapists over the cultural and gendered assumptions of their therapeutic orientation. She both identified and was probably perceived as an advocate for the women clients she interviewed. On the other hand, her position as nontherapist meant that she could only sympathize with the women's accounts rather than answer their questions about the services. In the second study, conducted by Noreen Sheikh, the researcher was positioned as a coprofessional, researching with women working in similar positions and with similar issues. This gave rise to a sharing of strategies and experiences, alongside an exploration of cultural and historical as well as professional differences between them.

The third, Gill Aitken's, project was perhaps more complicated. She was positioned as a training professional (in the same profession as the therapist whose practice she studied) as well as a researcher; and she was therefore explicitly institutionally allied with the therapist as well as positioning herself as politically allied with the client. She drew on her professional knowledge to interpret the accounts of the therapist-client relationship, and could appreciate and discuss professional dilemmas posed for the therapist over pressure from the client for disclosure of political affiliation or departure from current models. A major issue for the researcher here concerned the withholding of information, such as not prematurely closing the client's concern with the political orientation of the therapist by reassuring her that the therapist was in fact at the forefront of antiracist initiatives in her profession. Indeed it would be a sobering research topic to explore how a therapist's felt and active commitment may fail to be conveyed to her client.

Hence the particular cultural and professional positions of the researchers—as espoused by or imposed upon them—all interacted in vital ways to determine their particular realization. It is impossible to speculate whether "the same" issues would or could have arisen had the studies been conducted by three other women drawn from either similar or different cultural-political backgrounds (or indeed, supervised by someone else). Such would be to engage in the scientific discourse of reliability, replicability, and so on. At another level, scientific psychology's response is not only facile, but—as ever—misses the point. The point here is that, irrespective of the particular configurations of relationships, it is inevitable that issues of radicalized and gendered positions (and many others too) will enter into therapy and research relationships—not only in prescribing their initial form but as a vital and intersecting feature of the research/therapeutic power relation.

It is also inevitable and often desirable that research has "effects"; not only do we have to admit that as researchers we too (like those we research) have passions and commitments, but that no research is devoid of these, so the sooner we sort this out and take responsibility for what we do, the better. Finally, we may be researchers and therapists, but we also always inhabit other identities and positions—of gender, "race," class, and sexuality, for example. These enter into not only the what and why of our work, but also the how: how we act and how we are perceived. It is unhelpful and sometimes racist and sexist, for example, to abstract categories of identity and presume that in any particular setting, one (e.g., professional) position takes priority over another. On the other hand, it can be equally racist and sexist to presume that it cannot. Both can happen, especially when we consider research as a relationship, a process with history and duration and thus with lots of scope for fluctuation and change within albeit socially determined positions. When we depart from the precepts of scientific psychology we are no longer bound by the principle of noncontradiction. Indeed it seems that it is only by admitting such contradictions that we will begin to do justice (in more senses than one) to the complexity and contested character of the cultural-political relations within which we exist.

CHALLENGING THE "DRESS CODE"

So far I've talked about how conceptual debates about method connect with some examples of mental health research. Let me now return to consider how the issues encountered in these projects can inform our (apparently) methodological debates to see how these figure in un/scientific psychology.

Method Codes for Politics

I want to end by cautioning against the dressing up of antiracist work as "qualitative" psychology. Debates about the adequacy of qualitative methods are all too often equated with resistance to challenges to dominant knowledges and practices posed by their exposing structures of marginalization. It seems that in Britain the cutting edge of those debates lies within clinical psychology and psychotherapy. Of the three studies I have discussed in this essay, I want to finish with some comments about the process of Gill Aitken's project, which illustrates so clearly the possibilities of working across radicalized and professional differences. This study is of particular importance to my concerns here because, as a project conducted as part of a clinical psychology training, it became the site of a protracted struggle. This was notwithstanding the outstanding success of the project as a piece of action research and the fact—perhaps also as an indication of how little work is done on "race" and cultural issues in clinical psychology—that Gill was rapidly enlisted into many of the committees and training fora in this area that exist within clinical psychology in Britain.

Doubtless the fact that the course had recently shifted from an exclusively behavioral to a cognitive behavioral orientation and (unlike other British clinical psychology courses) that there was no prior history of any qualitative research (hence my involvement as an external supervisor) made this clearly a test case. As if to concentrate the examiners' critical gaze further, the clinical psychology qualification was in its first phases of moving from master's to doctorate status (part of the current drive for professional upgrading), with the key difference supposedly arising from some ineffable (and undefined) admixture of the length and quality of the dissertation. While this is a particular story, I tell it in the belief that it is an index of both what we have to struggle against and what we can do: of regulation and resistance.

It seems no accident that it was in this specific context of professionalization that debates about "method" became so vexed and vicious. Indeed, that this challenge goes beyond this individual study was highlighted by a three-day conference specifically concerned with qualitative research in clinical psychology, held in Wales in September 1997, in which Gill and I both participated. But the key point I want to make here is that the struggle over methods was merely the domain over which the battle over power relations and critical interventions in clinical psychology was being played out. The key political issue is whether and how clinical psychology can address the conceptual and practical problems of the cultural limitations of its models, modes of delivery, and even access for black people.

The suppression of critical and participatory approaches to research threatens to marginalize further the vital debate on racism in psychological practices. However, we do a disservice to the interventions this critical qualitative research seeks to initiate if we allow the struggles involved to remain presented as a problem of *methodological* credibility (Burman, 1996). There is clearly much more at stake. If we get diverted into merely defending a methodological approach, then not only have we committed the classical political error of mistaking strategy for principle, but we have also colluded in diverting the key arena of contest from politics to method. An unscientific psychology should be a politics of psychology, not a methodological approach to it.

Beyond Cozy Collusions

If qualitative research is to fulfill the radical claims made for it, then researchers need to attend to two key issues. First, they should recognize their progressive politics as driving, rather than already structured within, their methods. There is indeed no necessary antithesis—in either political direction—between quantitative and qualitative research. Both are potentially as "scientific" or "unscientific" as each other. Rather, the issue becomes how we choose to use them, and what we do.

Second, sameness is not a prerequisite for successful research or therapy. My accounts of these research projects have, I hope, indicated how difference can be the starting point from which joint identifications can be forged. The conception of identifications as intersecting—that is, as multiple, fluid, and negotiated across different axes of power—affords ways of representing personal and political change that do not necessarily lead to the disappearance of political agency but, rather, produce varieties of agencies and provisional alliances.

I have tried to show how postmodern and feminist accounts of subjectivity as fragmentary and relational can be useful resources for analyzing research and therapeutic relationships. Taking difference as the starting point highlights the negotiated and unstable character of alliances, and their status as never entirely secure. However, in a divided, unstable, and contested world, working with this framework may be the best we can do, so that acknowledging these differences of identification and power can strengthen and develop feminist and antiracist practice in psychology and psychotherapy.

NOTES

1. I want to acknowledge here the innovative and courageous work of Gill Aitken, Kuljeet Sangha, and Noreen Sheikh, whose studies inspire my comments here. Their comments on this essay have also improved it, helping me to

think again about working (including writing) in this complicated field. Our thanks go also to their anonymous but central research participants. Finally I want to acknowledge Jaya Gowrisunkur, who acted as clinical supervisor to Kuljeet and with whom I am now developing further work in this area.

REFERENCES

Adelman, H. (1995). Servants and sexuality: Seduction, surrogacy, and rape: Some observations concerning class, gender and race in early modern Italian Jewish families. In T. Rudavsky (Ed.), *Gender and Judaism: the transformation of tradition*. New York and London: New York University Press.

Aitken, G. (1996a). The covert disallowing/discrediting of qualitative research: Exploring black women's referrals to, and engagement in, clinical psychology services. *Changes: An International Journal of Psychology and Psychotherapy* (Special Issue: Tensions and Debates in Qualitative Research), *14(3)*, 192–198.

Aitken, G. (1996b). *Exploring "race" and gender in referrals to, and engagement in, clinical psychology services*. Thesis submitted to University of Manchester for Clinical Psychology Doctorate, UK, submitted July, awarded March 1997.

Aitken, G. (1996c). Issues for clinical psychology training in relation to people of African Caribbean and Asian origins. Unpublished Small Scale Research Project No. 2, held at Department of Clinical Psychology, University of Manchester, UK.

Aitken, G. (1996d). "Racial"/ethnic/cultural issues in relation to clinical psychology service provision within Central Manchester—a preliminary study. Unpublished Small Scale Research Project No. 2, held at Department of Clinical Psychology, University of Manchester, UK.

Aitken, G., and Burman, E. (1999). Keeping and crossing professional and radicalized boundaries: Challenges and possibilities for feminist practice. *Psychology of Women Quarterly* (Special Issue: Innovative Issues in Feminist Research), *23*, 277–297.

Aitken, G., and Other (in preparation). Introducing the social into CAT (Cognitive Analytic Therapy).

Anthias, F., and Yuval-Davis, N., with Cain, H. (1993). *Radicalized boundaries: Race, nation, gender, color and class and the antiracist struggle*. London: Routledge.

Bhavnani, K., (1990). What's power got to do with it? Empowerment and social research. In I. Parker and J. Shotter (Eds.) *Deconstructing social psychology*. (pp. 141–152). London: Routledge.

Bhavnani, K., and Phoenix, A. (Eds.). (1994). *Shifting identities, shifting racism*. London: Sage.

Bonnett, A. (1997). Constructions of whiteness in European and American antiracism. In P. Werbna and T. Madood (Eds.), *Debating cultural hybridity: Multi-cultural identities and the politics of anti-racism* (pp.173–192). London: Zed Books.

Brah, A. (1996). *Cartographies of diaspora: Contesting identities*. London: Routledge.

Burman, E. (1996). Psychologizing "race"and gender. Paper presented at British Psychological Society Annual Conference, Brighton (April).

Burman, E. (1997). Minding the gap: Psychology and the politics of qualitative research. *Journal of Social Issues, 53 (4)*, 785–801.

Burman, E., Gowrisunkur, J., and Sangha, K. (1998). Conceptualizing radicalized and gendered identities in mental health services. *European Journal of Psychotherapy, Counselling and Health, 1(2)*, 231–256.

(charles), H. (1992). Whiteness—the relevance of politically coloring the "non." In H. Hinds, A. Phoenix, and J. Stacey (Eds.), *Working out: New directions in women's studies* (pp. 29–35). London: The Falmer Press.

Cochrane, R. (1977). Mental illness in immigrants to England and Wales: An analysis of mental hospital admissions. *Social Psychiatry, 12*, 23–35.

Dawes, A. (1986). The notion of relevant psychology with particular reference to Africanist pragmatic initiatives. *Psychology in Society, 5*, 28–48.

Fernando, S. (1991). *Mental health, race and culture*. London: Macmillan.

Fernando, S. (1995). *Mental health in a multi-ethnic society*. London: Routledge.

Frankenberg, R. (1993). *White women, race matters*. London: Routledge.

Gowrisunkur, J., (in preparation). Managing organizational change towards the promotion of multicultural psychotherapeutic practice.

Gowrisunkur, J. and Burman, E. (in preparation). Ethnic minority women and psychological treatments: Shifting stances towards equitable practice.

Haraway, D. (1991). Situated knowledges: Feminist epistemology and the privilege of partial perspective. In *Simians, cyborgs and women*. London: Verso.

Harding, S. (1993). Rethinking feminist standpoint epistemology: What is strong objectivity? In L. Alcott and E. Potter (Eds.), *Feminist epistemologies* (pp. 48–82). London: Routledge.

Henwood, K., and Phoenix, A. (1996). Race in psychology: Teaching the subject. *Ethnic & Racial Studies, 19 (4)*, 841–863.

Holland, S. (1995). Interaction in women's mental health and neighbourhood development. In S. Fernando (Ed.), *Mental health in a multi-ethnic society* (pp.36–50). London: Routledge.

Kareem, J. (1992). The Nafsiyat intercultural therapy centre: Ideas and experience in intercultural therapy. In J. Kareem and R. Littlewood, (Eds.),

Intercultural therapy: Themes, interpretations and practice (pp. 14–37). Oxford, UK: Blackwell.

Kareem, J., and Littlewood, R. (Eds.). (1992). Intercultural therapy: Themes, interpretations and practice. Oxford, UK: Blackwell.

Kelleher, D., and Hillier, S. (Eds.). (1996). Researching cultural differences in health. London: Routledge.

Kurtz, S. (1992). All the mothers are one: Hindu India and the cultural reshaping of psychoanalysis. New York: Columbia University Press.

Kovel, J. (1990). What is true mental health? Paper presented at Social services in changing South Africa, OASSSA Fourth National Conference Proceedings. Johannesburg: Organization for Appropriate Social Services of South Africa.

Lewis, G. (1996). Situated voices: Black women's "experience" and social work. Feminist Review, 53, 24–56.

Littlewood, R. (1992). How universal is something we call therapy? In J. Kareem and R. Littlewood, (Eds.). Intercultural therapy: Themes, interpretations and practice (pp.38–56). Oxford, UK: Blackwell.

Littlewood, R. (1995). Psychopathology and personal agency: Modernity, culture change and eating disorders in South Asian societies. British Journal of Medical Psychology, 68, 45–63.

Mama. A. (1995). Beyond the masks. London: Routledge.

Marshall, J. (1995). Heavy periods: The process of collusion and compromise in research. In E. Burman, P. Alldred, C. Bewley, B. Goldberg, C. Heenan, D. Marks, J. Marshall, K. Taylor, R. Ullah and S. Warner. Challenging women: Psychology's exclusions, feminist possibilities (pp. 73–89). Buckingham, UK: Open University Press.

McClintock, A. (1995). Imperial leather: Race, gender and sexuality in the colonial contest. London: Routledge.

Mercer, K. (1987). Race and transcultural psychiatry. In P. Miller and N. Rose (Eds.). Power of psychiatry (pp. 111–142). London; Routledge.

Opie, A. (1992). Qualitative research: Appropriation of the "other" and empowerment. Feminist Review, 40, 52–69.

Parpart, J. (1995). Deconstructing the development "expert": Gender, development and the "vulnerable groups." In H. Marchand and J. Parpart (Eds.). Feminism/Postmodernism/Development (pp. 221–243). London: Routledge.

Pugh, A. (1990). My statistics and feminism: A true story. In L. Stanley (Ed.) Feminist Praxis. London: Routledge.

Ratna, L., and Wheeler, M. (1995). "Race" and gender issues in adult psychiatry. In C. Burck and B. Speed (Eds.), Gender, power and relationship (pp. 136–152). London: Sage.

Reason, P. and Rowan, J. (Eds.) (1981). *Human inquiry: A sourcebook of new paradigm research*. Chichester, U. K.: Wiley.

Reay, D. (1996). Insider perspectives or stealing the words out of women's mouths: Interpretation in the research process. *Feminist Review, 53*, 57–73.

Rose, N. (1990). *Governing the soul*. London: Routledge.

Sangha, K. (1996). *Asian women and psychotherapy: Professional and client perspectives*. Unpublished dissertation for MSc Psychology (by Research), The Manchester Metropolitan University, Manchester, UK.

Sangha, K., Burman, E., and Gowrisunkur, J. (1996). Asian women and psychotherapy: A meeting of minds or a clash of cultures? Paper presented to the Psychotherapy Research Association, Ravenscar, UK, March.

Sashidaran, S., and Francis, E. (1993). Epidemiology, ethnicity and schizophrenia. In W. Ahmad (Ed.). *"Race" and health in contemporary Britain* (pp. 96–113). Buckingham: Open University Press.

Sheikh, N. (1996). *Black women professionals in mental health services: An interview study*. Dissertation in part fulfillment of MSc Psychology, The Manchester Metropolitan University, Manchester, UK.

Sivanandan, A. (1985). RAT and the degradation of black struggle. *Race and Class, XXVI(4)*, 1–33.

Stowell-Smith, M. (1995). *Race, psychopathy and subjectivity*. Unpublished PhD thesis, The Manchester Metropolitan University, Manchester, UK.

Sue, S., and Zane, N. (1987). The role of culture and cultural techniques in psychotherapy: A critique and reformulation. *American Psychologist, 42*, 37–45.

Tharp, R. (1991). Cultural diversity and treatment of children. *Journal of Counselling and Clinical Psychology, 59(6)*, 799–812.

Thomas, L. (1995). Psychotherapy in the context of race and culture: An intercultural therapeutic approach. In S. Fernando (Ed.), *Mental health in a multi-ethnic society: A multidisciplinary handbook* (pp.172–192). London: Routledge.

Tyler, F., Susswell, D., and Williams-McCoy, J. (1985). Ethnic validity in psychotherapy. *Psychotherapy, 22*, 311–320.

Ullah, R. (1995). Black parent governors: A hidden agenda. In E. Burman, P. Alldred, C. Bewley, B. Goldberg, C. Heenan, D. Marks, J. Marshall, K. Taylor, R. Ullah and S. Warner. *Challenging women: Psychology's exclusions, feminist possibilities* (pp. 90–105). Buckingham, UK: Open University Press.

Ware, V. (1992). *Beyond the pale: White women, racism and history*. London: Verso.

Wheeler, E. (1994). Doing black mental health research: Observations and experiences. In H. Afshar and M. Maynard (Eds.), *The dynamics of "race" and gender* (pp. 41–62). London: Taylor & Francis.

Wilkinson, S., and Kitzinger, C. (Eds.). (1996). *Representing the other: A feminism & psychology reader*. London: Sage.

Yuval-Davis, N. (1992). Fundamentalism, multiculturalism and women in Britain. In J. Donald and A. Rattansi (Eds.), *"Race," culture and difference* (pp. 278–292). London: Sage.

Yuval-Davis, N. (1997). *Gender and nation*. London: Routledge.

Zack, N. (Ed.). (1996). *Race/sex: Their sameness, differences and interplay*. London: Routledge.

Performance, Criticism, and Postmodern Psychology

Lois Holzman

THE FOLLOWING REMARKS were prompted by what has been, over the past five years, a growing interest in performative psychology in general and performance social therapy in particular among psychologists and psychotherapists from a broad range of traditions and orientations. (The 1997 "Unscientific Psychology: Conversations With Other Voices" conference/retreat was, in retrospect, a pivotal moment.) No longer do those of us who practice and advocate for a new performance-based study of human action speak only to ourselves; the circle is widening. Nowadays, my colleagues and I regularly meet psychotherapists and university professors who, stumbling across improvisation or some other performance work, seize upon it to breathe new life into their work with clients and students. Less frequently, yet still more than in the early 1990s, we meet philosophically and theoretically oriented psychologists who have become intrigued by the challenges performance presents to the foundational issues of both modernist psychology and its postmodern critique.

Along with interest come questions (some put forth explicitly and others more a subtext of a conversation) that might not have occurred to those of us practicing performative psychology, but which have turned out to be key issues to engage in exploring postmodern psychologies as societal practice. Such was the case with a talk delivered by Will Wadlington as part of a symposium entitled "Toward a Postmodern Humanistic Psychology: The Performative Paradigm" presented at the 107th Annual Convention of the American Psychological Association (APA) in 1999. Wadlington, Associate Director of the

Center for Counseling and Psychological Services at Pennsylvania State University and active member of the Humanistic Psychology division of APA, organized the session as part of the dialogue that has been going on for a few years within humanistic psychology on post-modernism, performative psychology and performance social therapy. His presentation, "Social Therapy as Revolutionary Activity: Implications for Humanistic Psychology," reviewed Fred Newman's and my book, *The End of Knowing* (Newman and Holzman, 1997) and provided: "a phenomenological description of my experience as a naïve learner-performer of social therapy, and a participant-observer account of the learning-development community in which this approach comes to life" (Wadlington, 1999, p. 2).

I was very moved by Wadlington's portrayal of our work and his experience of it; what he said about what he sees was extremely thoughtful and complimentary (and, from my point of view, accurate). And what was fascinating was that he didn't give his opinion—not once—and yet the audience learned much about how and what he thinks. It's unusual and refreshing to hear someone discussing someone else's work without presenting points of agreement and disagreement, cataloguing what's right and what's wrong, and backing those opinions up with appropriate references. One focus of his talk was the blaming and shaming that characterize intellectual activity in epistemologically-based environments epitomized by schools and universities (including those that mouth the liberal credo: "There is no right answer"). It was this, in particular, that led me to look at our performatory (nonepistemologically-based) practice in a new way. Is it possible to be critical in/of performance social therapy? In calling for "the end of knowing," are Newman and I also calling for the "end of criticism?" Can you engage in criticism without being a knower?

Questions of this sort came up several times during the remainder of the APA gathering. One instance occurred at a performative psychology symposium chaired by Kenneth Gergen (the fifth such symposium of this type Gergen has organized at APA annual conventions under the sponsorship of the APA Divisions of Psychology and the Arts and Humanistic Psychology). Entitled "Performative Psychology: Knowledge and Representation," the session included five performative presentations (poetry, painting, dance and movement, mime, and stand-up comedy). In the discussion that followed, audience members initially shared their enthusiasm and support for what was, to most of them, a new format and an experience of learning in a new way. When someone asked: "What is the role of criticism in performative psychology?" the conversation shifted to the relevance of measurement and evaluation and the role of scientific and aesthetic criteria.

I welcome the opportunity these questions offer to pursue further the methodology of postmodern psychology-in-the-making, particularly its political and moral dimensions and the implications of giving up knowing in favor of performance.

KNOWING AND PERFORMING

In recent years, Fred Newman and I have been writing about the work we do and the community that we, along with hundreds of others, have been building for the last twenty-five years. We write with the hope of shaping a *methodological* focus for dialogue on postmodern psychologies. For example, *The End of Knowing* (1997) is meant to challenge our postmodern colleagues to turn their attention from theorizing about alternative epistemologies (ones more social and/or cultural than that of mainstream psychology) to giving up epistemology altogether. The book argues that in these postmodern times the relevant ontological unit for psychology is *activity*, which requires a nonepistemological (nonobjectivist, noncognitive) methodology. We use the term activity in its Marxian sense— "revolutionary, practical-critical activity" (Marx, 1974, p. 121)—and not as a general reference to human action and/or agency, as many social constructionist and sociocultural psychologists do. *Revolutionary, practical-critical activity* is human practice that is fully self-reflexive, dialectical, transformative of the totality, and continuously emergent. It is human practice that "abolishes the present state of things" (Marx and Engels, 1974, p. 57) by the continuous transformation of mundane specific life practices into new forms of life. This conception of activity as revolutionary activity is key to understanding Newman's and my calling for a nonepistemological approach for studying human life. As Newman discusses elsewhere in this volume, revolutionary activity is not a *kind* of activity; it is a new methodology for a new kind of political-psychological practice: "Marx is urging us to consider the need for an activity revolution" (Newman, this volume, p. 174).

The End of Knowing grows out of our efforts to create the conditions for "an activity revolution." Since the 1970s we have created and sustained the building of an ever-expanding, diverse community of what is now tens of thousands of people and an interconnected network of cultural, psychological, educational, and political projects that support people to transform existing environments and ways of relating that they find oppressive, painful, and destructive of the human spirit into ones that meet their/human needs.[1] We have done this without *applying* any method, but (again, following Marx) by *practicing method*—an approach in which method is inseparable from the object to be studied. Lev Vygotsky, Marx's follower in the area of psychology, stated it this way:

> The search for method becomes one of the most important problems of the entire enterprise of understanding the uniquely human forms of psychological activity. In this case, the method is simultaneously prerequisite and product, the tool and the result of the study. (Vygotsky, 1978, p. 65)

Vygotsky is saying that human activity cannot be studied apart from creating the very tools with which to study it. It cannot be studied instrumentally, that is, by applying an existing or even newly created method. It cannot be studied epistemologically. "Method as simultaneously tool and result" is dialectical practice, not a new method but a new *conception of method*—method as the practice of dialectics. Method and object are a totality, a dialectical unity. The entire enterprise—human life and its study—is a search for method. Newman and I coined the term *tool-and-result methodology* for Vygotsky's (and our) practice of method in order to distinguish it from the *instrumental tool for result methodology* that characterizes the natural and social sciences (Newman and Holzman, 1993). Our community-building and the projects that comprise it—the East Side Institute for Short Term Psychotherapy, the East Side Center for Social Therapy and affiliated centers in other cities, the Castillo Theatre, the All Stars Talent Show Network, the Development School for Youth, and so on—are practices of this methodology.

The human capacity to perform, that is to be both who we are and who we are not at the very same time, is central to our practice. Performance is, we have come to believe, the revolutionary activity by which human beings create their lives (develop)—qualitatively transforming and continuously reshaping the unity that is *us-and-our environment*. Over the last two decades we and our colleagues have learned an enormous amount about performance from the dozens of projects we have created for and with young people and adults. Our therapeutic practice, performance social therapy, is based in the power of performance as revolutionary activity. We believe that talk therapy helps people grow emotionally to the extent that "the talk" is performatory; more specifically: "some kind of development takes place in the process of ensemble, collective performance of not just someone else's play, but the performance of our own discourse with each other" (Newman, 1999, p. 130).

A note is warranted here about development, a term currently out of favor with postmodern and critical psychologists alike (Burman, 1994). Newman and I agree with our colleagues that development, as defined and studied by psychology, has little constructive to do with human life; however (and fortunately), human beings *do* engage in developmental activity, that is, abolish the present state of things, transform totalities. It is this concept of developmental activity that we want to bring to the forefront of any new postmodern psychological practice.

EPISTEMIC AND PRACTICAL-CRITICAL CRITICISM

Critiques are based in knowing. Criticism, as typically understood and done in our culture, is the exercise of one's cognitive faculties in the service of what is "true" and who is "right." This kind of objectification—an appeal to something *outside* and *other*—is essential to criticism and its usual form, the debate. Social-therapeutic practice has little interest in this sort of criticism (modernist criticism). Aside from the inevitable shaming (of the one who is "wrong"), it is problematic to us because it's not a creative, or building, activity. Modernist epistemologically-based critique is not developmentally driven or change-oriented; that is, it's not meant to transform anything qualitatively and, not surprisingly, rarely does anything transformative come of it.

Nevertheless, criticism is an ongoing and very important part of the practice of performance social therapy—but it's not criticism as it is commonly known. We deal with criticism methodologically, not epistemologically. Our approach is based in activity and is concerned completely with change. We do criticism as the exercising of everyone's performative faculties in the revolutionary activity of transforming the totality and creating something new.

Our work to go beyond an objectivist truth-referential framework builds on a long tradition within psychology and philosophy to construct subjectivist accountings of truth. Most recently, postmodernism has taken the lead in battling objectivity and Truth on philosophical grounds. Within postmodern psychology, social constructionists search for forms of dialogue alternative to objectivist-based criticism. Aligned with this antipositivist tradition, we are sympathetic to its subjectivist and relational accounts. Yet there is, we believe, a qualitative difference between positing subjectivist accountings of truth (many truths, all with a small "t") and rejecting truth (in both its upper- and lowercase forms) in favor of activity. The ontological shift to activity, among its other significant impacts, transforms criticism from an epistemological appeal to an objective (outside) Truth/Reality (or truths and realities) to an activisitic, self-reflexive engagement of what is/is becoming. No longer a knower, the critic is fully engaged as an integral part of the activity being studied/performed. It is from this vantage point that we applaud all efforts to create *non*-truth-referential ways of talking, for we have come to see how growthful the subversion of truth-based discourse can be.

In this essay, I will try to bring this characterization to life by sharing some of our development community's history in relation to criticism. It may be helpful to keep in mind that our activity-based critical practice has the following features: it is methodological, transformational of the totality, involves a process of completion, and has developmental use.

We—and here I mean not just the East Side Institute or social therapy centers but the wider development community of which they are a part—are no strangers to criticism. This "community without membership" (Wadlington, 1999) is an ever-expanding and diverse group of ordinary people, which means we're as opinionated as everyone else. What's different is the value placed on these opinions and how they are related to. In our community, opinions matter to the extent that something can be created with them. In this sense, one could argue that we take opinions more seriously than modernist epistemological criticism on which very little hinges except people's egos. We use criticism to produce change, to produce something relevant to a humanistic developmental practice.

In the case of the origin and development of performance social therapy, a practice had already existed by the time trained professionals became interested in it. In the 1970s, Fred Newman and a few lay therapists he had trained were practicing a Marxist-based therapy that was connected to left political activism. The work attracted, among others, me—a developmental psychologist in the Vygotskian, sociocultural tradition; a few other social scientists; and many therapists with different theoretical orientations—analytic, object relations, behavioral, radical community social work, antipsychiatry, feminist, and black psychology among them. We were miles apart on what we thought therapy—and psychology—should be. Our earliest debates were over which was the right theory, persisting in the conviction that there must be one. Relatively soon, we transformed these epistemic debates into developmental and nonobjective questions: What can we build that can be of help to people emotionally? What does psychology need to be in order to reinitiate people's development, given how oppressive and nongrowthful societal conditions are?

Our critical posture took shape in the completion of the debate as a community practice. As we built our therapy and research centers, we brought the debate out into our community and to the people of New York City through public forums (including a monthly speaker series that lasted for three years). Leading progressive psychologists, psychotherapists, psychiatrists, educators, social scientists, and community activists (among them, psychologists Michael Cole, Michelle Fine, Howard Gadlin, and Robert Wozniak; psychiatrist Joel Kovel; economist Michael Tabb; sociologist Stanley Aronowitz; and radical feminist Ti Grace Atkinson) would debate to a diverse audience of mostly nonacademics and nonprofessionals. The experience of the mix—ordinary people hearing the experts talk about issues in their lives and having a chance to respond—was enormously educational and developmental (empowering) for the audience and some, but not all of, the speakers. (Some of the more academic speakers, not used to hearing from "the community" on its own terms and turf, were quite offended to find themselves challenged by folks who didn't possess "knowledge" and who didn't adhere to proper debate form.) These dialogues (often less than friendly) played an activistic role in the development of both social therapy and the larger community of which it is a part. They were, to use a characterization of continuous emergent process, a "completion" of the debate (Vygotsky, 1987; Newman and Holzman, 1997).

Even today, epistemic debates and academic critique such as those that appear in the pages of this book are given expression in the learning/development community. Topics such as postmodernism, dialectics, epistemology, language games, social constructionism, and so on, are part of the everyday conversations in social therapy groups, among the youth of the All Stars Talent Show Network, and at meetings of the Castillo Theatre staff.

The Castillo Theatre is an Off-Off-Broadway theatre in New York City noted for its experimental productions, populist political concerns, and postmodern sensibility (Friedman, in press, a & b). Castillo was born in the early 1980s out of criticism from artists who were attracted to our work because of how it linked grassroots political organizing and social change to the subjectivity of the mass. But as artists, they weren't interested in becoming therapists and, more important, they believed that culture plays at least as significant a role in shaping mass psychology as does psychology. They thought we were missing the boat (or at least one of the boats).

There was a period of intense debate. The artists who founded Castillo in the early 1980s came from the broad-based left cultural movement that had fallen apart—in no small part because none of the diverse groups could work together, and years of debating theory and political positions had taken their toll. Among them were those in the Brechtian, avant-garde, and labor theater traditions, black nationalist writers, feminist painters, and performance artists of various identities and ideologies. They continued debating when they began to work with us, for a while in the same epistemic way (What is *true*? there must be an answer that is *knowable*). Some fought for a street-theater agitprop approach; others who were deeply influenced by the avant garde argued for a more sophisticated art-based theater; still others who glorified "folk art" argued for making street performers and youth hip-hop performers the core of the cultural work. Then there was a shift—from epistemic debating in order to find correct answers *relative to varying objective criteria*, to practical-critical debating in order to create something *relative to the particular people involved in a specific revolutionary task*, that is, building a new cultural center and gaining support for *independent* culture. (To us, independent culture refers to a way of seeing not overdetermined by the marketplace and created self-consciously by a community defined only by its ongoing activity.)

What we did was to bring into existence a theater that reorganized this debate and gave it life. This reorganizing connected to ordinary people the artists' debate over what constitutes progressive culture and political art.

Initially we went to those involved in our development community (who by and large knew nothing about theater and had no interest in it) for support. We literally built the audience for the theater out of this public performance of a transformed theoretical debate. We had to win people in our community over to the activity of creating independent culture. What this looked like was women and men with diverse cultural traditions and identities—working-class African-Americans from Harlem and Latinos from the Bronx, political activists in women's, lesbian and gay, and civil rights movements, radical therapists, leftists, welfare recipients, and so on—coming to see theater and view gallery shows that they would never dream of spending their time and money on, except that they were organized to do so as the activity of bringing into existence a new independent cultural center. We also canvassed door to door in New York City and its suburbs and stood on street corners asking people we'd never met to support this new independent cultural project. This was our way of insuring Castillo's independence from government and corporate foundations—an organizing activity that built a financial base of support and also created the Castillo audience, as many supporters became theater-goers.

All areas of our work have this feature—the transformation from "What's the right answer here?" "Whose opinion is going to win the day?" "What is theoretically sound?" into "How's this debate itself of value to the ongoing process that is our community?" No small part of our history, in retrospect, has been the continuous process of transforming modernist critique and abandoning epistemic debate. This activity has been transformative of the total environment—not in the narrow sense of the community directly involved in our projects; I mean the totality that includes mainstream psychology, mainstream culture (including their left/alternative/avant garde wings), their critiques, and their consumers and audiences.

Two Paradigms of Understanding

Giving up the knowing paradigm and epistemic critique and debate is understandably hard to contemplate (and even more difficult to do). Giving up objectification means that there is nothing outside of the activity to appeal to. Gone is the objective distance (the theoretical stance, the ideological position, even the so-called real world) that is foundational to theory building, psychological practice, scholarly critique, and academic debate. It is our experience that this distance just isn't useful in the kind of self-reflexive environment we have built. What matters is how to continue to create tools that have some developmental value—therapy, theater, education, politics in which people can, in whatever ways they choose, participate in social transformation, recreating subjectivity (creating culture and creating psychology, which, to me, amount to the same thing). In this environment, needing to know which was more politically correct—the antipsychiatry or Marx-Freud synthesis movement in the case of the institute—or who was more culturally radical—Brecht or Artaud in the case of Castillo—became nonissues because resolving these debates would not move us forward. Instead, we brought everything we had, including our opinions, to the activity of building the institute and the Castillo Theatre.

Our belief that there is nothing social, cultural, or historical other than what we human beings create requires that we give up the deeply rooted Western assumption that we can distance ourselves enough from our activity to study it scientifically (Newman and Holzman, 1996). It requires that we stop imposing objectification onto what we do. It requires Vygotsky's search for method, the ongoing process of changing totalities—revolutionary activity. What it doesn't require is a theory of truth. Elsewhere in this volume, John Morss suggests "a significant rethinking of the important but flawed idea of the social construction of truth" (Morss, this volume, p. 20). We completely agree that such a rethinking is necessary if postmodern psychology is to become a relevant force in social-cultural transformation. Social constructionism's libertarian relativism (equating truth with consensus) is no less a theory of truth for being subjective. We have come to believe that truth claims, no matter how relativistic, are oppressively authoritarian. Finally, studying activity does not require, as far as we can tell, the kind of knowing that psychologists (and critics in all disciplines) tend to do. Such knowing tends to put a stop to further developmental activity.

This radical abandonment of modernist critique, objective distance, and theories of truth is no small part of our controversiality. After all, if you call for the end of knowing, especially among professional knowers, you should be prepared for people to be provoked; it comes with the territory. Over the years we've gotten all kinds of reactions, from admiration, serious interest, and intelligent critique, to ambivalence, to blatantly hostile attacks. The attacks (many of which are discussed in Chapter 1 of Holzman, 1999) are a fascinating challenge for us. In each case, the critic applies one or more objective criteria (for example, a definition of dialectical materialism, the golden rule about boundaries in psychotherapy, what true multiculturalism is). But we don't take objective criteria to be valid tools to evaluate us! We don't accept the terms of the debate. Objective distance is precisely what we are critiquing, in practical-critical fashion, by building environments that do not depend on or have use for it. Our response is our activity—the Institute, social therapy centers, the Castillo Theatre, the development community—which (by its very nature) cannot satisfy this requirement of modernist critique.

How do our critics respond to this? Those who are open to the issues our practice raises find this nonepistemological response intriguing, if not completely satisfactory, and see us as an unusual kind of community. Others, who cling to the modernist necessity of objective criteria, find it completely unacceptable. They conclude from our insistence that there is nothing outside of activity that we must be a cult (completely insular know-it-alls). Thus a dilemma faces us all: two different paradigms of understanding, one based in epistemology and the other based in practical-critical activity, are available: which is to be used to resolve *this* debate and how can *this* be decided? We have no answer. In our view, the debate is resolvable only historically. I think this gives us an advantage over our modernist critics for, unlike them, we have no need of an answer. As methodologists (revolutionary-activityists) who are postmodernizing Marx, we have nothing to prove. But there is always something new to build.

Acknowledgments

My thanks to Fred Newman for his assistance in conceptualizing this discussion.

Notes

1. See Newman and Holzman 1996, 1997; and Holzman, 1997, for discussion of the origin and evolution of the development community and its projects.

REFERENCES

Burman, E. (1994). *Deconstructing developmental psychology*. London: Routledge.

Friedman, D. (in press a). Castillo: The making of a postmodern political theatre. *Theatre Symposium 1999*.

Friedman, D. (in press b). "Performance of a Lifetime": Interactive growth theatre and the development of performance in everyday life. *Theatre InSight*.

Holzman, L. (1997). *Schools for growth: Radical alternatives to current educational models*. Mahwah, NJ: Erlbaum.

Holzman, L. (Ed.). (1999). *Performing psychology: A postmodern culture of the mind*. New York: Routledge.

Holzman, L., and Newman, F. (1979). *The practice of method: An introduction to the foundations of social therapy*. New York: Institute for Social Therapy and Research.

Marx, K. (1974). Theses on Feuerbach. In K. Marx and F. Engels, *The German ideology*, pp. 121–123. New York: International Publishers.

Marx, K. and Engels, F. (1974). *The German ideology*. New York: International Publishers.

Morss, J. (1996). *Growing critical: Alternatives to developmental psychology*. London: Routledge.

Newman, F. (1999). A therapeutic deconstruction of the illusion of self. In L. Holzman (Ed.), *Performing psychology: A postmodern culture of the mind*, pp. 111–132, New York: Routledge.

Newman, F., and Holzman, L. (1993). *Lev Vygotsky: Revolutionary scientist*. London: Routledge.

Newman, F., and Holzman, L. (1996). *Unscientific psychology: A cultural-performatory approach to understanding human life*. Westport, CT: Praeger.

Newman, F., and Holzman, L. (1997). *The end of knowing: A new developmental way of learning*. London: Routledge.

Vygotsky, L. S. (1978). *Mind in society*. Cambridge, MA: Harvard University Press.

Vygotsky, L. S. (1987). *The collected works of L. S. Vygotsky*. (Vol. 1). New York: Plenum.

Wadlington, W. (1999). Social therapy as revolutionary activity: Implications for humanistic psychology. Delivered at the 107th annual convention of the American Psychological Association, Boston.

II

FROM

IDENTITY

TO RELATIONSHIP:

POLITICS

AND

PARTICIPATION

The contributors to Part I have been primarily concerned with psychology's encounter with postmodernism. The contributors to Part II concentrate on the nature and implications of postmodern psychologies for societal practices and political life.

Weaving its way throughout their discussions of psychology, society, culture, and politics is the concept of performance as a method for a new way of understanding/being/becoming, that is, for transforming human social relations. At issue is: Can we create new performances of our sexuality, our meaning-making, our emotionality, our identities, our politics, our lives? Performance, the authors imply, becomes unstoppable.

Performance is not just the first night of the show, the polished (perhaps) and single-voiced human pyramid that is the orthodox Western (and Eastern) theater. The stage lights show you what you are meant to see and how your are meant to see it, just like a conventional conference presentation. Performance in that sense— the performance of *Cloud Nine* at the Royal Court Theatre or of *The Lion King* on Broadway, official performance as sanctified by the institution of the theater—is no more than the tip of the iceberg. That kind of performance is essentially repetitive, even if it closes after the first night, and even if it's been arrived at through the actors improvising in a workshop.

Performance, we think, is better revealed by the rehearsal. Here the nuts and bolts are in clear sight, yet the performance aspects are just as much present as on opening night. Actors are working in rehearsal to create collectively something new, not to display a finished product. Rehearsals lurch awkwardly between technical precision and tedium. They may stop and start unexpectedly. At one and the same time some people are performing on stage, some are chatting about the performance, the play, the director, or the acting, while others argue about where they will have dinner after the show.

This is the performance that our contributors find relevant—even essential—to the transition from (modernist) identity to (postmodern) relationality, from a psychology of adaptation to a psychology of transformation. Their essays can also be viewed as a rehearsed performance of the possibilities afforded by the postmodernization of psychology. The implication, the authors suggest (passionately), is that such a transformation of psychology is helping to make possible a social/political/cultural transformation that goes far beyond the borders of a particular discipline. Performance, as a method and as a form of life, can restructure and rebuild how it is that we are together.

Women

as

Spectacle[1]

Mary Gergen

[As the house lights dim, and the spotlight falls upon me, I begin.[2] I carry a pink boa and a gold lamé purse. A sign with the printing "FEAR IS THE MOST DANGEROUS WEAPON" is placed on the stage, facing away from audience. I place a chair center stage. A music stand holds the script.]

POMO: *[Chewing gum, blowing bubbles, takes it out and sticks it under the chair. Poses with my gloves]*.

Limelight, ah, that turns me on. *[Waves for light.]* Basking in that warmth of the spotlight. What a place for a lime-starved kid. *[Stretching out.]*

Kid, I said. Do I hear some snickering? Who is she kidding? She may not be an old goat, but kidhood is long since past for her. This week Beatrice Wood, the Mama of Dada, died in her studio in California, just days after she gave a party in honor of the director of Titanic. The obituary said she was 105, but she quarreled with that calculation. She always said that if scientists had showed that time was relative, then she was thirty-two. Longevity for her depended on two things: chocolate and young men. I want to dedicate this performance to the Mama of Dada, wherever she may be.

Age is a social construction. . . . So like Beatrice, I'm somewhere between six and sixty today, depending on how we get along together. We'll see what the relationship will bring.

Still, at whatever age, this is a pretty formidable place to be standing, with you out there—a real live audience—expecting something from the latest dance troupe perhaps. It's a big space to fill. I'll give it a whirl. *[Swirling around big space with arms out.]*

Before I get too far along, let me just thank you for coming, and joining in the performances . . . I couldn't be standing up here without you. And, of course, if you are wondering how come you are watching me, then you just better reflect back and consider what you did to deserve me. Cause I certainly didn't make this up all by myself.

But you might ask: What is this Woman-as-spectacle thing all about? What is she going to do? and Why? Here I am, a nice girl (formerly) of Lake Wobegon, looking like a raspberry shortcake, and Mardi Gras is already over. Heck it's Lent already. What's the psychology of being outlandish . . . outside the customs, peculiar, . . . provocative . . . a woman on the edge of feminine respectability . . . or way over the line?

One thing for sure—I'm here to amuse you . . . bemuse you, and confuse you. All those ooze words . . . is that sexy or what?

Over there is an imaginary circle of my textual friends, my social ghosts, they warn me of the dangers of what I am trying to do. Mary Russo[3] has said: "Making a spectacle out of oneself seem[s] a specifically feminine danger. The danger . . . of an exposure . . . women who make spectacles of themselves have done something wrong, had stepped, . . . into the limelight out of turn—too young or too old, too early or too late—and yet . . . any woman can make a spectacle out of herself if she is not careful."

[*pause* . . .] WHAT IS THE WORST SPECTACLE YOU MADE OF YOURSELF? (*Pointing at individual audience members.*)

Arguing with somebody more important than you in public?

Belching or, God forbid, farting in company, or even alone?

Getting caught eating like you were hungry? Not a bad idea.. [*digs in purse, brings out donut.*]

Being rude to somebody, even if he was trying to molest you?

DO YOUR CHEEKS BURN TO THINK OF IT? EVERYBODY WHISPERING BEHIND YOUR BACK . . . HOW EMBARRASSING . . . IF ONLY YOU COULD DISAPPEAR INTO THIN AIR. (IF ONLY I HAD NOT BROUGHT IT UP!)

[*Pauses, points.*]

Peggy Penn, over there in my magic circle, has spelled out one of those moments in a poem called "Omen for Women." Here she describes her first moments of menstruation:

At twelve my russet blood rolled out,
everyone on the bus to Latrobe, PA. saw it.
they whispered, "See, her eggs are multiplying!
her insides sloughing off! See! its dripping on her
knees![4]

Is there no recourse but to relive our endless anguishes or try to forget?

Peggy saves her humiliation this way:

Leaving a trail
for you to find me in eleven years.

[*Motion of looking at trail of blood behind me.*]

(There's a positive spin if I've ever seen one. A Hansel and Gretel fairytale: follow my droplets and you'll find your way home.)

COULD *YOUR* SPECTACLE EVER BE REVALUED? MIGHT THERE BE SOMETHING TO SALVAGE IN YOUR STORY? EVEN POLITICAL POTENTIAL? (Or is this feminist jive?)

Mary Russo also said: " In contemplating these dangers, I grew to admire . . . the lewd, exuberant . . . Mae West.

. . . her . . . feminine performance, imposture, and masquerade . . . suggest cultural politics for women."

[*Taking out flask, has a drop of schnapps.*]

bell hooks[5]—an outlandish African American star—concurs: "When we give expression . . . to those aspects of our identity forged in marginality, we may be seen as 'spectacle.' Yet, . . . it is a means by which culture is transformed and not simply reproduced with different players in the same game."

Transformation, re-creation, even recreation, the politics of fun. Let us women move from living with *fear, the most elegant weapon*, as Jenny Holzer's neon sign proclaims [*takes out sign and holds it up*] to a raucous appreciation of our violations of the codes by which we live. [*Tears it up.*]

If we want to strip away the bars holding us in place, the corset stays of respectability [*opening coat*], and tease the audience with our unbounded flesh, how shall we begin? [*takes off coat, revealing her outfit.*] We walk a thin line in this little striptease . . . we must be careful that the seams of sentences all run smoothly into one. We don't want to snag our stockings, stub our toes, on the runways of our stage of life.

[*Checks nylon seams leg on chair.*]

Beryl Curt warns that . . . words . . . beguile the listener . . . into believing they are merely mirroring the world "as it really is," and obscure their ability to glamour that reality into being"[6].

I am guilty. I do wish to glamour a reality into being, preening these words into worlds. You have been forewarned. [*Waves her scarf.*]

The spectacle under construction needs more introduction. Over there are people who would want to strip me of my style. At my age, (chronological, that is) I am meant to disappear. I should have been gone long ago. In the dance of the life cycle, I am being propelled against the wall. Centripetal forces spin me to the chairs, from which I rose so long ago. Arms that circled me and kept me on the floor. Oh, how I could dance. [*A bit of waltz.*] Now they've let me go. My dance card is empty.

Now I'm—melding with the walls, pressing into paper . . . melting with the glue . . . stuck, not pinned and wriggling like Eliot's Prufrock, but misting into mottled lavender, without a muscle's twitch. [*Places scarf of sheer purple silk over head.*]

This is the fate woman of a mature age endures. She is somewhere over forty, and about as useful as a fruit fly. [At least they have the courtesy to die swiftly when their breeding days are done.] If she cannot procreate, she is lifeless, you see, but not dead. She never should attract attention. She learns to be the antispectacle. [*Removes scarf.*]

Such hatred we sometimes feel for her. [*Wrings scarf.*] That shameful blot on the image of our youth? Couldn't we just wring her neck? Be done with her. No one needs her. Hoarder of Medicare, Social Security, our tax dollars.

But lest we discard her so quickly, she is also me, and perhaps you. She is our destiny, us of the female persuasion. Ugghhh, should we call for our pills, our drugs of convenient forgetting?

[*Takes another sip from the flask.*]

Is there anyone to call?

Today, she is a creature under construction.

And I, in my spectacular role, a Postmodern Mama, with nothing to lose but my invisibility, I challenge those who wish to erase these *fine lines*. [*Takes off next jacket.*]

On the face of it, it's a challenging task. How do we claim a space on the floor when we are told that the music has stopped? How can we face up to this rejection? It is a challenging task.

We spin over possibilities.

Who else can we become?

Is this only a Midsummer Night's Dream?—we struggle with meaning and mistaken identity.

In this masquerade, where parody is paramount, we must fake it as we go. Well at least we have some talent and experience there.

In the politics of spectacle, we will reclaim a space.

[*Pause*]

[*Points, and seems to listen*]

The man on the aisle wonders what all the fuss is about. Why fight the inevitable? Go gracefully into the night. Why blame men if we are swayed by the beauty of fair young maidens. We are mere animals, after all. Yearning to spread our seeds abroad. Nature's call is wild. It's not political, its biological.

In the dominant world of science, support for the gentleman endures. Doctor Freud had this to say: "A man of about thirty seems youthful. . . . A woman of about the same age frequently staggers us by her psychological rigidity. . . . There are no paths open to her for further development"[7].

Sociobiologists are crawling out from under every rock, claiming that our fates are in our genes, and they ain't talking Levis.

As evolutionary psychologist David Buss has said: "All around the world men are more interested in the youth and beauty of their sexual partners and less discriminating in their choice of partners than women are."

We hear feminist researchers lament the discourse of science on our wallflower women: "Images of disease and deficiency . . . become the basis of discourse about women's lives in general"[8].

"Every woman over fifty years of age becomes a patient."

The disease, of course, is menopause. I always say the best treatment, next to chocolate and young men, is a fan. [*Removes one from bag and fans self.*]

Well, let's not wait for Science to come to its senses. We haven't got all day. We must deface its smug veneer.

Yet, how is it possible?

Here, the other voices [*points*] suggest scripts for us to follow.

They can help us to blast out of our prisons of ladylikeness. There are . . . ruses, diversions, and ways to resist.

It is time for glamouring, for mystery, for puckish surprises, for carnival.

Can making a spectacle create cultural change?

As Michelle Fine and Susan Gordon suggest, we: "need to disrupt prevailing notions of what is inevitable what is natural, . . . to invent and publish images of what is not now, and what could be"[9].

(We need to draw dirty pictures . . . do unruly things . . . un-ruly . . . against the rulers, against the rules.)

Topsy-turvy, let's turn the world order upside down . . .

[*Some kind of straddling . . . the chair. Sits backwards on it.*]

Woman on top . . . controlling the pace . . . taking in as much as she wants.

A missionary in her position, evading the law.

A butterfly wing stroking in sweet rebellion. Stirring up the airwaves in spunky surrender.

The image of the disorderly woman stirring the cauldron.

Lady Godiva rides, and politics proliferate.

Let's make some "gender trouble," as Judith Butler says.

Let us fool with Mother Nature: rub on the line that divides the sexes. (Mmmmmm that always feels good to rub on that line.)

Cross over the line, erase the line, blur the line? Is there a politics of lines?

[*Gets up.*]

If gender is performance, we become the dramatic effect of our performances. We act out the bodily gestures of gender and age. We are fantasies whose bodies are inscribed through our performances.

We, whoever we are, can affirm ourselves, while destabilizing the ideal of female beauty and realigning desire.

Although we are trapped in social orderings, tattooed with our proper place . . . in outlandish moments we are freed to create the possibility of cultural change. . . . Let us go on from here.

To revel in our specialness. Never to blush again. To hold our heads up and be proud, no matter where and how we are.

To celebrate the lifted yoke of fertility and rejoice in our wholeness again. Like girls, to prance in moonlight and in sun.

To remember that the calendar is only one—bureaucratic—measurement of time. It cannot tell the age of spirit, heart, and mind.

Our spectacles are opportunities to glamour into being other forms of life. As we soar over the edge of respectability (with a bow to Thelma and

Louise), let us make a joyful noise and be glad of our excesses. Let us dare to strut our stuff and when we die, die laughing.

NOTES

1. I have presented various versions of this performative piece on several occasions.

2. I am wearing a bright-red sheath dress covered by a fuschia cape, a big curly platinum blond wig, and a variety of other accessories that are costume-overkill.

3. Russo, M. (1986). Female grotesques: Carnival and theory. In T. de Lauretis (Ed.). *Feminist studies, critical studies.* (pp. 213–229). Milwaukee: University of Wisconsin Press.

4. Penn, Peggy. "Omen for women," received New Years, 1996.

5. hooks, b. (in Bordo, p. 164). *Feminist Studies*, Spring, 1992.

6. Curt, B. C. *Textuality and tectonics. Troubling social and psychological science*, p. 14. Buckingham, UK: Open University Press.

7. Freud's *New Introductory Lectures*, no. 33.

8. Rostosky, S. S. and Travis, C. B. (1996). Menopause and the dominance of the biomedical model 1984–1994. *Psychology of Women Quarterly, 20*, pp. 285–312 (p. 288).

9. Fine, M. and Gordon, S. (1991). Effacing the center and the margins: Life at the intersection of psychology and feminism. *Feminism & Psychology, 1*, pp. 19–28.

From within Our Lives Together:

Wittgenstein, Bakhtin, and

Voloshinov and the Shift

to a Participatory Stance

in Understanding

Understanding

John Shotter

> My participative and demanding consciousness can see that the
> world of modern philosophy, the theoretical and theoreticized
> world of culture, is in a certain sense actual, that it possesses
> validity. But what it can see also is that this world is not the
> once-occurrent world in which I live and in which I answerably
> perform my deeds.   *Bakhtin, 1993, p. 20.*

> Words have meaning only in the stream of life.
> *Wittgenstein, 1982, no. 913.*

> Living life has fled you, only the formulas and categories remain, and
> that, it seems, makes you happy. You say there's more peace
> and quiet (laziness) that way . . .
> *Dostoevsky's answer to a critic, quoted in Bakhtin, 1984, p. 97.*

A WOMAN FRIEND APPROACHES ME, downcast; I take her hand, and just as
I feel something of her in her hand, so she feels something of me in mine.[1]
I feel her hand in mine as soft, small, limp, and lifeless, and in an attempt
to cheer her up, I look into her eyes, smile, and squeeze her hand. But for
her, as we approach each other, I seem to loom over her, blotting out her

light, intruding into her grief. She feels my hand as strong and rough, as vigorously moving in a way that is, so to speak, "out of tune" with the "tone" expressed in hers. She feels I'm in a hurry to be elsewhere. I feel I'm not "getting through," and we stand for a moment wondering if we are still friends. She feels somehow that her feelings have not been properly respected; I feel I have (morally) failed her in some way. Feeling concerned (but also obligated), I say: "Can I help? . . . We can go and have a coffee if you like, I can do my stuff some other time." She smiles, and we go off to talk. And in this initial part of our meeting, as a result of our reactions and responses to each other's expressions, we each gain a vague, outlined sense of the current "shape and vectors," so to speak, of each other's unique "inner world": besides the sensitivities we share, there are things she notices to which I am insensitive, things which she connects that are unconnected for me, and vice versa. And as our talk continues, focused more but not wholly on her inner world rather than mine, its initial vague outline—as a world of grief and suffering—will be internally articulated and developed further. Perhaps, even, between us, we will create some new pathways within it, leading out into a new, less grief-stricken world.

In what follows below, I want to explore those aspects of the work of Wittgenstein, Bakhtin, and Voloshinov that bear on our coming to a more well-oriented grasp of our experiences in involvements with the Others (and othernesses) around us, such as the one above—where, by the phrase "more well-oriented grasp," I do not mean an increased ability to make truth claims *about* such phenomena that others cannot gainsay, but an increased *practical* ability to conduct our own human affairs without, as Wittgenstein puts it, becoming "entangled in our own rules" (1953, no. 125). For, as we know, it is only too easy for us to set out explicit rules and principles and then, in our attempts to follow them, to find things not turning out in our daily affairs as we had assumed from our academic inquiries they should.

Spontaneous Orientations While "at Home" in Our Everyday Lives

Mostly, however, in our daily affairs, we do not need to make any reference to any explicit guides; mostly we are able to conduct our unfolding performances without it being necessary for us to pause for more than a few brief moments to gain the orientation we need to take our next steps. We see the ways "forward" offered or "afforded" us (to use the term given currency in Gibson's (1979) "ecological" approach to psychology) by our surroundings, directly and immediately, from within our living involvements with them. Indeed, just as in driving my car I see the other cars around me each moment, directly, as *near* and *far* (rather than just as large or small[2]) and can orient my own car in relation to them accordingly, so it is the same in my human affairs.

As long as I am engaged or involved with those around me, I can, so to speak, get a sense of how, to some extent, to "go on" in my own unfolding activities in ways appropriate to *our* shared circumstances at each moment. I do not just experience the scene before me as a dead shape or form needing deliberate interpretation by me, but as spontaneously offering me, as it were, a set of "action-guiding advisories," a "shaped and vectored sense" of where I am, where I have come from, and where I can (and should) go next. What is "in front" and what "behind" me, what is "in reach" and what "out of reach," and so on, is immediately apparent to me; I see objects in terms of what aspects they will present next as I move in relation to them—only if I am brain-damaged is this shaped and vectored orientation to my surroundings lost (Merleau-Ponty, 1962). It is as if each event in my involvements with them comes, so to speak, with "strings attached" to it, with a sense of "what can go with, or leads to, what," a "grammar." At each moment it is as if there are rules as to what I should do next, but they are of a kind such that, when I obey them, I do so immediately and spontaneously in a way that is "*not* an *interpretation* but which is exhibited in what we call 'obeying the rule' and 'going against it' in actual cases" (Wittgenstein, 1953, no. 201). The rule is of a kind such that, when I obey it, "I do not choose. I obey the rule *blindly*" (no. 219).

It is, I think, the achievement of Wittgenstein, Bakhtin, and Voloshinov to have all, in their own different ways, brought to our attention the architectonic importance of this special kind of *practical-moral*[3] understanding: the fact that we continually and spontaneously "shape," "build," or "construct" our performances in our daily affairs as we act "into" the opportunities offered us by our surroundings. The kind of understanding we display in such activity is an active, *relational-responsive* kind of understanding that, unlike the *representational-referential* form of understanding more well known to us, gives rise to more than just a "picture" of the speaker's meaning in another person's head.[4] It spontaneously shapes our practices, and is "carried" in them, so to speak, in such a way that we can "carry across" a certain way of acting from one situation into another.

This is where the importance of Wittgenstein's work lies. He has emphasized the importance of the fact that, as we have seen, events within the stream of our living involvements with those around us carry with them their own "logical grammar," as he terms it. Thus, from within each such involvement, each aspect of our surroundings does not lie "dead" before us—as would a car, if we saw it merely as small or large rather than as also "advising" us of its nearness to or distance from us—but it also points "outside itself to a reality beyond" (Wittgenstein, 1981, no. 236). Thus, in spontaneously responding to such events, we do not act just in terms of what, objectively, they are, but also in terms of the next possible actions they offer or make available to us. The meaning of what we do in so reacting is in what we *achieve* in what we say or do, by the *use* to which we put our actions. Although often ignored, we are in fact never not embedded in such an action-shaping flow of activity. And it is Wittgenstein's achievement alone to have developed a number of *methods* for bringing the architectonic influences at work within this flow into rational visibility when required.

He has brought to our notice a vast array of continually changing "action-guiding advisories" spontaneously at work everywhere in both our ordinary, everyday activities and in our academic disciplines; influences that, so to speak, are hidden from us only "because of their simplicity and familiarity. (One is unable to notice something—because it is always before one's eyes.)" (Wittgenstein, 1953, no. 129). And in his work, he wants to bring to our attention subtle and fleeting events occurring in and around us that we currently tend to ignore; "distinctions which our ordinary forms of language easily make us overlook" (no. 132). Indeed, he wants to suggest to us that, to the extent that understanding each other linguistically is a human achievement—something that we do between ourselves spontaneously, without noticing—it is not something for which we need a special explanation. It is something that in one sense is already known to us, something of which we need to remind ourselves. Thus, he suggests: "if it is asked: 'How do sentences manage to represent?'—the answer might be: 'Don't you know? You certainly see it, when you use them?' For nothing is concealed. How do sentences do it?—Don't you know? For nothing is hidden" (no. 435). It is just that we need to attend to events that usually pass us by unnoticed (see Shotter, 1996, and Shotter and Katz, 1996, where several of Wittgenstein's methods for bringing the relevant events to our notice are outlined in some detail).

Crucial in these methods is the emphasis on the fact that the ceaseless flow of spontaneous background activity between us is *dialogically structured*,[5] a fact brought to our attention by both Bakhtin and Voloshinov. Dialogically-structured activity can be understood neither in cause-and-effect terms nor in terms of logic or systems of calculation, nor reasons and interpretations. It is a *sui generis* realm of living activity with its own special, open, only partially specified or primordial nature, such that the reactions and responses occurring to us within it have the form of prototypes or candidates for all our more well-developed, separately characterized, deliberately conducted activities: all that we ever do or say in the special disciplines, in the arts, humanities, or sciences, has its origins in this ceaseless flow of dialogically-structured activity occurring between us. Wittgenstein's methods depend on it having this originary, primordial character.[6] Thus, taken together, the work of these three can, I think, show us a whole new approach to what we think of as our problems in psychology, an approach so new and strange that, as I see it, it marks a radical break with what has gone before. It is this new approach that I want to try to outline.

Rather than an *objective* approach, intended to increase the different representational knowledges "about" the *nature* of things acquired by the exercise of a research expertise, knowledges that to an extent we can each come to possess independently of who or what we are, that is, which are "external" to our being, so to speak, it can be called a *participative* approach. Its primary concern is with our constructing *ways of relating* ourselves to each other and the rest of our surroundings, which are not only of *use* to us in some way in "pointing outside themselves to a reality beyond," but which are also "internal" to who and what we are—in other words, rather than being concerned with bodies of knowledge having to do with an external reality, which, in being "set over against us" as "dead" bodies of objective knowledge, still require our "interpretation" if we are to apply them.

This approach is concerned, as we shall see, with our coming to feel and to know how to act in ways more "at home" in our own humanly made surroundings than at present—where those who all live in a common home implicitly know directly, *from within it*, its exits and entrances; its front and back, where guests are likely to appear; its upstairs and downstairs; its placement in relation to the rest of its surroundings; what things there are inside it; where they are; and how to help others confused for a moment to reorient themselves appropriately, as well as knowing that they know of things in the "outside" world in a way different from those within their home.[7] Those who know how to think participatively, notes Bakhtin (1993), "know how not to detach their performed act from its product, but rather how to relate both of them to the unitary and unique context of life and seek to determine them in that context as an indivisible unity" (p. 19). They know how to think of things from within "a domain of intimacy" (Bachelard, 1992, p. 12) with them, from within a totalized space of involvement that "calls out" certain actions from us. It is to the dialogically-structured character of this living context as an indivisible unity that I will now turn.

FROM WITHIN THE DIALOGICALLY-STRUCTURED CONTEXT OF LIFE

Bakhtin (1984) introduces the *sui generis* nature of dialogic or dialogically-structured relations to us by asking us to consider the two judgmental utterances: "Life is good" and "Life is bad." As he points out, considered logically, one is simply the negation of the other, and between them as they stand "there are not and cannot be any dialogical relationships; they do not argue with one another in any way. . . . Both these judgments must be *embodied*, if a dialogic relationship is to arise between them and toward them" (p. 183, my emphasis). When that is the case, when these two judgments issue from the mouths of two different people, one in response to the other, then they can come to play very different and unique roles in people's lives. For example, someone who cannot see a single, available step ahead of them to take may say, ironically, "Life is good"; another, who appreciates the gravity of his or her position says, by way of admonishing the other for inappropriate irony, "Life is bad, my friend . . . let's face it." Indeed, one can imagine an indefinite number of dialogical scenarios in which the second judgment is uttered in response to the first, with a very different use being served by each utterance on each occasion, each contributing to many different overall achievements—where people's living, responsive understandings of each other's utterances do not depend on the passive recognition of samenesses from the position of a spectator, but the active noticing of differences and othernesses from within an ongoing, living involvement with each other. Indeed, this is why in the exchange above, it is people's *embodied* judgments that are crucial, for it is only in our living, embodied relations to each other that we are spontaneously responsive to each other's activities—we cannot not be. But this does not mean, of course, that we understand each other completely and immediately in such exchanges, only that at each moment a sufficient understanding is achieved to make the next move in a still ongoing dialogue. Thus, as Bakhtin (1986) sees it, dialogically-structured understanding is not something that occurs in an instant, but is constructed or developed over time by both participants from within their unfolding, mutual involvement with each other.

And from within that unfolding involvement, when a:

> listener perceives and understands the meaning (the language meaning) of speech, he [or she] takes an active, responsive attitude toward it. He [or she] either agrees or disagrees with it (completely or partially), augments it, applies it, prepares for its execution. And the listener adopts this responsive attitude for the entire duration of the process of listening and understanding, from the speaker's first word. . . . And the speaker himself is oriented precisely toward such responsive understanding. He does not expect passive understanding that, so to speak, only duplicates his own idea in someone else's mind. Rather, he [or she] expects response, agreement, sympathy, objection, execution, and so forth. . . . Moreover, any speaker is him- [or her-]self a respondent to a greater or lesser degree. He is not, after all, the first speaker to disturb the eternal silence of the universe. And he presupposes not only the existence of the language system he is using, but also the existence of preceding utterances. . . . Any utterance is a link in a very complexly organized chain of other utterances. (Bakhtin, 1986, pp. 68, 69)

Thus what is developed here, in the back-and-forth of agreement, disagreement, supplementation, execution, augmentation, application and so on, is a practical understanding negotiated between participants as adequate to current purposes—where such an understanding may still not be a complete and final, cognitive understanding (an exact correspondence between the speaker's and listener's inner mental representations). But what can also be developed here, if we attend to the uniquely spontaneously responsive aspects of our dialogically-structured utterances, is a "shaped sense," so to speak, of each other's "inner world." And it is this grasp of the "inner" structure, so to speak, of an alien world, its "shaped and vectored" form, that is of central interest to Bakhtin, and to us in our inquiries into our own socially constructed worlds.

To introduce the dialogically-structured nature of our involvements with our surroundings through the use of examples drawn solely from spoken dialogues between us, however, is to court the danger of focusing too narrowly on speech communication alone to the exclusion of the larger context of our involved bodily activities. Through my office window the other day I watched four telephone workers erect a four-legged "pergola" structure over an open manhole: two held two of the uprights each, while the other two lowered and slotted a four-limbed "roof structure" onto them. It was all over in about five to ten seconds, but their wordless responsive-responding to each other as they coordinated their collective endeavor was also a perfect example of dialogically-structured joint action. Clearly, people who are in living, embodied, responsive contact with each other's activities in this way do not coordinate their activities cognitively and deliberately, continually having to stop to "work out" what to do next according to a theory-like structure, but are interrelating their activities in an immediate, precognitive and spontaneous, feelingful way: they feel resistances to their pulling in the pushes of the others, they look to where the others are looking to find "where the collective action is," and so on, in terms of a myriad of small and detailed events.

In other words, joint or dialogically-structured activity occurs whenever a first-person *I* is responsively sensitive in his or her living bodily actions to how the second-person *yous* around him or her are bodily responding to what he or she does (or says). Indeed, as soon as a second living human being responds to the activities of a first, then what the second does cannot be accounted as wholly his or her own activity—for the second acts in a way that is partly "shaped" by the first (while the first's acts were responsive, not only to the existence of the language system he or she is using, but also to the existence of preceding utterances, as Bakhtin points out above). It is this that makes the dialogically-structured nature of the background flow of spontaneous activity between us so special.

In the past in social theory, we have focused on the two major realms of human activity most visible to us as individuals: supposedly natural happenings (Behavior) and the actions (Action) of individuals. Dialogically-structured or joint activity, however, cannot be assimilated to either of these two categories. It cannot be understood simply as *Action*, for it is not done by individuals alone, and cannot be explained by giving any person's *reasons* for it[8]; nor can it be treated as a "just happening" event, for, although very like such events, it is intelligently "shaped" to fit the circumstances of its occurrence, and thus cannot be explained as a naturally happening regularity in terms of causal principles either. In fact, what is produced in such dialogical exchanges is a very complex mixture of not wholly reconcilable influences—as Bakhtin (1981) remarks, at work at the same time in every one of our utterances are both "centripetal" tendencies inward toward order and a unitary language, as well as "centrifugal" ones outward toward diversity and heteroglossia.

It is thus next to impossible definitively to characterize the nature of dialogically-structured, joint activity: it has neither a fully orderly nor a fully disorderly structure, neither a completely stable nor an easily changed organization, a neither fully subjective nor fully objective character. More than just a static kind of complexity, dialogically-structured activity has a dynamic, continually changing, oscillating, pulsating character, such that its structure at any one moment is very different from its structure at another. Indeed, it would not be going too far to say that it is its very lack of specificity, its lack of any predetermined order, and thus *its openness to being specified or determined yet further only by those practically involved in it*, that is its central defining feature. So, although in one of its aspects—in terms of its centripetal tendencies— it can be seen as an endless repetition of already existing forms, in another—centrifugally—it can be seen as the endless emergence of unrepeatable novelty. This will be crucial when we come to examine Wittgenstein's work below.

Another crucial feature important at this juncture, however, arises from the impossibility of being able to trace the overall outcome of any exchange back to the intentions of any of the individuals involved in it: because of this, the "situation," the "dialogical space," or the "reality" constructed between them, is experienced as, to an extent, an "external" reality or as a "third agency" with its own (ethical) demands and requirements. "Each dialogue takes place as if against the background of an invisible third party who stands above all the participants in the dialogue (partners)" (Bakhtin, 1986, p. 126). Thus instead of acting within a neutral (mechanistic) reality, we find ourselves within a "living" reality with an agency of its own, an agency that can make claims on us, demands of an ethical kind, an agency that "calls" in a vectored way for us to respond to it. This arises out of the fact that, if you respond to me in a way sensitive to the *relations* between your actions and my responses to them and I respond to you in a way sensitive to the *relations* between my actions and your responses to them, then we can act together as a "collective we"; but if I sense you as not being sensitive in that way, as not responding to my responses to you, then I feel immediately offended in an ethical way—I feel that you lack a proper care or respect for "our" joint "goings on." As Goffman (1976) puts it, the maintaining between us of our "joint spontaneous involvement" (to use his phrase) requires that we continually satisfy various "involvement obligations." I will return to this issue again in a moment, for it leads, as we shall see, to a number of very important points to do with the *necessary* spontaneity of our background activities, but for the moment, let me remain with related but somewhat more basic issues.

ANSWERABILITY WITHIN "ONCE-OCCURRENT EVENTS OF BEING"

Dialogically-structured activities come into being only when agents go out to meet and to interact, actively and bodily, with aspects of their surroundings. Only then is it possible for them to get a sense of the relations between their outgoing activity toward the othernesses around them and the incoming activity that results. But to be able to do that, agents must be able to distinguish between those aspects of their outgoing activities for which they themselves are responsible and direct toward an other (its "addressivity"[9] to use Bakhtin's [1986, p. 95] phrase), and those aspects of their activities that merely happen irrespective of their agency. Just as in feeling one of our fingers over another, it is the shape of the passive finger which is felt through the agency of the active one (not the shape of the active finger through "impressions" received by the passive one); or in a handshake, the shape of the *other's* hand is felt through *our* handshaking activity, while he or she feels the shape of *ours* through his or hers; or from within a greeting, we get a sense of an other's attitude toward us in his or her reply (whether friendly or hostile, joyous or downcast) while he or she gets a sense of ours toward them, so in all such encounters in which we take up an active, living, unfolding involvement with our surroundings, we get a sense of what our surroundings mean for us from within those of active relations toward them for which we ourselves are responsible (Shotter, 1974, 1975, 1984).[10]

The basic structure displayed here, in our responsible engagements with our surroundings, is the *from-to* structure of "tacit knowing" as outlined by Polanyi (1963): we attend *from* a secondary or subsidiary awareness of the moment-by-moment unfolding *details* of the relations between our outflow of responsible activity toward an other and the inflowing results, *to* an *overall* focal awareness of the continuously changing, "vectored shape" disclosed in those relations—its *physiognomy*, as both Polanyi (1963, p. 12) and Wittgenstein (e.g., 1953, p. 210) call it. We attend *from* bodily processes occurring within us *to* qualities in our surroundings; these qualities are what the internal processes *mean* to us. In doing so, we tend not to notice what is going on in our own bodies.[11] We displace the qualities disclosed away from ourselves, and locate them out in that aspect of the world from which the incoming responses to our outgoing activities emanate.

A paradigm instance of such a displaced and vectored form of disclosure is our sense, say, of us as feeling the road "dangerously slippery" beneath our tires when driving on a wet day, and the mood of apprehension, along with the now careful movements of the steering wheel, such a sense calls out from us as a result. What the details are to which we are sensitive in such circumstances would be difficult to say—and it must be emphasized that all such sensitivities take time to develop and seem to be developed only by those "interested" in driving well—but there is no doubt that it is not too difficult for us to learn what they can "mean" or "point to" for how we should handle our driving in such situations. And in the light of this example, we can now, perhaps, see that the sense in which we do respond responsibly is not (at least, not immediately) anything to do with being responsible to others but to do with being responsible, so to speak, to the "call" coming from our circumstances to act in a particular way. Hence the importance of being "interested" in driving well.

Bakhtin (1993) calls such a form of responsibility an act's *answerability*: "In its answerability, the act sets out its own truth [*pravda*] as something to-be-achieved—a truth that unites both the subjective and the psychological moments, just as its unites the moment of what is universal (universally valid) and the moment of what is individual (actual). . . . The actually performed act in its undivided wholeness is more than rational—it is *answerable*. Rationality is but a moment of answerability . . ." (p. 29). Without an immediate and unequivocal responsive understanding that, on at least some occasions, a person's current response is (or is not) answering what questions put to him or her "call for," and us "going on" with them, practically, on that basis, rational discussion amongst us would be impossible. "The end is not," says Wittgenstein (1969), "certain propositions striking us immediately as true, i.e., it is not a kind of *seeing* on our part; it is our *acting*, which lies at the bottom of the language-game" (no. 204). It is in how we "go on" with people that we display our relationally responsive understandings.

But just as we may turn to or go up to someone or something, so we may also turn from or go away from someone or something, and cease our responsible, responsive actions toward them, and become involved elsewhere. Our involvements need not be continuous nor solely of one kind; they have the form of events with a beginning, middle, and an end. Because of their unique, unrepeatable character and because, even if the world around us was utterly static and unchanging, we would change and develop as a result of our encounters with it, Bakhtin (1993) calls the time period when we are in a state of responsible or answerable involvement with an aspect of our surroundings a "once-occurrent event of Being" (p. 2). What is crucial about such events is that it is only from within them, from within their unfolding and from within their unfolding alone, that we can bring the past into contact with the present in a way shaped by the anticipation of a particular future: we can bring an already determined and integral aspect of ourselves, or of the world, or of both into contact with a unique, never-before-existing and never-to-be-repeated, lived experience; we can bring an objective and general domain of culture into relation with a set of unique, concrete circumstances; we can bring "the already spoken" into contact with the "not yet said" (Bakhtin, 1981, p. 28); and "in the novel," which is of course of special interest to Bakhtin (1981): "the 'already bespoke quality' of the world is woven together with the 'already uttered' quality of language, into the unity of the world's heteroglot becoming, in both social consciousness and language" (p. 331). In all these cases, within once-occurrent events of Being, we can bring a whole range of diverse influences into relation with each other, to bear on each other not in a logical or causal way, but in a moving, living, dialogically-structured fashion.

> The answerability of the actually performed act knows a unitary plane, a unitary context in which [a] taking-into-account is possible—in which its theoretical validity, its historical factuality, and its emotional-volitional tone figure as moments in a single decision or resolution. All these moments, moreover (which are different in their significance when viewed from an abstract standpoint), are not impoverished, but are taken in their fullness and in all their truth [*pravda*]. The performed act has, therefore, a single plane and a single principle that encompasses all those moments within its answerability. (Bakhtin, 1981, p. 28)

But so far, it will have been noticed, within the plane of the once-occurrent event of Being, we have considered mostly the experience of a single agent becoming involved with an aspect of his or her surroundings, and have not yet begun properly to consider the relations within such events when two (or more) consciousnesses become involved with each other. As Bakhtin (1984) points out: "It is one thing to be active in relation to a dead thing, to voiceless material that can be molded and formed as one wishes, and another thing to be active *in relation to someone else's living, autonomous consciousness*. This is a questioning, provoking, answering, agreeing, objecting activity; that is, it is a dialogic activity no less active than the activity that finalizes, materializes, explains, and kills causally, that drowns out the other's voice with nonsemantic arguments" (p. 285); that is, arguments (from within a speaker's own scheme of abstractions) that do not arouse a responsive understanding of any kind in their listeners, that lie "dead" before one. It is once we begin to consider the relations between two (or more) consciousnesses and the ability of another's voice to "call out" responses from us, whether we like it or not, that we can begin to examine more closely people's practical understanding of each other's actions and to turn toward issues to do with people appreciating both each other's "inner" lives and their own.

For, just as in touching and caressing another's hand, although we mostly feel his or her hand and not our own, he or she will react to ours as rough or smooth, as fleshy or bony, as strong or weak, and so on, and we get to know about our own hand through his or her responses to it, so we can get to know more about other aspects of ourselves through the responses of others to our responses to them. Indeed, as Bakhtin (1984) remarks: "I am conscious of myself and become myself only while revealing myself for another, through another, and with the help of another. . . . I cannot manage without another, cannot become myself without another; I must find myself in another by finding another in myself (in mutual reflection and mutual acceptance)" (p. 287). But it is only from within once-occurrent events of Being, those events in which we are involved with or engaged with the others around us, that the possibility of me coming to be conscious of myself arises. It will be useful to dwell for a moment on the relation of such events to our already existing practices.

Unrepeatable, First-Time Reactions in Relation to "Regular Ways of Action"

Central to Bakhtin's, Voloshinov's, and Wittgenstein's accounts of meaning and understanding is the fact of our living, bodily *responsiveness* to events in our surroundings. For them, meaning and understanding are not first to be found inside people's heads and then, later, in their actions, but the other way around: what is later to be found in their heads appears first in their actions. "To understand another person's utterance means to orient oneself with respect to it, to find the proper place for it in the corresponding context. For each word we are in the process of understanding, we, as it were, lay down a set of our own answering words. . . . *Any true understanding is dialogic in nature.* Understanding is to utterance as one line of dialogue is to the next" (Voloshinov, 1929/1986, p. 102). As Wittgenstein sees it: "The origin and primitive form of the language-game is a reaction; only from this can more complicated forms develop. Language—I want to say—is a refinement, 'in the beginning was the deed'" (1980, p. 31). By the word *primitive* here, Wittgenstein means that " . . . this sort of behavior is *prelinguistic*: that a language-game is based *on it*, that it is the prototype of a way of thinking and not the result of thought" (1981, no. 541).

Such living, bodily responses are thus the primitive beginnings from which our more refined and elaborated meaningful behavior and our understandings of it are developed. It cannot be emphasized too much that at the heart of us becoming language users is us being trained by those around us to react and respond in various ways, spontaneously and directly. Where training us to respond in this way does not depend on our first understanding, but rather, our later understanding depends on it. At the heart of all our "mental" activities are our practices, practices that meet certain public norms and criteria of successful performance. "Only in learning a foreign language does a fully prepared consciousness . . . confront a fully prepared language which it need only accept" suggests Voloshinov. "People do not "accept" their native language—it is in their native language that they first reach awareness" (1929/1986, p. 81).

Let me emphasize the radical nature of what all three are claiming here. Rather than beginning with anything in our heads, they are suggesting that the origin or source of everything that is meaningful for us can be found out in the world between us, in our living, bodily reactions to events in our surroundings. What may seem to end up residing inside our individual heads, in our minds, and to have its whole existence there without any obvious relation to our surroundings, starts out in the living, bodily responsive relations between us and the world around us. And furthermore, our meaningful ways of so acting are in fact sustained in existence by our unceasingly exhibiting in our spontaneous responsive reactions certain characteristic ways of acting and forms of expression, in relation to certain very general facts of nature:

> If there were, for instance, no characteristic expression of pain, of fear, of joy; if rule became exception and exception rule; or if both became phenomena of roughly equal frequency—this would make our normal language-games lose their point. The procedure of putting a lump of cheese on a balance and fixing the price by the turn of the scale would lose its point if it frequently happened for such lumps to suddenly grow or shrink for no obvious reason. (Wittgenstein, 1953, no. 142).

It is not that we have certain "instincts," as if we were automatons who exhibit fixed and innately patterned sequences of behavior, released from us solely by the occurrence of specific stimuli. It is just that the immensely varied relations between us and our surroundings depend on our being able to depend on certain regularities, sureties, certitudes, in the world around us—where these everyday certitudes and sureties are not claims to knowledge, in the sense that we can offer criteria for our belief in them, but are, once again, the basic but ungrounded terms which are constitutive for us of who and what we are; they are the terms in which we make sense of everything else around us; they constitute "the element in which [our] arguments have their life" (Wittgenstein, 1969, no. 105). Hence, in contrast to the Cartesian claim that any proper knowledge of things must begin in doubt, Wittgenstein suggests: "The primitive form of the language-game is certainty, not uncertainty. For uncertainty could never lead to action. I want to say: it is characteristic of our language that the foundation on which it grows consists in steady ways of living, regular ways of acting. . . . The basic form of the game must be one in which we act" (1993, p. 397). "What has to be accepted, the given, is—so one could say—*forms of life*" (Wittgenstein, 1953, p. 226).

Thus, as we have seen, Bakhtin, Voloshinov, and Wittgenstein all draw our attention to the fact that, whether we like it or not, we live our lives embedded within one or another strand of a ceaseless flow of living, unrepeatable, dialogically-structured activity where: "this chain of ideological creativity and understanding, moving from sign to sign and then to a new sign, is perfectly consistent and continuous: from one link of a semiotic nature (hence, also of a material nature) we proceed uninterruptedly to another link of exactly the same nature. And nowhere is there a break in the chain, nowhere does the chain plunge into inner being, nonmaterial in nature and unembodied in signs" (Voloshinov, 1929/1986, p. 11). And it is only *from within* our own living, spontaneous involvements or engagements within such a chain of activity that we can make sense of what is occurring around us. Indeed, as we are socialized into such activity-flows, into the already established practices going on around us, we become trained in the practical, relationally responsive forms of understanding required in spontaneously "going on" with those who are already "at home," so to speak, within such practices.

"Individuals do not receive a ready-made language at all, rather, they enter upon the stream of verbal communication; indeed, only in this stream does their consciousness first begin to operate" (Voloshinov, 1929/1986, p. 81). To repeat, such spontaneous ways of acting, with their "grammar," are thus *constitutive* for us of who and what we are and what counts for us as the stable, repeatable, and significant forms within that flow; and as such, they cannot be explained, for they constitute the basis in terms of which all our explaining of things to each other is done. For us they are foundational.

This, however, is what is so difficult for us to accept. If Wittgenstein is right, then our actions are not rooted or grounded in any supposedly already existing, objective structures out in the world, nor in any subjective structures in our minds, but simply in the "grammars" currently existing in our forms of life, that is, in the immediate and "blind" but sure and unquestioned, ways of acting, in terms of which we spontaneously relate to the Others and othernesses around us. In other words, our ways of acting are not themselves based on grounds; they are not reasonable (or unreasonable); they are simply "there" as an aspect of our lives together. And their "grammar," their physiognomy, the set of "action-guiding advisories," the "shaped and vectored sense" of where I am, where I have come from, and where I am going to that they continuously provide to us from within our participation in them is crucial in giving intelligible shape to everything we do. Thus, as Wittgenstein remarks, "grammar tells us what kind of object anything is" (Wittgenstein, 1953, no. 373). But as we have seen, in lived space, objects are known to us in terms of what aspects they will present to us next as we move in relation to them. In other words, as Wittgenstein puts it, his investigations are not so much directed toward phenomena in themselves, but: "as one might say towards the '*possibilities*' of phenomena. We remind ourselves, that is to say, of the *kind of statement* that we make about phenomena. . . . Our investigation is therefore a grammatical one" (1953, no. 90). It is to do with the *possible* connections and relations between things, whether already realized or not.

"GOING ON" FROM WHERE WE ARE

In the past we have developed our language-game-entwined forms of life collectively, without being aware of how (or why) we have brought about such changes from the primitive and myth-laden forms of earlier times to what they are today in all their complexity and refinement. What Wittgenstein's work now allows us to do, however, is to come to a much more aware grasp of how such changes occur. This is crucial. For, although our language-game-entwined forms of life may seem to be utterly arbitrary and without foundations and thus just to be "there" without any explanation, this does not mean to say that we cannot, from within our living of them, criticize or improve them. Indeed, just as we argue that the transition from our seeing our world in terms of myths of our own devising to seeing it in the more objective terms of science was an improvement in that we now orient ourselves toward our "external" world in less confusing, more instrumentally effective ways, so we can argue that Bakhtin's, Voloshinov's, and Wittgenstein's work can help us orient ourselves in similar more "vectored," less confused, and confusing ways "inside" our social lives together. Thus, even though their work cannot be justified in terms of any explicit foundational principles, it can nonetheless still be counted as critical, and their attention-directing statements as not simply arbitrary, if in their application they can lead to forms of life that, by comparison, can be accounted better than previous forms.

But more than just at this global level, their work is also crucial in bringing to our attention the importance of details; they have made rationally visible to us the immensely varied and subtlety detailed ways in which it is possible for us to bring about such changes in our forms of life. Above I have emphasized the importance of the steady ways of living and regular ways of acting within which our language is rooted. If we lived in a wholly mechanistic world, that would once again be an invitation to focus on the importance of repetitions and regularities—for in a world in which earlier states can be repeated exactly, all traces of the passage of time could be eradicated. But in a living world in which time is real and irreversible, so that the world as a whole can never take up again a previous configuration, to sustain repeatability at least within portions of it takes energy and effort.

In other words, as we are now beginning to realize from, say, Prigogine's (1980; Prigogine and Stengers, 1984) work on what he calls "dissipative structures" and other work in complexity and chaos theory (Waldrop, 1992), living stabilities are dynamic stabilities sustained within a constantly changing, unrepeatable, surrounding flow of activity, and as such are in fact, strangely, sources of ceaseless novelty (see Shotter, 1984, p. 197). For there must be an irreducible, qualitative difference between the successive moments of such a stability for it to be recognizable as a flowing (rather than frozen) stability. As Wittgenstein (1980) puts it: "Life's infinite variations are essential to our life. And so too even to the habitual character of life" (1980, p. 73). We thus find that what is repeated in "once-occurrent events of Being" are not dead, identical forms, like each tooth of a cogwheel, but unique living events that, although all different from each other, can be "counted as" the same as each other; they are such that we can spontaneously respond to each in the same way (but that we can, should we so choose to orient ourselves differently, respond to differently also).

Everyone's voicing of the greeting "Hello," for example, is different from everyone else's; and we can recognize a friend's voice as greeting us while knowing that other greetings are uttered by strangers. But, as Bakhtin points out, what makes an utterance an utterance, and not just the voicing of a linguistic form, is *"the possibility of responding to it* or, more precisely and broadly, of assuming a responsive attitude toward it (for example, executing an order)" (1986, p. 76). That is, it is in the realm of doings and deeds that an utterance has its being. And as speakers we not only express our own particular position and evaluative attitude toward both the topic and our addressee (friendly-unfriendly, official-intimate, etc.) in the ongoing action between us, but we determine in our tone their responsive position (subservient, equal, superordinate, etc.).

In being shaped in accord with a speaker's responsive relations to their surroundings, every utterance expresses in its intonation a speaker's momentary *evaluative orientation* and, in so doing, also *positions* listeners in relation to it. And listeners respond accordingly from within the position they now find themselves placed. Thus, rather than first recognizing the repetition of a regular form, and then going on to interpret its particular meaning in a particular context, the opposite is the case: as living beings, we first find ourselves spontaneously responding to another as friendly or unfriendly, as of higher or lower social rank, as keeping us at a distance or as being intimate with us, and so on, without it at all being apparent to us precisely what it is in the *form* of their behavior that positions us in relation to them. As we have seen above, such spontaneous responses are the primitive beginnings from which most refined and elaborated understandings are developed.

To emphasize the point again: these initial forms of response do not depend on cognitive acts occurring inside our individual heads, on thought, understanding, or acts of interpretation. Rather, our individual acts of cognition depend on our acting—"in the beginning was the deed." Thus, as Voloshinov puts it:

> The basic task of understanding does not at all amount to recognizing the linguistic form used by the speaker as the familiar, 'that very same,' form, the way we distinctly recognize, for instance, a signal that we have not quite become used to or a form in a language that we do not know very well. No, the task of understanding does not basically amount to recognizing the form used, but rather to understanding it in a particular, concrete context, to understanding its meaning in a particular utterance, i.e., it amounts to understanding its novelty and not to recognizing its identity. . . . Thus the constituent factor for the linguistic form, as for the sign, is not at all its self-identity as signal but its specific variability; and the constituent factor for understanding the linguistic form is not recognition of 'the same thing,' but understanding in the proper sense of the word, i.e., orientation in the particular given context and in the particular, given situation—orientation in the dynamic process of becoming and not 'orientation' in some inert sense. (1929/1986, pp. 68, 69)

Thus, just as I recognize that it is "your" voice as my friend on the telephone now, and not that of a stranger, irrespective of what you might say, or you recognize that it is "my" writing, irrespective of what is actually written there, so we recognize in the continuously changing "vectored shapes" disclosed *in* the events occurring around us a *physiognomy*, a quality to which we can orient—like suddenly hearing our native tongue spoken in a foreign land. Here is something very particular to us, something we are "at home" in, to which we can relate, something that gives us a set of possible paths forward. We feel that we have a sense of what to do next, that here is a situation in which we know how to "go on." As intellectuals and academics, due to our mechanistic upbringing, we think that without an accumulated experience of very general repetitions, we lack all orientation; like Descartes, we feel "as if [we] have fallen unexpectedly into a deep whirlpool which tumbles [us] around so that [we] can neither stand on the bottom nor swim up to the surface" (1968, p. 16).

But this is to forget the anchoring that we can have in certain situations, in our sense of our responsibility for our own actions: we need to remind ourselves of the fact that we can distinguish in at least some cases those occurrences for which we, and we alone, can be said to be responsible from those just naturally happening, and from the protophenomena making this possible. It is this which allows us to orient ourselves, even in what are for us unique, first-time events. For to repeat: "The actually performed act in its undivided wholeness is more than rational—it is *answerable*. Rationality is but a moment of answerability. . . . " (Bakhtin, 1993, p. 29). And it is in spontaneously finding ourselves answerable to specific "calls" coming to us from our surroundings, along with (more or less elaborated) "action guiding advisories" of some kind, their "grammar," that gives us the orientation we need. To that extent, even as very young babies, we are never not oriented, to put the matter rather awkwardly. Indeed, as is well known, babies react to complex qualities, such as friendliness and joy, unfriendliness and anger, long before they distinguish between simple forms, such as triangles and squares.

What cultural and linguistic *forms* are seen and accounted by us as constant in our lives, are achieved by us. So, while we may be tempted to suggest that the norm is constancy, and that it is in *variations* from the norm that we can express our own, unique "inner lives," ourselves, more properly we should say that variation is the norm, and that exceptionally, besides expressing our own uniqueness, we can on occasions, if we have been trained properly so to respond, understand in another's unique behavior aspects of it which we all share, which we can count as constant. What is important to us in our lives together, then, are the fleeting, on-off, unique, unrepeatable events, events that, as Garfinkel so wonderfully puts it, continually occur for yet "another first time" (1967, p. 9). It is "within" these unique, first-person expressions, these once-occurrent events of Being, that we make our "inner" lives "visible" to the others around us. We become present to each other "from within" them, "from within" our ongoing involvements with each other, "from within" our forms of life.

Conclusions: The Shift into a Participatory World

Instead of attempting to provide any new theories, then, of the supposed mechanical and repetitive realities underlying our behavior, Voloshinov, Wittgenstein, and Bakhtin focus on the amazing and almost infinitely complex nature of what previously has passed us by unnoticed, in the background to our lives: the flow of spontaneously responsive, living, relational activity within which everything we do in our ordinary, everyday lives is embedded. The perspective—no, the form of life they offer us, is one very different from the essentially Cartesian form of life we have adopted and trained ourselves in, in our intellectual inquiries in modern times. Primarily they have shifted our attention away from what is supposed to be *radically hidden* inside us somewhere, and toward what occurs out in the world between us, which is hidden from us only because we fail to attend to it. They have also drawn our attention to the fact that, as living beings, we cannot not be responsive to our surroundings and are thus always in one or another living relationship to them. They have also shifted our whole standpoint from that of disengaged, outside observers to being interested, involved participants. Indeed, a whole galaxy of changes is involved—a shift into a world very different from the modern, "external" world in which we have now lived for three hundred years or so. We can list some of the more prominent changes, that is, those that most clearly contrast with (almost as mirror images of) our current assumptions:

1. There is something quite special about us being alive and embodied.[12]
2. We cannot not be spontaneously, that is, directly, responsive to each other and our surroundings in one way or another.
3. There is a complexity and fullness, so to speak, of those fleeting moments when we are in a direct, living contact with others or an otherness in our surroundings.
4. We live as responsive parts of a larger, living, responsive whole.
5. Among the consequences of our being immersed in such a flow of living activity is the fact that everything we do and say has its being and makes sense only *from within* this unceasing stream of life in which we also have our being.
6. Indeed, in "calling out" certain actions rather than others from us, we spontaneously find ourselves oriented within the flow.

7. The focus on events within the stream of life leads people to emphasize *internal* rather than *external* relations: that is, while the parts of a dead structure have a nature to them whether a part of the structure or not, those of a living, organic unity owe their very nature at every moment not only to their relations to the other parts within the whole, but also to its earlier parts from which they have developed—thus, as well as their momentary spatial relations, their temporal (historical, developmental) relations are of importance also.

8. To adopt this stance, to distinguish between internal and external relations, is to distinguish between those aspects of a scene which stand before us "dead," so to speak, and those which "call" something from us, to which we are "answerable."

9. Also, to adopt this stance toward living things and activities is to adopt what Bakhtin (1993) calls a "participative" (p. 8) or "unindifferent" (p. 44) style of thought. It means that whatever one might say with respect to our communicative activities, for instance, must be said *from within* one's living involvement in them, rather than as a disinterested external observer of them.

10. The ultimate realm in which we live and have our being, and in which we must find the final arbitration as the value of our achievements, is the realm of doings and deeds.

11. All this finally leads to what we might call a *performative* mode of inquiry, a mode of inquiry in which "the proof" of a result, an outcome, is not in participants now being able to make true claims to knowledge, but in them now being able to carry out new practices successfully between them. To repeat: "the end is not certain propositions striking us immediately as true, i.e., it is not a kind of *seeing* on our part; it is our *acting*, which lies at the bottom of the language-game" (Wittgenstein, 1969, no. 204).

To these themes in common, Bakhtin and Voloshinov add, as we have seen, another, quite distinct, *dialogical* theme:

12. In bridging the momentary "gaps" occurring between us as we turn from "addressing" others to "inviting" them to address us, the outcomes of the responsive activity occurring between us have a special kind of unique, open, complex, and mixed quality to them

that makes them utterly distinct from any other kind of events in existence.

Clearly, as Bakhtin, Voloshinov, and Wittgenstein see it, the spontaneously responsive relations that we have to each other and to the rest of our surroundings, which are prior to and provide the background for everything else of a more self-conscious and deliberately controlled kind that we do as individuals, have a very special nature: in being protophenomena, candidates for later, more well-defined forms of behavior, they have what we might call a *primal*, *originary* or *constitutive* character. It is this which makes them amenable only to a certain kind of understanding: what, as we have seen, Bakhtin (1993) calls a *participatory* style of thought and understanding. And I would like to end this article with some comments as to its nature.

In the past, we have thought of our inquiries as making reality apparent to us, with the hope that if we knew the true nature of our surroundings, we could act in ways better fitted to them. Thus, as uninvolved, disinterested, objective observers, we could just pass on the results of our findings for everyone's benefit. But it is impossible for us to conduct any inquiries without at some point voicing claims, opinions, theories, and so on, as to their nature. And as Bakhtin remarks:

> An utterance is never just a reflection or an expression of something already existing and outside it that is given and final. It always creates something that never existed before, something absolutely new and unrepeatable, and, moreover, it always has some relation to value (the true, the good, the beautiful, and so forth). But something created is always created out of something given (language, an observed phenomenon of reality, an experienced feeling, the speaking subject himself, something finalized in his world view, and so forth). What is given is completely transformed in what is created. (Bakhtin, 1986, pp. 119, 120)

In other words, because we live in a world of dialogically structured events, people's utterances always and inevitably make a difference in and to our lives: they make history. They cannot be unsaid. It is not a matter simply of us possessing, or not, a certain body of knowledge. Another kind of understanding is at work. It is not the kind of understanding that can be formulated in terms of general facts or theoretical principles; it is not a "knowing that" (Ryle, 1949). But neither can it be the understanding of a particular skill or craft, a "knowing how." For clearly, it is a kind of understanding which is uniquely relevant only to the particular concrete, dialogically structured situation within which it makes its appearance. It has its being only within our ongoing, living, participative relations to others. As such, it depends on our grasp of particular, only once-occurrent connections and relations *internal* to the specific situation in which we are involved, and because they occur only once, unrepeatably, we can never gain an explicit, systematic understanding of such relations within a unitary order of connectedness. As I have suggested elsewhere (Shotter, 1993a and b), it can be called a "knowing-from-within," a kind of understanding that one has only from within a social situation and which, in being answerable to its situation, takes into account (and is accountable to) the *others* in the situation within which it is applied. Indeed, it is a codeveloped, dialogically-structured kind of understanding, an understanding of a participatory kind that we can come to only as a result of our responsive contact with the others and othernesses around us. It does not give us what we have sought in the past, an objective, independent picture of "how it is."

But that monological, representational-referential form of understanding, as we have called it, into which we were trained as stand-alone, Cartesian thinkers, gives us its supposed, objective pictures only against the background of, or in relation to, the unceasing flow of spontaneous, living activity between us which constitutes for us the basic social reality within which we all live our lives.[13] Within that reality, the relational-responsive kind of understanding we employ is more than the passive picturing of a state of affairs. It is the articulating or disclosing further, over time, in an active and dialogical fashion, from within our living involvements with the others and othernesses around us, the "vectored shape" of the initial living impulses "called out" in us by those involvements. And it is a kind of understanding that is improved by "seeing connections" not noticed before (Wittgenstein, 1953, no. 122). For the seeing of such connections orients us in how further we might "go on" with what or who is in our surroundings. Indeed, due to its origination in living impulses of one kind or another, such a form of understanding always *matters* to us, it "always has some relation to value (the true, the good, the beautiful, and so forth)" (Bakhtin 1986, p. 120). It is the ineradicably *evaluative* and *orientational* aspect of our living relations to our surroundings below that distinguishes the embodied, *participatory* stance Bakhtin and Wittgenstein take in their studies, which contrasts markedly with the disembodied, disinterested, disengaged ways of being currently demanded of us by our training as objective scientists. But it is precisely this which allows us continually to improve it from with our involvements in it.

Thus, to summarize the general shift in stance entailed in moving from a disengaged, Cartesian stance toward a more participatory style of thought, we can say: it entails a shift from the attitude of the uninvolved, disinterested, external observer to that of the engaged, interested partic-ipant in a language-game-entwined form of life. Where, within such forms of life, participants are interested, at any one moment, in grasping (perceiving) in an action-relevant manner, what can be effected within them, the possibilities for action they *allow* or *afford* us. For we want to act in ways that are not at odds with our surroundings, in which, among the many other barriers to effective and proper action, we do not become entangled in our own rules. Where, in the long term, of course, we are interested in extending what abilities we have to move in ways that are "in tune with" our own immediate surroundings, out further into the larger world around us. In other words, as a participant in all aspects of human life at large, I want, as Wittgenstein put it, to "know my way about" (1953, no. 123), unendingly, inside more and more aspects of it. I want to be more "at home" in the complicated "landscape" of human phenomena without the continual need to consult and puzzle over maps—to be "at home" in human life at large in ways that I can contin-ually extend as I actively engage myself in elaborating yet further the "calls" I receive from my surroundings.

NOTES

1. Helen Keller, it is said somewhere, could recognize people again up to two years after having shaken their hands just once (remember, she was deaf and blind). However, this is no more remarkable than those of us who are hearing people being able to recognize people again from their voices.

2. This is an experience I had once when, after having broken a lens in my eyeglasses, I tried driving with just one lens: although the cars around me were clearly different distances from me, I found myself feeling very unsure of what,

for driving purposes, that distance was. And it was of course impossible to puzzle it out consciously in a way that gave me any surety in my driving. There is also the experience related by Helmholtz somewhere, that when young, while out in the town square with his mother, he noticed some workmen high up on the church: he asked his mother to reach down some of the "little dolls" for him to play with.

3. This is Bernstein's (1983) term. He links it to Aristotle's notion of *phronesis*, which is that kind of practical knowing, "which is not detached from our being but is determinative of what we are in the process of becoming" (Bernstein, 1992, p. 25).

4. This is the kind of *passive* understanding familiar to us in our current, *mechanistic* theorizing in psychology and other social sciences: we assume the passive reception of inputs or impressions from the external world, and their "understanding" is said to depend on certain relations holding between what is "out there" and the "inner mental states" these inputs are said to *cause* in us. We have no initially *active* relation to such inputs prior to their "understanding."

5. Elsewhere, I have called this kind of activity *joint action* (Shotter, 1980, 1984, 1993a and b, 1995).

6. We can think of it as containing not only a protologic, a protophysics, a protodrama, literature, and poetics, and especially a proto-civil law, but also as continually giving rise to entirely new and unique relations between us, such that from within them, we can also come to a grasp of alien worlds previously utterly unknown to us (Shotter, 1998). Often, when faced with such a circumstance, "our mistake is to look for an explanation where we ought to look at what happens as a 'proto-phenomenon'" (Wittgenstein, 1953, no. 654); i.e., we look for repetitions of what already exists, rather than for something unique and novel.

7. Of great relevance here are Bachelard's (1992) claims that "the house is one of the greatest powers of integration for the thoughts, memories and dreams of mankind" (p. 6), that "it is the human being's first world" (p. 7), and his designation of certain spaces as "domains of intimacy" (p. 12) that, in imaginatively returning to them, allow us to relive, phenomenologically, certain experiences—for example, the polarity of the cellar and the attic, what is up, airy, clear, and light compared with what is dark, damp, down, and mysterious (the one-sided walls that have the entire earth hidden behind them). There is insufficient space to explore the power of these images further here.

8. Functionalist accounts attempt to explain human phenomena in terms of basic human interests and needs people's actions *must* satisfy if they are all to fit together into a systematic whole. Neither Bakhtin, Voloshinov, or Wittgenstein is a functionalist. Indeed, Wittgenstein expresses his antifunctionalism (and

antifoundationalism) thus: "You must bear in mind that the language-game is so to say something unpredictable. I mean: it is not based on grounds. It is not reasonable (or unreasonable). It is there—like our life" (1969, no. 559).

9. Bakhtin also talks of addressivity as "the quality of turning to someone" (1986, p. 99). Wittgenstein makes a similar observation in noting that he wants to say: "When we mean something, it's like going up to someone, it's not having a dead picture (of any kind). We go up to the thing we mean" (1953, no. 455).

10. "We all distinguish, and indeed if we are to be accounted reasonable human beings we all *must* be able to distinguish, between that for which we as individual personalities are responsible and that which merely happens irrespective of our agency. This distinction is *fundamental* not only in everyday life but also in science . . . lacking any sense of their own functioning scientists would be unable to do experiments" (Shotter, 1974, p. 57).

11. "Our own body is the only thing in the world which we normally never experience as an object, but experience always in terms of the world to which we are attending from our body. It is by making intelligent use of our body that we can feel it to be our body, and not a thing outside us" (Polanyi, 1963, p. 16).

12. "Our attitude to what is alive and what is dead, is not the same. Our reactions are different" (Wittgenstein,1953, no. 284).

13. "What determines our judgment, our concepts and reactions, is not what *one* man is doing *now*, an individual action, but the whole hurly-burly of human actions, the background against which we see any action" (Wittgenstein, 1981, no. 567).

REFERENCES

Bachelard, G. (1992). *The poetics of space*. Boston, MA: Beacon Press.

Bakhtin, M. M. (1981). *The dialogical imagination*. Edited by M. Holquist, trans. by C. Emerson and M. Holquist. Austin, TX: University of Texas Press.

Bakhtin, M. M. (1984). *Problems of Dostoevsky's poetics*. Edited and trans. by Caryl Emerson. Minneapolis: University of Minnesota Press.

Bakhtin, M. M. (1986). *Speech genres and other late essays*. Trans. by Vern W. McGee. Austin, TX: University of Texas Press.

Bakhtin, M. M. (1993). *Toward a philosophy of the act*, with translation and notes by Vadim Lianpov, edited by M. Holquist. Austin, TX: University of Texas Press.

Bernstein, R. J. (1983). *Beyond objectivism and relativism*. Oxford, UK: Blackwell.

Bernstein, R. J. (1992). *The new constellation*. Cambridge, MA: MIT Press.

Descartes, R. (1968). *Meditations on first philosophy: With selections from objections and replies*. Translated by J. Cottingham, with an introduction by B. Williams. Cambridge, UK: Cambridge University Press.

Garfinkel, H. (1967). *Studies in ethnomethodology*. Englewood Cliffs, NJ: Prentice-Hall.

Gibson, J. J. (1979). *The ecological approach to visual perception*. London: Houghton Mifflin.

Goffman, E. (1976). *Interaction ritual: Essays on face-to-face behavior*. Harmondsworth, UK: Penguin.

Merleau-Ponty, M. (1962). *Phenomenology of perception*. C. Smith (Trans.). London: Routledge and Kegan Paul.

Polanyi, M. (1963). *The tacit dimension*. London: Routledge and Kegan Paul.

Prigogine, I. (1980). *From being to becoming: Time and complexity in the physical sciences*. San Francisco: Freeman.

Prigogine, I., and Stengers, I. (1984). *Order out of chaos: Man's new dialogue with nature*. New York: Bantam Books.

Ryle, G. (1949). *The concept of mind*. London: Methuen.

Shotter, J. (1974). What is it to be human? In N. Armistead (Ed.), *Reconstructing social psychology*. Harmondsworth, UK: Penguin.

Shotter, J. (1975). *Images of man in psychological research*. London: Methuen.

Shotter, J. (1980). Action, joint action, and intentionality. In M. Brenner (Ed.), *The structure of action*, pp. 28–65. Oxford, UK: Blackwell.

Shotter, J. (1984). *Social accountability and selfhood*. Oxford, UK: Blackwell.

Shotter, J. (1993a). *Cultural politics of everyday life: Social constructionism, rhetoric, and knowing of the third kind*. Milton Keynes, UK: Open University Press.

Shotter, J. (1993b). *Conversational realities: Constructing life through language*. London: Sage.

Shotter, J. (1995). In conversation: Joint action, shared intentionality, and the ethics of conversation. *Theory and Psychology, 5*, pp. 49–73.

Shotter, J. (1996). Living in a Wittgensteinian world: Beyond theory to a poetics of practices. *Journal for the Theory of Social Behavior, 26*, pp. 293–311.

Shotter, J. (1998). Social construction as social poetics. In B. Bayer and J. Shotter (Eds.) *Reconstructing the psychological subject: Bodies, pracitces and technologies*. London: Sage.

Shotter, J., and Katz, A. M. (1996). Articulating a practice from within the practice itself: Establishing formative dialogues by the use of a "social poetics." *Concepts and Transformations, 2*, pp. 71–95.

Voloshinov, V. N. (1929/1986). *Marxism and the philosophy of language*. L. Matejka and I. R. Titunik. (Trans.). Cambridge, MA: Harvard University Press.

Waldrop, M. M. (1992). *Complexity: the emerging science at the edge of order and chaos*. New York and London: Simon and Schuster.

Wittgenstein, L. (1953). *Philosophical investigations*. Oxford, UK: Blackwell.

Wittgenstein, L. (1965). *The blue and brown books*. New York: Harper Torch Books.

Wittgenstein, L. (1969). *On certainty*. Oxford, UK: Blackwell.

Wittgenstein, L. (1974). *Philosophical grammar*. Oxford, UK: Blackwell.

Wittgenstein, L. (1980). *Culture and value*. P. Winch. (Trans.). Oxford, UK: Blackwell.

Wittgenstein, L. (1981). Zettel (2nd ed.). G.E.M. Anscombe and G.H.V. Wright (Eds.). Oxford, UK: Blackwell.

From

Identity

to Relational

Politics

Kenneth J. Gergen

Social construction and identity politics form a pair of star-crossed lovers, entwined in a relationship suffused with passion, provocation, and perfidy. No easy relationship, this, but one in which deep intimacy has given birth to an enormously influential array of movements across the land. As I presently see it, however, the fecundity of this union is rapidly diminishing. The tensions between these erstwhile intimates have burst into bitterness. Their love children now tread very mean streets—with damaging countercritique, derision, disregard, and disaffection on every darkened corner. With identity politics under siege, social constructionism now seems a suspicious ally—if not, indeed, an assassin. Can identity politics sustain its course successfully, and should its relationship with social construction be maintained? In what follows, I shall propose that identity politics cannot continue successfully in its existing modes of action and that, indeed, we find a movement struggling toward reformation. Similarly, constructionist dialogues are entering a new phase of development. The new turn in constructionist endeavors can and should play a key role in the future evolution of identity politics. We are poised, then, for a rekindling of the passions, in what I will call a *relational politics*.

Although the phrase "identity politics" has served many different purposes, for the present I will take it to stand for a mode of political activism—typically though not exclusively initiated by groups excluded from traditional mainstream politics. Such marginalized groups generate a self-designated identity (group consciousness) that is instantiated by

the individual identities of its constituents. Identity politics differs from many social movements, such as left-wing or fundamentalist Christian activism, in that the constituents of the former—such as women, Afro-Americans, gays—are politically marked as individuals. Politics and personal being are virtually inseparable. This inseparability is owing largely to the natural production of the political categories. One may by virtue of reason or impulse join the National Rifle Association or the Praise the Lord Club. Not so with being a Native American or a Black Muslim. One simply is, by virtue of nature, tradition, or thrown condition, an Asian-American, a lesbian, or a member of the lower class. And finally, it is largely by virtue of the "natural" condition of its members that the groups lay claim to certain inalienable rights—for example, equal opportunities, equal treatment, freedom to practice, participation in democratic governance.

For present purposes we may see social constructionism as a range of dialogues centered on the social genesis of what we take to be knowledge, reason, and virtue, on the one side, and on the other the enormous range of social practices born and/or sustained by these discourses. In its critical moment, social constructionism is a means of bracketing or suspending any pronouncement of the real, the reasonable, or the right. In its generative moment, constructionism offers an orientation toward creating new futures, an impetus to societal transformation.

Why a love affair between identity politics and social constructionism? There are many reasons. Among them, the generalized shift toward social construction in the academy furnished a powerful justificatory basis for political and moral activism. For the better part of the century, the academy basked in what it believed to be an ideological nonpartisanship. Epitomized by the positivist-empiricist stance in the natural and social sciences, it held that the function of inquiry is to determine what is objectively true. Moral and ideological commitment obfuscate the quest, it was said, yielding bias and misinformation. ("Proper scholarship is about truth, not the good.") However, as constructionist critique challenged claims to objectivity—truth beyond cultural standpoint—so did it eradicate the is-ought divide. Not only did the discourses of truth, objectivity, and rationality cease to be commanding rhetorics, but their claimants seemed guilty of either ignorance (lack of reflection on implicit ideology) or exploitation (masking self-serving ideology in the cloak of neutrality). The constructionist assault, then, led to a slow dete-rioration of authority, with the simultaneous liberation of politically and morally invested inquiry. If one's professional work is inevitably politi-cal, as constructionists reason, then the academician is furnished a new and inspiring telos. Rather than generating knowledge that may or may not be used by those making decisions for the society—as the pure sci-entists envisioned their goal—the knowledge-generating process becomes itself a means of creating the good society. (Women's studies, black studies and queer studies are exemplary of this impulse.)

Not only did constructionism thus help to incite the political impulse, but it has also generated a powerful set of implements for societal cri-tique. Constructionist inquiry has demonstrated how claims to the true and the good are born of historical traditions, fortified by social net-works, sewn together by literary tropes, legitimated through rhetorical devices, and operate in the service of particular ideologies to fashion structures of power and privilege. For the sophisticated constructionist, there are no invulnerable or unassailable positions, no foundational war-rants, no transcendent rationalities or obdurate facts in themselves. Most important for the present, many of these modes of deconstructing the opposition are "street-ready"; they can be (and are) paraphrased easily in the daily argots of political activism.

THE UNRAVELING OF IDENTITY POLITICS

You will not be mistaken if you recognize in these remarks a soupçon of nostalgia. These have been times of dizzying excitement, crashing idols, scintillating discussion, and epiphanies of virtue. I scarcely think the implications are yet fully explored, nor their action potential exhausted. However, in my view the enormous force of identity politics, aided and abetted as it has been by constructionist dialogues, has begun to sub-side. In large measure, this deterioration of efficacy can be understood in terms of cultural change, change that can in part be traced to the influ-ence of identity politics itself. To take a constructionist stance in this analysis, let me focus only on the rhetoric of identity politics.

From the outset, the prevailing rhetoric has been of little influence outside groups of the already-committed. For the targets—those most in need of "political education"—such rhetoric has more often been alien-ating or counterproductive. By and large, identity politics has depended on a rhetoric of blame, the illocutionary effects of which are designed to chastise the target (for being unjust, prejudiced, inhumane, selfish, oppressive, and/or violent). In Western culture we essentially inherit two conversational responses to such forms of chastisement—incorporation or antagonism. The incorporative mode ("Yes, now I see the error of my ways") requires an extended forestructure of understandings (i.e., a history that legitimates the critic's authority and judgment, and that renders the target of critique answerable). However, because in the case of identity politics there is no preestablished context to situate the target in just these ways, the invited response to critique is more typically one of hostility, defense, and countercharge.

Such antagonistic replies are additionally invited by virtue of the differing discourse worlds of the critic and target. What are viewed as "exploitative wages" on the one side are branded as "just earnings" on the other; "prejudicial decisions" on the one side are exonerated as "decisions by merit" on the other; attempts to combat "exclusionary prejudices" are seen as disruptions of "orderly and friendly community;" "rigid parochialism" for the critic is understood as "love of enduring traditions" by the target. Under such conditions, those targeted by the critiques are least likely to take heed, and most likely to become galvanized in opposition. As Mary Ann Glendon (1991) argues in *Rights Talk*, the rhetoric of rights "polarizes debate; it tends to suppress moral discussion and consensus building. Once an agenda is introduced as 'right,' sensible discussion and moderate positions tend to disappear."

It should be added that this antagonistic animus is not limited to the relationship of critic to target but, rather, has carried over significantly into many of the political movements themselves. With the rhetoric of blame a favored option for dealing with others, it also becomes a hammer for fixing what is wrong within the political movements. Any movement that targets the culture as guilty of suppressing voices will soon find that within its own ranks some voices are more equal than others. In the thrust toward economic equality, women turn on men for their patriarchal disposition; in the drive toward gender equality, white women are found guilty of silencing the black voice, the educationally privileged guilty of elitist and exclusionary language, the straight for politics inimical to the lesbian, and so on. To illustrate, prominent black intellectual Patricia Hill Collins (1990) writes of the necessity for a specifically black feminist movement. However, she also advocates a "critical posture toward mainstream, feminist, and Black scholarly inquiry" more generally (p. 12). Here she joins other prominent black thinkers, along with a cadre of Hispanic, Native American, and Asian-American women in challenging feminism for its implicit racism and its overarching concern with white, middle-class women's issues.

Not only is the dominant rhetoric of identity politics divisive in its effects, there are important respects in which it has lost its efficacy by virtue of its profusion. The rhetoric of rights, for example, has traveled weightlessly across contexts of contention. Where the most celebrated battles for equality were fought within the domains of class, race, and gender, the forms of rhetoric have become available to all who suffer. Rapidly the big three were joined by Native Americans, Asian-Americans, Hispanics, the aged, the homeless, ex-mental patients, the disabled, gay and lesbian enclaves, along with advocates for the right to life and children's rights. We also find litigation based on claims to a right to higher education, death row inmates to reproduce, and women's rights to urinate in any public facility. As Amitai Etzioni (1993) proposes: "The incessant issuance of new rights, like the wholesale printing of currency, causes a massive inflation of rights that devalues their moral claims." Glendon (1991) adds that rights talk contains the "unexpressed premise that we roam at large in a land of strangers, where we presumptively have no obligations toward others except to avoid the active infliction of harm." Other critics are far more scathing. National columnists have even spoken of "the rights babble."

Finally, given its relatively long-standing presence in cultural life, there has been ample time for the development of effective counterrhetorics. As Hirschman (1991) points out in *The Rhetoric of Reaction*, discursive attempts to thwart social change have a rich history. However, the past several decades have stimulated a new range of self-insulating rebuttals. There is, for example, the redoubt of "victimization," which proposes that claims to being a victim of oppressive circumstances are merely excuses to cover failures of inaction or irresponsibility. Reactionary critic Charles Sykes (1992) proposes that we have become a "nation of victims," and that the rhetoric of rights and blame is responsible for a "decay in the American character." In his volume, *The Abuse Excuse*, Alan Dershowitz (1994) claims that we have become a nation of "sob stories." One of the most powerful rebutting rhetorics, owing to the fact that it has been appropriated from identity politics itself, is that of political correctness. So trenchant are the minorities' critiques of established policies and practices that, in the targets' eyes, they take on a tyrannical demeanor—thus violating *their* rights to tradition and voice. As one commentator recently noted, it may be one of the first times in the nation's history in which both sides of political debate lodge their defense in civil liberties. Finally, as antiliberalist critics such as Michael Sandel (1982) have begun to dismantle the justification of individual rights, the way has been paved for a rhetoric of responsibility to replace that of rights. It is this latter rhetoric that has enabled the communitarian movement to gain such high cultural visibility.

THE CONSTRUCTIONIST CONUNDRUM

If identity politics were not sufficiently embattled by the vicissitudes of cultural history, it has also begun to feel a certain suffocating presence from its constructionist paramour. For, while social constructionism supplies vibrant discursive resources for building internal strength and undermining the opposition, it also plays havoc with central tenets of identity politics. In particular, constructionism offers strong arguments against the realism, essentialism, and ethical foundationalism endemic to much of the discourse of identity politics.

In the first instance, the social critiques developed within identity politics are typically lodged within a realist discourse, a discourse that privileges its critique with the capacity for truth beyond perspective. In characterizing the barriers of class, the glass ceiling, homophobia, the effects of pornography on rape, and the embryonic fetus as a human being, for example, claims are being made about the state of nature independent of our interpretive proclivities. For the constructionist, of course, such claims are not so much reflections of nature as the outcome of social process. The descriptions are inherently positioned both historically and culturally, and myriad alternatives are both possible and creditable from other societal locations. The realist posture is all the more ironic, the constructionist reasons, because such critiques are often coupled with a deconstruction of the opposition's objectivity. The constructed character of the dominant discourse is used by the identity politician to pave the way for the marginalized alternative, with the latter position then treated as if transparent.

Closely related to a problematic realism is the essentialist presumption implicit in much identity politics. To make claims for the rights of women, children, the aged, the poor, the insane, and so on typically implies the existence of an essential entity—a group unified by its distinctive features. The group name is treated as referential—derived from characteristics existing in nature, independent of the name itself. For the constructionist, of course, reference is preeminently a social achievement and thus inherently defeasible. The reality of history, ethnicity, class, and so on is generated within contemporary cultural life, and could be otherwise. As Henry Louis Gates (1994) proposes, blackness is "not a material object, an absolute, or an event," but only "a trope." And lodging the argument in social process, he goes on: "Race is only a sociopolitical category, nothing more." As this sociopolitical category is applied to individuals, it also acts as a reductive agent, circumscribing one's identity, and reducing one's potential to be otherwise. In his *Reflections of an Affirmative Action Baby*, Stephen Carter (1991)proposes that such labels operate as problematic stereotypes, covering over complexities and generating misleading social policies (see also Calhoun, 1994).

Finally, constructionist thought also militates against the claims to ethical foundations implicit in much identity politics—that higher ground from which others can so confidently be condemned as inhumane, self-serving, prejudiced, and unjust. Constructionist thought painfully reminds us that we have no transcendent rationale upon which to rest such accusations, and that our sense of moral indignation is itself a product of historically and culturally situated traditions. And, the constructionist intones, is it possible that those we excoriate are also living within traditions that are, for them, suffused with a sense of ethical primacy? We find, then, that social constructionism is a two-edged sword in the political arena, potentially as damaging to the wielding hand as to the opposition.

THE RELATIONAL TURN IN SOCIAL CONSTRUCTION

As many now propose, identity politics is reaching an impasse. No longer does it seem an effective means of securing voice, dignity, and equality. Should social constructionism now content itself with a more sedentary scholarly role, circulating filigreed obscurities among its own kind—culture critique without audience, commentary without commitment? My response is already foreshadowed in the phrasing of these questions. I have cherished the gains achieved by identity politics, and grieve its failings; and for me, if constructionism ceases to be politically engaged, it will lose its essential élan. More positively, however, I see significant signs of transformation in both identity politics and in social constructionism. In the political arena, for example, left-wing activist Todd Gitlin (1993) despairs of what has become of identity politics, the proliferation of which, he says: "leads to a turning inward, a grim and hermetic bravado celebrating victimization and stylized marginality" (p. 173). Black intellectuals—Cornell West, Toni Morrison and Henry Louis Gates—have also turned critical toward the past political postures, and now resonate with many others seeking an evolution in identity politics. Let me, then, describe what I feel to be a central outgrowth of contemporary constructionist thought. We may then consider how this movement lends itself to a re/visioned political agenda.

Since their emergence as a self-conscious force (most prominently in the 1970s), social constructionists have largely been deconstructive in their aims and effects. By demonstrating the social, linguistic, rhetorical, ideological, cultural and historical forces responsible for generating the world of knowledge—both professional and everyday—they have challenged all claims to authority, truth, rationality, and moral superiority. They have been highly effective forces for extending rights for negotiating the real and the good. But while this enterprise must and should continue, alone it is insufficient. It is insufficient in part because its primary role is symbiotic; critique remains dormant until the fools begin to dance. At the same time, as constructionist discourse is placed into orbit, as it begins to insinuate itself into the ways we describe and explain, so does it invite alternative forms of action—new patterns of relationship. In certain respects, these patterns represent dislocating alternatives to traditions of centuries-long duration. In effect, constructionism harbors enormous revolutionary potential for our cultural forms of life. In the exploration of this potential, constructionist inquiry moves from a symbiotic to a productive posture—from deconstruction to reconstruction.

I have said much about these positive outcomes in an earlier work

(Gergen, 1999). However, for present purposes, I wish to focus on only one emerging development, namely that of relational theory and practice. Constructionist dialogues consistently underscore the significance of relationship as the matrix from which meaning is derived. It is in the generation of coordinations—of actions, words, objects—that human meaning is born. In this sense, meaning does not originate in individual minds but in relationships among persons. To say that "I know" is but a derivative of what has already been achieved within relationship.[1] All that we take to be true of nature and of mind, of self and others, thus finds its origins within relationship. Or, in Martin Buber's terms, "In the beginning is the relationship." It is this line of reasoning that has played a spirited counterpoint with the conceptual movement from individual to relational selves (Gergen, 1999) and with the therapeutic movement away from exploring individual minds and toward co-constructed realities (McNamee and Gergen, 1994). This turn in constructionist thought is not toward the enunciation of a new truth, that of relationship. Rather, this turn in sensibilities opens a new space for innovation and transformation.

TOWARD RELATIONAL POLITICS

If these are the implications of the relational metaphor, what are the implications for identity politics? In my view the potentials are substantial. Indeed, I believe that we find here the seeds for both revitalization and transformation of the most profound variety. Let me cast such a transformation in terms of *relational politics*—a politics in which neither self nor other, we nor them, takes precedence, but in which relational process serves as the generative source of change. I am not speaking here of a mere fantasy, another grand but unworkable design hatched in the ivory tower. Rather, I believe that relational politics are already in evidence—not altogether self-conscious, but struggling in multiple sites toward common intelligibility. Here I wish to touch on only three specific sites of development: the revisioning of self and other, discursive practice, and social action.

RE-THEORIZING SELF AND OTHER

In important degree, identity politics is a descendent of Western, individualist ideology. It is not the single individual who commands our interest in this case; rather, individual identity is conflated with group identity. Individual and group interests (and rights) are one. In this way, the group replaces the individual as the center of concern, but the discourse of individuality is not thereby disrupted. Rather, the group is treated discursively in much the same way as the individual: imbued with good and evil intent, held blameworthy, deemed worthy of rights, and so on. In spite of the shift toward the social, we thus inherit the problems of individualism yet once again—simply one step removed. Rather than a society of isolated and alienated individuals—a potential war of all against all in the individualist sense—we have a battlefield of antagonistic groups. As James Hunter (1991) has put it, we are now engaged in "culture wars."

Advocates of identity politics have become keenly aware of the problematics of separation. As they point out, the dominant culture is already prone toward objectification of the Other. In du Preez's (1980) terms, the Other is forced into *identity traps* that confirm the dominant culture's sense of superiority and self-righteousness. It is in this light that we can understand the attempt by black intellectuals to blur the boundaries of ethnic, sexual and political identity. For example, in *Race Matters*, Cornell West (1993) warns against the delineation of a distinct black culture and seeks a: "frank acknowledgment of the basic humanness and Americanness of each of us." Similarly, Stanley Crouch (1990), in *Notes of a Hanging Judge*, argues that politics must involve African-Americans "not as outsiders"—a distinct group unto itself—but as participants in broad-ranging enclaves of society, for example as "voters, taxpayers, and sober thinkers." In a similar vein, Todd Gitlin (1993) speaks of *commonality politics*, oriented around understanding differences "against the background of what is *not* different, what is shared among groups" (p. 173).

These are salutary invitations to subvert the traditional binary and to reconceptualize self and Other. Given the constructionist shift toward a relational sensibility, I believe we are poised for just such a revisioning. We confront the possibility of developing intelligibilities that go beyond the identification of separable units—I versus you, we versus them—and that may create reality of relatedness, the palpability of inseparability. How might a relational intelligibility be articulated? There are several current attempts to achieve this end, each of which contributes significantly and differentially to a relational consciousness.

There is, first, a bustling renaissance of interest in Vygotsky's (1978) inquiries into cognitive development (see, for example, Wertsch, 1991; Newman and Holzman, 1997). The significance of this work is largely owing to its dislodgment of psychology's long-standing investment in autonomous, or self-contained, cognitive processes, in favor of a profoundly more socialized conception of self. For the Vygotskian, to paraphrase John Locke, there is nothing in thought that is not first in society. Or, to extend the implications, the concept of the autonomous agent is a myth: each of us is constituted by the other; we cannot deliberate or decide without implicating otherness. While Vygotskians do retain a strong interest in individual functioning, more fully relational is a range of work conceptualizing the self as dialogically constituted (see, for example, Shotter, 1993; Sampson, 1993a; Hermans and Kempen, 1993). In this case, drawing significantly from Bakhtinian semiotics, the individual is conceptualized as inseparable from ongoing social process (with *the conversation* featured as the dominant metaphor). Within this frame, individual psychological process is typically granted ontological status but, similar to the Vygotskians, only as a private stand-in for public conversation.

My own endeavors, perhaps constituting a radical relationalism, have followed a third route (see Gergen, 1994). My attempt has been to make intelligible a range of *microsocial scenarios*, or relational forms in which individual action derives its sense or meaning from its placement within the extended interchange. Thus, for example, an expression of anger is nonsense if isolated from a scenario of relationship. One cannot sensibly be angry without a preceding action that grants anger meaning as a supplement. And once anger is expressed, there is only a limited number of meaningful moves available to the target (e.g., apology, explanation, hostility). If apology is the subsequent move in the dance, there is only a limited number of options then rendered plausible as replies. In effect, actions such as anger and apology gain their meaning from the broader relational scenario in which they are embedded. Individual bodies may bear the signifiers into action, but the moves (anger, apology, etc.) are not thereby possessions of individuals. They are constituents of the relational dance.

These efforts to articulate relational being are in their infancy. We have yet to fully explore, for example, Davies's and Harré's (1990) conception of self-positioning, Taylor's (1989) "webs of interlocution" (p. 36), and Baudrillard's (1994) selves as terminals of multiple networks. Many moves in the postmodern register also offer fertile sources of rhetorical enrichment. I think here especially of images of selves as *multiple-partials*, that is, selves as constituted by multiple facets, each reflecting a different domain of human relationship and each representing but a partial aspect of the whole. Here Connolly's (1991) *Identity/Difference* and Judith Butler's (1990) *Gender Trouble* come quickly to mind. In each case we find a rich range of images that could substantially alter our interpretation of social life. As the reality of relationship becomes increasingly intelligible, we find substantial implications for future deliberation on identity politics. To scan the horizons briefly, we are invited to consider the possibility that:

- There is no natural (biological, genetic) basis for intergroup antagonism (as sociobiologists, ethologists, and Freudians are wont to argue). Violence is a meaningful integer in a relational dance; this dance is rooted in historical convention and is subject to change both on the grassroots and policy levels.
- Prejudice does not originate in the individual mind. Prejudicial action is a meaningful move within a variety of cultural scenarios. As the scenarios unfold, so is prejudicial action invited. Given a modicum of participation in the culture (including its mass media), all of us are capable of such actions. By the same token, we are all capable of loving, caring, and societally responsible action. All actions, in effect, are by-products of existing relational forms.
- Identity—whether individual or group—is not derived from the nature of the world. (There are no necessary or natural distinctions among persons or groups). Rather, identity is a relational achievement. Individuation (or unitization) is only one of many ways in which we might describe or explain the world. And such forms of discourse obscure the more essential domain of human connection.
- There is no means of ultimate victory (politically, economically, militarily) if winning means eradication of the Other (or the Other's position). To condemn, excoriate, or wage war against a constructed Other in our society is inherently self-destructive; for in a fundamental sense, we are the Other. We are born of our relationship and derive our sense of identity from relationship.

- Societal transformation is not a matter of changing minds and hearts, political values, or the sense of the good. Rather, transformation will require unleashing the positive potential inherent in relational process. In effect, we must locate a range of relational forms that enable collective transformation as opposed to alienated dissociation. This latter point will become amplified in what follows.

TOWARD RELATIONAL DISCOURSE

In addition to the development of new conceptions of self and Other—with its associated array of provocative logics—relational politics invites the exploration of alternative modes of talking/acting with others, and particularly those with whom we otherwise disagree. This is not because we require prettier, sharper, or more sophisticated words in which to wrap the case. I am not speaking here of "knockdown arguments" or a "better spin." Rather, discourse is important because it is itself constituent of relationship. As social action, discourse serves to form and sustain our forms of relationship; a shift in mode of speaking or writing stands as an invitation to alter the character of relationship. Here we have glimpsed some of the ways in which traditional rhetorics—for example, claims to truth, claims to moral authority, and critical attack—function to alienate, antagonize, and escalate conflict. An effective relational politics requires, then, a poetic leap into new forms of discourse and, more specifically, forms that invite broader opportunities for mutual sustenance. Or as David Goldberg (1993) puts it, required is a new range of *incorporative metaphors*, not in this case for purposes of theoretical development, but serviceable in the hurly-burly of daily interchange.

It is in this context that a number of colleagues have joined Sheila McNamee and me (McNamee and Gergen, 1999) to explore the potentials of *relationally responsible* discourse. As reasoned in this case, if we place a value on the process of meaning-making—essentially that process without which there would be no domain of political value—then our attention is drawn to forms of discourse that sustain as opposed to subvert this process. In what ways can we speak, it is asked, such that our capacities for the productive (as opposed to destructive) generation of meaning are sustained? In our view, one major discursive ritual that often destroys the grounds for sustained interchange is that of individual blame. When the discourse of blame is set in motion, the target is typically degraded, set apart from the community of the good, and thus alienated from it. In the process of blame, the vast sea of complexity in which any action is submerged is denied, and the single individual serves as its sole origin. In terms of relational responsibility, the challenge is that of locating alternative forms of discourse that can serve as replacements for the ritual of blame and recrimination. How else can we talk under such conditions that might serve the ends of altering or terminating the unwanted action but simultaneously sustain a relationship of mutual respect?

While the aforementioned volume (McNamee and Gergen, 1999) is focally concerned with this issue, one of the options is of special relevance to moving from an identity to a relational politics. As we saw, many onetime identity politics advocates are moving away from rhetorics of antagonism and separation to articulate visions of unity. This is a move highly congenial to a relational politics. The discursive shift from *me versus you* to *we* has enormous consequences for political process. The construction of separation gives way to one of shared investments. In our discussion of relational responsibility, we treat this move in terms of "crafting conjoint relations." All units of social life—from the individual person to the community and nation state—are relational constructions. They typically require conversational coordination to bring them into recognition as units. Thus, wherever there is antagonism—the recognition of *me versus you*—we confront the opportunity of creating a transcendent discourse of the *we*. To replace the ritual of blame, a relationally responsible inquiry might be launched into how the untoward act has been jointly achieved. How did we *together* create a situation in which an intolerable act has resulted? Not only does such inquiry enable participants to remain creatively connected, but so are new lines of inquiry opened. It is not simply that the single individual must "correct his ways," but rather, there is an exploration of cooperative opportunities.

Let me illustrate in a homely way: several years ago Mary and I were driving on a dangerous cliffside road in southern Europe. The rain was pelting, visibility was minimal, the traffic was treacherous, and we were late for an appointment. We were both highly tense, and as my driving was less than flawless, Mary became increasingly critical, and I became increasingly irritated and resentful of her blame. Soon it was not only the road we had to fear, but ourselves. After a breathtaking near-collision, I pulled the car over to the side of the road so we could collect ourselves. Here we decided to reconceptualize the drive. Rather than defining me as "the driver" and her as the "endangered passenger," we decided it would be better to share the roles. *We* would drive and *we* would criticize together. She became an added pair of eyes on the road; I developed a self-critical posture. The results were gratifying; not only did we avoid shredding our relationship but we lived to tell the tale.

On a more general scale, however, with the flourishing of a discourse of conjoint relations we confront the possibility that political parties could desist in blaming each other for various governmental or social failings. As many see it, the ritual of mutual recrimination has undermined the potentials for effective policy-making at the national level. Virtually all preferences in one political party are automatically targets of critique by the opposing party; virtually all claims to achievement are degraded; all failings are traced to origins in the opposition. With the shift toward conjoint realities we open a space for alternative conversations. How have "we together" created the conditions of failure; how have these achievements been jointly wrought; and is it possible that differing preferences can be conjoined in new and creative ways? A relational politics need not obscure or eradicate differences; however, there is much to be gained by seeing these differences as derived from relational process as opposed to independent origins. We have scarcely tapped the possibilities for "actionable" vocabularies of relational responsibility; the future remains open. Let us finally turn to more direct forms of political action.

THE POLITICS OF RELATIONAL PRACTICE

A transformation in theoretical resources and discursive practices is scarcely sufficient. Most acutely needed are innovative forms of political action. In my view, one of the most significant innovations derived from the identity politics movement was to broaden extensively the arena of the political. In particular, political practice ceased to be reserved for the arena of politics formally considered—campaigning, voting, office-holding, and so on—and it ceased to be hierarchical, with the flow moving from the top echelons down to the grass roots. Rather, the doing of politics became everyone's business in the arenas of the local and the immediate—in the streets, the classrooms, business, and so on. Further, as we have slowly learned, particularly from feminist activists, there are no everyday activities that are not political in implication—from the cartoons our children watch to our purchase of shampoo and shirts. In this sense, political action does not require either aggressive championing of specific agendas or party partisanship to be effective. It seems to me that the future of relational politics might promisingly be shaped by conjoining these realizations: we may view relational politics as *defused* (in terms of a reduction in aggressive or hegemonic pursuits) and *diffused* (in terms of an expansion into all forms of relationship). Politics in the relational mode may be subtle, fluid, and unceasing—not the work of specific groups on specific sites identified as "political," but the work of us all, in all relationships.

My special concern here is with forms of practice informed by or congenial with the relational turn in constructionist theory. How can we move from argumentation, agitation, and litigation to ordinary but unceasing forms of mutually sustaining activity? What forms of practice may be generated that move away from isolation and insulation and toward the cross-fertilization of identities, the intermingling of practices, the interweaving of selves, and ever-broadening forms of coordinated action? I do think such practices are possible, and, indeed, there are numerous instances of just such innovation. The constructionist move in therapy has successfully shifted the focus from defective individuals to relational processes. The shift is away from who or what is defective, to how it is we come to interpret life patterns as defective and what alternative forms of construction may enable relations to proceed more congenially. Therapy, then, is not intent on locating evil (disease, dysfunction) and correcting it, but on coordinating meanings within relationships such that the discourse of evil is rendered obsolete. In the case of education, we discussed newly emerging practices of collaborative learning, critical reflection, polyvocal literacy, and dialogic evaluation. Again, I see such practices as relational politics in action.

There is principally no limit to the forms of action that can be generated in the service of relational politics. Every form of human coordination offers opportunities for innovation. However, a few concerted attempts—among them some of my favorites—will round out the discussion.

Community-Focused Institutes

I am deeply impressed by the activities of many therapeutically oriented institutes to move outward into community work—not in the name of a specific political advocacy, but for purposes of crossing boundaries of divided discourse and value. Prominent, for example, is the work of Sallyann Roth and Laura and Richard Chasin and their colleagues at the Public Conversations Project (Chasin and Herzig, 1992), where the attempt has been to bring together leaders from warring ideological camps—for example, pro-choice and pro-life, or straights and gays. The purpose of these interchanges is not to champion one cause over the other, not to impugn the intelligibility of either tradition or to dismiss the conflict. Rather, by suppressing various forms of divisive rhetoric and simultaneously giving voice to narratives of lived experience ("my experience with abortion," "what it is like for me to be gay"), the attempt is to open a way of incorporating the Other, of appreciating the situated character of the perspectives in question. No, the ideological conflict is not thereby dissolved, but the outcome appears to be far more humane modes of relating to the Other. I also think here of the impressive work of Fred Newman and Lois Holzman (Newman and Holzman, 1996, 1997) and their colleagues at the East Side Institute for Short Term Psychotherapy in Manhattan.[2] Going far beyond therapeutic practice, the institute helps ghetto youth to organize talent shows, offers public dialogues between blacks and Jews, and has run a multiracial elementary school in Harlem. Even those who seek treatment in therapy are encouraged to join in community action. Such action may be political and specifically of the kind that might alter the conditions responsible in creating their problems.

Appreciative Inquiry

In the domain of organizational management, David Cooperrider (1990) and his colleagues at Case Western Reserve have developed a form of organizational intervention called *appreciative inquiry*. When organizations confront conflict—between management and workers, men and women, blacks and whites, and so on—appreciative inquiry shifts the focus from who is right and wrong, fostering tolerance, or developing rules of proper conduct, to modes of collaborative action. More specifically, the attempt is to work with the organization to locate instances of desirable or ideal relations—cases in which groups work well and effectively with each other. Further, as these appreciated instances are brought into public consciousness, the organization is brought into discussion of the kind of future it might build around such cases. In the very process of instancing the positive and forging an image of a desirable future, the divisive constructions lose their suasive capacity. This orientation to positive collaboration has also been extended to processes of community-building, interreligous integration, education, elder care, police training, and more.[3] And, under the direction of Bliss Brown and her colleagues, citizens of Chicago are being united to create a new future together. Their program, Imagine Chicago, has fostered appreciative and growth-directed dialogue not only within numerous Chicago communities but across diverse economic and ethnic groups.[4]

These relational innovations have been party to constructionist dialogues. However, there are additional movements of note, which are not so much informed by relational conceptions as they are congenial. Here I would include the enormous growth over the past decade of *private voluntary organizations*—grassroots organizations devoted to humane and life-giving practices. There are now some 20,000 of these organizations operating on a transnational basis, coordinating participants from around the globe in reducing hunger, curing disease, controlling AIDS, saving the environment, helping children to survive, and so on. As Cooperrider and Dutton (1999) propose, there are "no limits to global cooperation." The mushrooming of *virtual communities* on the Internet also represents a potential contribution to relational politics. There are now almost five million users of the Internet, a large proportion of whom take part in small, loosely linked communities of meaning. Cutting across racial, ethnic, age, gender, geographical, and religious lines, such communities enable dialogue on innumerable issues, both profound and personal. I am also impressed with the attempt toward full ecumenicalism among world religions, as realized, for example, in the recent Parliament of World Religions. This meeting, in Chicago, brought together 8,000 people from 150 faiths around the globe into mutual inquiry. In each of these cases, the signifiers cross boundaries and begin to play in new arenas.

In conclusion, I do not wish to abandon the existing tradition of identity politics, the discourses of oppression, justice, equality, rights, and so on, nor the *in-your-face* activism that we have come to know so well.[5] The point is not to eradicate existing vocabularies of action. Rather, my hope is that we are now participating in the generation of a new vocabulary, a new consciousness, and a new range of practices—a relational politics that will be incorporative, pervasive, collaborative, and unceasing. As lesbian feminist Shane Phelan (1989) proposed, "identity politics must be based not only on identity, but on an appreciation for politics as the art of living together" (p. 170). Relational politics is precisely the attempt to realize this art.

NOTES

1. For a sharpening of the issues, see Chapter 11 in Gergen, 1994.
2. Also see http://www.EastSideInstitute.org.
3. For ongoing discussion of these applications and extensions, consult the newsgroup by writing to www.appreciative-inquiry.org.
4. See also http://www.imaginechicago.org.
5 See Sampson, 1993b, for a positive account of traditional identity politics at work.

REFERENCES

Baudrillard, J. (1994). *Simulacre and simulation*. Ann Arbor: University of Michigan Press.

Bruffee, K. A. (1993). *Collaborative learning*. Baltimore, MD: Johns Hopkins University Press.

Butler, J. (1990). *Gender trouble: Feminism and the subversion of identity*. New York: Routledge.

Calhoun, C. (1994). Social theory and the politics of identity. In C. Calhoun (Ed.). *Social theory and the politics of identity*. Oxford, UK: Blackwell.

Carter, S. L. (1991). *Reflections of an affirmative action baby*. New York: Basic Books.

Chasin, R., and Herzig, M. (1992). Creating systemic interventions for the sociopolitical arena. In B. Berger-Could and D. H. DeMuth (Eds.). *The global family therapist: Integrating the personal, professional and political*. Needham, MA: Allyn and Bacon.

Collins, P. H. (1990). *Black feminist thought*. New York: Routledge.

Connolly, W. (1991). *Identity/difference: Democratic negotiations of political paradox*. Ithaca, NY: Cornell University Press.

Cooperrider, D. L. (1990). Positive imagery, positive action: The affirmative basis of organizing. In S. S. Srivastva and D.L. Cooperrider (Eds.). *Appreciative management and leadership*. San Francisco: Jossey-Bass.

Cooperrider, D. L., and Dutton, J. E. (Eds.). (1999). *Organizational dimensions of global change*. Thousand Oaks, CA: Sage.

Crouch, S. (1990). *Notes of a hanging judge*. New York: Oxford University Press.

Davies, B. and Harré, R. (1990). Positioning and the discursive production of selves. *Journal for the Theory of Social Behaviour, 20*, 43–63.

Dershowitz, A. M. (1994). *The abuse excuse*. Boston: Little Brown.

du Preez, P. (1980). *The politics of identity*. New York: St. Martin's Press.

Etzioni, A. (1993). *The spirit of community*. New York: Crown.

Gates, H. L. Jr.(1994). *Colored people: A memoir*. New York: Knopf.

Gergen, K. J. (1994). *Realities and relationships*. Cambridge, MA: Harvard University Press.

Gergen, K. J. (1997). The place of the psyche in a constructed world. *Theory and Psychology, 7*, 723–746.

Gergen, K. J. (1999). *An invitation to social construction*. London: Sage.

Gitlin, T. (1993). The rise of "identity politics." *Dissent, 40*, 172–177.

Glendon, M. A. (1991). *Rights talk: The impoverishment of political discourse*. New York: Free Press.

Goldberg, D. T. (1993). *Racist culture*. Oxford, UK: Blackwell.

Hermans, H. J. M., and Kempen, H. J. G. (1993). *The dialogical self*. San Diego, CA: Academic Press.

Hirschman, A. O. (1991). *The rhetoric of reaction*. Cambridge, UK: Belknap.

Hunter, J. D. (1991). *Culture wars*. New York: Basic Books.

Leo, J. (1991). The lingo of entitlement. *U.S. News and World Report*, October 14, p. 22.

McNamee, S., and Gergen, K. J. (Eds.) (1994). *Therapy as social construction*. London: Sage.

McNamee, S., and Gergen, K. J. (1999). *Relational responsibility*. Thousand Oaks, CA: Sage.

Morgan, R. E. (1984). *Disabling America: The "rights industry" in our time*. New York: Basic Books.

Newman, F., and Holzman, L. (1996). *Unscientific psychology: A cultural-performatory approach to understanding human life*. Westport, CT: Praeger.

Newman, F., and Holzman, L. (1997). *The end of knowing: A new developmental way of learning*. London: Routledge.

Phelan, S. (1989). *Identity politics*. Philadephia, PA: Temple University Press.

Sampson, E. E. (1993a). *Celebrating the other*. Boulder, CO: Westview Press.

Sampson, E. E. (1993b). Identity politics: Challenges to psychology's understanding. *American Psychologist, 48*, 1219–1230.

Sandel, M. (1982). *Liberalism and the limits of justice*. Cambridge, UK: Cambridge University Press.

Shotter, J. (1993). *Conversational realities*. London: Sage.

Sykes, C. J. (1992). *A nation of victims: The decay of the American character*. New York: St. Martins.

Sternberg, U. (1989). *The ethnic myth*. Boston: Beacon.

Taylor, C. (1989). *Sources of the self*. Cambridge, MA: Harvard University Press.

Taylor, T. (1992). *Mutual misunderstanding*. Durham, NC: Duke University Press.

van Dijk, T. A. (1989). *Elite discourse and racism*. Newbury Park, CA: Sage.

Vygotsky, L. (1978). *Mind in society: The development of higher psychological processes*. Cambridge, MA: Harvard University Press.

Wertsch, J. V. (1991). *Voices of the mind: A sociocultural approach to mediated action*. Cambridge, MA: Harvard University Press.

West, C. (1993). *Race matters*. New York: Vintage.

Race,

Identity,

and Epistemology

Lenora Fulani

As an African-American child growing up in Chester, Pennsylvania, I (not surprisingly) never heard the word epistemology, rarely heard the word identity, and frequently heard the word race. My race faced mistreatment, poverty, and poor education, and I decided that I was going to become a psychologist so that I could help people and so that together we could change the world. As an undergraduate I was immediately disappointed by what psychology had to offer, and disturbed (outraged, really) by the official assessment of the African-American community as a tangle of pathology. I soon became a militant Black Nationalist and immersed myself in black psychology. I still never heard anyone speak about epistemology, although just about everyone was talking about race, and we nationalists spoke about identity all the time. I rapidly developed one.

It was becoming a political activist, a Marxist, a social therapist, and a builder of a multiracial *development community*[1] that taught me about epistemology and its links to race and identity. Having learned what it is, I strongly urge that we get rid of it! In the following remarks, I will share some of what this has looked like in my work and, I hope, give some sense of the power there is in giving it up, especially (though not exclusively) for young people of color.

In *The End of Knowing: A New Developmental Way of Learning*, my colleagues Fred Newman and Lois Holzman provoke us into taking a hard look not just at so-called modernist epistemology and its oppressive and conservatizing force upon us, but at *all ways of knowing*, including some of the current postmodern alternatives (Newman and Holzman, 1997). To them, the problem we human beings face at this moment in history is our epistemic posture—whether individuated, social, cultural,

151

or relational. Challenging truth, reality, and objectivity but leaving *knowing* untouched won't do, they claim, as a tactic for world transformation. Don't we have to subject the notion of narrative itself to the same rigorous deconstruction as has been applied to modernism's grand narratives? And can we leave untouched the polarity of relativism/absolutism even as we reject the bipolar worldview that justifies and perpetuates the status quo? What about the concept of relationality—has it merely swept all the troublesome individual particulars (including individuated selves) under the rug? Finally, shouldn't we question the common assumption that socially constructed identity and identity politics were and remain a "natural" stage in the cultural-political process?

Coming as I do from a working-class African-American family and having become a Marxist after I developed a strong black identity, I find Newman's and Holzman's methodological challenges extremely helpful in understanding both the pulls of identity (especially racial identity) and how it is that, more often than not, I successfully resist them in my work, whether that is supporting black and Latino inner-city youth to create new performances of themselves or working within the mostly white Reform Party to restructure the American political process through the building of a viable independent party. We don't follow or apply a method (not even the method of Marxist praxis). What we do is practice method (Holzman and Newman, 1979; Newman and Holzman, 1993), and it is this nonepistemologically-based group activity that deconstructs identity psychology and identity politics. As I delineate the features of this method, I will illustrate with examples from my experiences with two New York City youth programs based on the practice of method about which Newman and Holzman write—the All Stars Talent Show Network, an antiviolence cultural organization, and the Development School for Youth, an after-school leadership training program for high-school-age students.

WHAT'S WRONG WITH IDENTITY?

Understood culturally rather than politically, the nationalism I embraced as a college student is the dominant tradition in the African-American community. Nationalist political beliefs—such as the establishment of a separate black state or a return to Africa—are not widely held in the African-American community, but a strong nationalist bias is apparent in the widespread belief that African-American *culture* is of great importance and must be expressed in a multitude of ways in daily life.

Racism, of course, historically forced the African-American community to create its own institutions (e.g., black colleges and black churches) and foisted on it a constant awareness of racial identification. We would expect the African-American community to be more eager than most for cultural norms based on race to disappear—but that is not the case. Since the postintegration 1960s, the African-American community has purposefully perpetuated its overidentification with race. This kind of cultural nationalism goes beyond knowing one's history and taking pride in it. It entails a set of postures, attitudes, and beliefs—for example, that the way to change institutions positively is to increase black presence in them—as well as language, gestures, dress, forms of music, and so on, that have become identified as "behaving black" and, therefore, in this racially identified context, as hip and cool. Parents implicitly and explicitly teach their children this nationalistic model as "the way to be" in the world.

The problem with this model of worldliness is that it's culturally and politically naïve. The postures, attitudes and norms that are hip and cool "in the hood" don't open doors outside the African-American community; they're less than helpful in navigating the complex network of societal institutions in our multicultural society. Ironically, while many black-identified cultural postures and attitudes have been adopted by white Americans to enhance their hipness, and by major clothing manufacturers to market a cultivated hip/black image to both white and black consumers, the African-American community, by virtue of the self-imposed narrowness of its cultural nationalism, has largely been unable to take advantage of this phenomenon.

To complicate matters, "behave black" isn't the only message conveyed (implicitly or explicitly) to children by African-American parents. At the same time, they also convey that it's necessary to assimilate in order for their children to become educated and get a good job. The contradiction between the cultural nationalism of the African-American community and its desire to see its children educated and succeed in mainstream culture is something with which most parents have not yet come to terms. Will children have to subvert their history and culture in order to "make it?" Will they have to deny who they are? Can the contradiction be resolved?

The work of Kwame Anthony Appiah is helpful on this issue. Appiah is Professor of African-American Studies and Philosophy at Harvard University whose recent works include *In My Father's House: Africa in the Philosophy of Culture* (1992), *The Dictionary of Global Culture* written with Henry Lewis Gates Jr. (1997) and *Color Conscious: The Political Morality of Race*, coauthored with Amy Gutmann (1996).

Like many scholars, Appiah argues that there is no such thing as race. Going beyond showing that there is no biological evidence for racial differences, he claims that race is not cultural either. The move to identify racial differences as cultural, according to Appiah, falsely suggests that people in one cultural grouping are the same as each other and different from people in other cultural groupings. Racism is then understood as stemming from cultural misunderstandings. But, Appiah points out (and I agree with him), black and white Americans understand each other just fine. Racism isn't a matter of cultural differences and misunderstandings; it's a matter of political power.

Appiah speaks of the need to get beyond what Sartre identified as antiracist racism—as exemplified, for example, in Black Pride and Pan-Africanism. The establishment of this kind of racial identity, he says, is a stage in a people's demand to be recognized. But there are problems that come with identity: it becomes categorical, defining, and rigid, signaling association with particular political or social agendas and particular beliefs. Like Ken Gergen (this volume), Appiah writes persuasively of the destructive effects of identity politics as identity-defined interest groups compete with each other for legislative initiatives and social policy on the basis of presumed shared characteristics and on their own behalf. Appiah recommends that we engage in "identity play"—that we step back from our identities, see that they are not always so important and not all of who we are, and move on to postracial identities. He describes this "moving on" as: "the . . . imaginative work of constructing collective identities for a democratic nation in a world of democratic nations, work that must go hand in hand with cultivating democracy here and encouraging it everywhere" (1996, p. 105).

Appiah is doing more than offering a practical way out. He is in fact hinting at a different methodological foundation for human social life. Within the model of cultural nationalism life is, methodologically speaking, fundamentally about being "who you are" (e.g., expressing one's "blackness"). Appiah is suggesting that it's time for the African-American community to "move on" to a life where we are not so narrowly defined, methodologically speaking, but are rather simultaneously "who we are" *and* "who we are not."

CULTURAL ACTIVITY

Taking this analysis as a starting point, I want to develop my argument against epistemology and identity. While I agree with much of what Appiah says, I do take issue with his view that establishing racial identity is a necessary stage in the process of challenging identity and, further, his appeal to dialectics in making the claim that *first* we have to establish our identity and then we can challenge it (Appiah, 1996). I see nothing natural or inevitable about this. The fact that historically this is what has happened is more an issue of a mistaken political tactic than the instantiation of the abstract thesis-antithesis-synthesis dialectic or an equally abstract stagist theory of human history. By relating to Marxism and to dialectics as epistemological rather than as methodological, Appiah misses the opportunity to subject identity to the radical deconstruction it deserves.

A book important in my own development, *Black Bolshevik*, is helpful here. In this autobiography, Harry Haywood, an African-American leader of the Communist Party USA in the 1930s and 1940s, writes about his struggles to come to terms with being black and being a communist (1978). Was he losing his black identity to his communist one? Which identity was dominant? Who was he . . . really?

As I have come to understand it, being a revolutionary (a "postmodern" Bolshevik, we could say) is not an issue of identity at all. A revolutionary is someone who carries out certain revolutionary activities—it has everything to do with what you're doing and nothing to do with who you are. It is the epistemologizing of Marxism—the distortion of Marx's method into categorization and abstraction—that makes it seem as if being black, being a woman, being gay, being working-class and being a revolutionary are identities and comparable.

Without epistemology, what is there? There is revolutionary activity. Marx's usefulness to me is located here—in the self-conscious and self-reflexive "changing of circumstances and of human activity" (Marx, 1974, p. 121). Without such a method to change totalities, to reshape the existing circumstances and create something new, *how* would one be, and *why* would one be a revolutionary in nonrevolutionary times such as the ones in which we are living?

In their 1993 book, *Lev Vygotsky: Revolutionary Scientist*, Newman and Holzman repeatedly pose this question. Their take on Vygotsky, unlike many of his contemporary followers, is that he is best understood as a revolutionary Marxist methodologist. From this activity-theoretic (as opposed to epistemological) perspective, one of the most important contributions Vygotsky has made is his specification of Marx's conception of revolutionary activity to human development and psychology.

In attempting to create a psychology that would not fall into the dualistic traps of existing theories, such as behaviorism or introspectionism, nor perpetuate the assumed bipolarities of individual-social, cognitive-affective, or biological-cultural, Vygotsky argued that *human social-cultural-historical activity* is the proper object of psychological study. He wisely realized that this new object of study required a new methodology—that you couldn't study activity with tools designed to study behavior. What was needed was not just new tools but new *kinds of tools*—ones that are of a dialectical unity with what they produce—or as he put it: "simultaneously the tool and the result of study" (Vygotsky, 1978, p. 65).

Newman and Holzman take this methodological discovery by Vygotsky and run with it. To them, tool-and-result methodology not only is what is required of revolutionary psychologists, but it is the ordinary, day-to-day process of how human beings learn and develop—unless societal conditions put a stop to it, as they have in the latter part of this century. Human beings create development and learning by creating the environments that make development and learning possible. In other words, we create developmental, revolutionary activity.

This understanding of development is a far cry from the linear, dualistic, stagist, individuated—and race-, gender-, and class-biased—theory I was taught in graduate school. Vygotsky's views on learning and development are refreshingly and radically monistic and antistagist. Development is not something that happens *to us* as we go about constructing a Kantian world, nor is it a prerequisite for learning, as it is for Piaget. Development and learning are sustained revolutionary activities—a dialectic unity in which *learning leads development*. Babbling babies become speakers of a language by participating with their caregivers in creating environments in which they learn in advance of their development—in simple terms, they do what they don't know how to do. They babble, adults talk back to them, they creatively imitate, and so on. There is no knowledge antecedent to this activity and no understanding separate from it. As some have pointed out, there couldn't be. Babies are related to as speakers, they perform as speakers—this joint activity *is and creates* a new speaker (Holzman, 1999; Newman and Holzman, 1993).

This learning-leading-development activity is key to the work of the East Side Institute and the programs that utilize its approach. Additionally, I think it's key to practicing postmodern revolutionary Marxism, whatever your affiliation. We believe that reinitiating developmental activity is what revolutionaries should be doing today. I think political activists of all kinds—those working against sexual oppression, against reactionary nationalist forces, those involved in antiracist work, those fighting class oppression, gay activists, those in democracy movements—need to become *activityists*.

As I understand it, to be an activityist is to be a nonknower and a performer. Methodologically, these two go together: we cannot *know* what developmental activity is; we have to perform it (Holzman, 1999; Newman and Holzman, 1997). Despite how rare and undervalued performance is in our culture, we human beings can, fortunately, reinitiate our performatory capacities with surprising ease. It is the social identities that stand in our way, locking us into acting in certain ways because "that is who we are."

From this perspective, cultural nationalism turns out to be a rather substantial impediment to the development of the black community, both individually and collectively—it's a particularly severe case of "that's who we are." To the extent that the cultural nationalism that pervades child-rearing among African-Americans reinforces identity, it undermines learning and development in the African-American community.

GROWING UP PERFORMED

My work with teenagers has been incredibly challenging, rewarding, and developmental. Traditional developmental theory calls adolescence a crucial stage in identity formation. But from an activityist perspective, identity is—if anything—as much a part of the problems of violence, drugs, teen pregnancy, and school failure as are economic and political factors. (Spend a little time with inner-city youth if you want to see how destructive and antidevelopmental identity can be.) Our youth projects might be said to be anti-identity—we have no interest in helping young people become possessors of different, more secure, and positive identities, because we believe that won't help them grow. Instead, we support them to create continuously their development through the creative, emergent activity of performing beyond themselves. The All Stars Talent Show Network and the Development School for Youth are cultural-performatory environments in which "identity play" and "performing ahead of oneself" can take place—not *after* or *in* these environments but, in tool-and-result fashion, along with their creation.

The All Stars Talent Show Network

The All Stars Talent Show Network is an antiviolence youth program that is made possible by grassroots fund-raising. Now in its fifteenth year, it involves some 30,000 children and teenagers. The young people, primarily from working class and poor black and Latino communities, produce talent shows in their neighborhoods (up to sixty-five shows a year) as an alternative to violence. Not only do they sing, dance, and rap in these shows, they take responsibility for producing them. Working with adults from the All Stars and from their own communities, they find locations for the shows (usually high school and junior high school auditoriums), sell the tickets, stage-manage, usher, emcee, run the light- and soundboards, and maintain security. They also build the audience and mentor younger children in the program. In the process, these young people not only learn all sorts of technical skills, they also learn to relate to kids from other neighborhoods, to work with adults, and to interact with their community's institutions (schools, churches, block associations, etc.). In short, they create an environment in which they can perform as leaders, and most of them, in fact, do.

Among other things, the All Stars can be viewed as a form of supplementary education, as this term has been popularized by Edmund Gordon, one of the founders and the First Director of Research for Project Head Start (Gordon, 1994). It is an educational activity organized outside the parameters of the public school system and engineered to address the particularities of the population it engages. Educators speak of supplementary education as everything from after-school literacy classes to parents taking their children to museums and concerts. Most supplementary education directed to working-class and minority youth has in recent years been cognitively based and focused on buttressing the young peoples' less-than-ideal academic skills. In contrast, the education the All Stars provides has more to do with *developing* than with *knowing*.

The All Stars builds on young peoples' strengths, including their connections to their communities. It begins with what most young working-class African-American and Latino youth are interested in, namely, hip-hop culture. Every individual or group who auditions, no matter the age or the nature of the act, must create and perform a skit or performance piece on a subject that he or she thinks is important to their community. These performance pieces are videotaped and shown on a big screen before an individual or group's live performance at a talent show. The creation of the skits not only gets young people articulating their views and experiences, it also helps them realize, in many cases for the first time, that they actually have something to say. In addition, the creation of dramatic skits expands the meaning of performance for the participants beyond singing, dancing, and rapping.

In our culture, inner-city youngsters are typically overidentified with destructive behavior and defined by others as having nothing to give, and all too many of them adopt the appropriate identity and act out the expected roles. Participating in the All Stars requires that they perform as builders and givers, and in doing so, they discover that they can. In this process, they create new options for who they are and how they want to be. They create opportunities to participate actively in ever-broadening arenas. For the past five years, the youth of the All Stars have produced the annual Phyllis Hyman Phat Friend Awards, in which they honor adults in government, education, entertainment, sports, and other fields whose work supports the development of young people. Last year, they cowrote and coproduced with the Castillo Theatre a play entitled *Crown Heights*, which brought black and Jewish youth together to reexamine the disturbances that took place in 1991 in Crown Heights, Brooklyn (a neighborhood shared uneasily by Hassidic Jews and blacks). In 1994, All Stars members traveled to Moscow, where they presented a symposium, "Developing in a Violent World," at an international conference of

Vygotsky scholars; in 1998, they went to Canada for the United Nation's Youth Vision Jeunesse Drug Abuse Prevention Forum and to Santiago, Chile, for the nineteenth World Scout Jamboree, where they displayed "development through performance" by creating a talent show with some of the 20,000 young participants.

At its best, the All Stars provides its participants with a worldliness that they previously lacked and, as part of that worldliness, with experience and skills in leadership. Its effect is the growth of the whole person. In the best sense of the term, the All Stars is about moral development. Its impact, therefore, goes beyond individual education, to influence the culture of the community.[2]

The Development School for Youth

This is a newer and smaller outside-and supplemental-to-school performance project. Launched in the spring of 1997, the program graduated over one hundred high school students in its first two years. Unlike the All Stars, which is an ongoing and continuous program (in which many youngsters have "grown up"), the Development School for Youth is a twelve-week program (with two cycles per year). There is, in addition, a summer program in which the teens are placed as interns in businesses in the New York metropolitan area (including Merrill Lynch, area banks, media, and other corporate environments).

During the twelve weeks, students work with program associates (these are financial donors to the program who additionally have volunteered to train and teach the young people how to perform in the culture of the donor's/associate's professional location, e.g., Wall Street, banking, entertainment, computer graphics, etc.). These sessions are structured as performances and challenge the deeply rooted assumptions about who teenagers are and the ambivalence about confronting the question of who these particular young people are becoming. Each week the stage is set, casting done, and directors chosen, and when the director calls "Curtain," the performance begins.

On a trip to Washington, D.C., the young people were directed to perform professionalism in the offices of Congress. They rehearsed looking a politician in the eye, shaking hands, and saying "My name is——. It's a pleasure to meet you." From an epistemological perspective, one might see this as a potential clash of identity for these mostly poor, very unprofessional kids. Are they subverting their class identity by being professional? Are they denying who they really are? And, if so, isn't this impositional? I don't think it's impositional. On the contrary, as I see it, identity is impositional—because it carries the presumption that one can know who these kids "really" are.

The challenge to identity begins before the start of the program, with both the recruitment and orientation process. We currently recruit at fifteen New York City high schools, and in our opening "speech" we (codirector Pam Lewis and I) talk to young people about development. Among the things we tell them is that we all hear people say how important it is to reach kids when they're young, and we're concerned that this sends a message that by the time you're thirteen or fourteen you're already formed, you're all you're going to be. We tell them we don't believe this, and that people can develop all through their lives. Fearful of making mistakes, all of us tend to do only what we know how to do, which is a surefire way to stop growing. We tell them that what's unique about our approach is that we create environments where they can make mistakes, fail, get up, and do it again and again. The Development School for Youth is a place where they can create without getting hung up on rightness and wrongness.

The current format for orientation illustrates the performatory approach we take to identity play. All incoming students, their parents, the workshop leaders, program associates, support committee members, and donors are invited to attend. At the most recent orientation, emceed by a longtime donor, I chose for my "development topic" the cultural nationalism of the black community and the work I had been doing in getting to know and prepare the program associates to work with young people whom they, by and large, either thought they already "knew" or were afraid to get to know. After my talk, the program associates (nearly all of whom are highly accomplished, top management professionals) got on the stage and performed a skit they had created entitled 1–800–THE GAME, in which they performed as young people "before" and "after" going through the program. Many of them "made fools of themselves" as they imitated teens describing what it was like to learn how to talk, dress, be on time, and so on. The young people then went to the stage one at a time and introduced themselves. They did this with widely varying levels of skill. Some wrote poems for the occasion, and others read poems written by others. Some were terrified and barely got out a sentence. Some were funny, while others were very serious. I remember particularly one seventeen-year-old African-American young man who got on stage and said: "When they asked me to introduce myself I realized I didn't know myself enough. I guess the reason I came to this program was to learn more about myself and what place I can have in this world."

In *Schools for Growth: Radical Alternatives to Current Educational Models* (1997), Holzman discusses performance in relation to education and institutionalized learning. She argues that current educational reforms (even radical ones) apply an epistemological paradigm. They misidentify the source of the educational crisis as stemming from either specific learning and teaching methods or strong ideological bias. They then focus on bringing into schools materials that tell the real (instead of the ideological) story and other ways of learning and teaching that are sensitive to culturally different ways of knowing. But the problem with schools, Holzman says (and I agree) is not a particular epistemological bias, but the bias *toward epistemology*. Schools separate learning from development. They discourage the creative joint activity of learning-leading-development; they wrench learning from this unity and attach it to the acquisition of knowledge.

If, as Holzman, Newman, and I argue, knowing has outlived its usefulness and actually gets in the way of growing, then efforts to create better knowers are doomed to failure. What should schools be in a culture where development has stopped? We need to transform schools into environments where developmental activity dominates. We need, above all, to teach development—a nonknowing performatory activity. Students should not be captured by culture but participate in creating it.

The strength of our activity-based youth programs lies in their capacity to reinitiate performance—that capacity to be who you and who you are not at the same time. This kind of developmental activity is vital to inner-city youth, who are trapped in very limited and too often negative social roles at an early age. How does a high school freshman with failing grades approach the principal of her school about using the auditorium for an All Stars show? By performing as a community organizer. How does a dance group with sharp, sophisticated moves come to teach them to kids with a shaky performance? By performing as mentors rather than competitors. How is it possible for twelve-year-olds to provide security for a show with forty acts and 2,000 in the audience? By performing the moral authority to provide leadership to the older kids and adults in attendance.

From a nonepistemological, activityist perspective, what's significant about our young peoples' performances of professionalism and leadership as producers of the All Stars, interns at Merrill Lynch, or guests of Congress is not that these young people now *have* a new identity, but that they have the capacity to *project it* and, given the opportunity and support, they do. This is what is developmental about performatory activity. And this is how, as I understand it, we cannot "move on," as Appiah urges, without getting rid of identity—and the epistemic posture that supports it and all of its weight.

NOTES

1. The development community (or developing development community) is what Newman and Holzman call the environment that we are continuously building, one "that is not overdetermined by epistemology and the varied institutional arrangements that perpetuate it" (Newman and Holzman, 1997, p. 47).

2. While it's impossible to measure the impact of a single program on the totality of a community with any exactitude, All Stars producer Pam Lewis feels that the program has been a factor in the gradual but clear shift away from crack cocaine and a glorification of violence among young people that characterized inner-city communities in the 1980s. While there are many factors that have contributed to the dramatic drop in violence in New York City over the last few years, statistics supplied by the All Stars indicate that those neighborhoods where the All Stars have had the longest and most consistent presence—among them Bedford Stuyvesant, East New York, and Brownsville in Brooklyn, Morrisania and Soundview in the South Bronx, Central and East Harlem, and Jamaica and Far Rockaway in Queens—have also had the biggest drop in violent crime.

REFERENCES

Appiah, K. A. (1992). *In my father's house: Africa in the philosophy of culture.* New York: Oxford University Press.

Appiah, K. A. (1996). Race, culture, identity: Misunderstood connections. In K. A. Appiah and A. Gutmann, *Color conscious: The political morality of race.* pp. 30–105. Princeton, NJ: Princeton University Press.

Appiah, K. A., and Gates, H. L. Jr. (1997). *The dictionary of global culture*. New York: Knopf.

Gordon, E. (1994). Too much schooling, too little education. *The Journal of Negro Education, 63 (3)*.

Haywood, H. (1978). *Black Bolshevik: Autobiography of an African-American Communist*. Chicago: Lake View Press.

Holzman, L. (1997). *Schools for growth: Radical alternatives to current educational models*. Mahwah, NJ: Erlbaum.

Holzman, L. (1999). *Performing psychology: A postmodern culture of the mind*. New York: Routledge.

Holzman, L., and Newman. F. (1979). *The practice of method*. New York: Institute for Social Therapy and Research.

Marx, K. (1974). Theses on Feuerbach. In K. Marx and F. Engels, *The German ideology*, pp. 121–123. New York: International Publishers.

Newman, F., and Holzman, L. (1993). *Lev Vygotsky: Revolutionary scientist*. London: Routledge.

Newman, F., and Holzman, L. (1997). *The end of knowing: A new developmental way of learning*. London. Routledge.

Vygotsky, L. S. (1978). *Mind in society*. Cambridge, MA: Harvard University Press.

The Performance

of Revolution

(More Thoughts

on the Postmodernization

of Marxism)

Fred Newman

> The economists express it like this: each person has her or his private
> interests in mind, and nothing else: as a consequence she or he
> serves everyone's private interests, i.e., the general interest,
> without wishing to or knowing that she or he is. The irony of
> this is not that the totality of private interest—which is the
> same thing as the general interest—can be attained by the
> individuals following her or his own interest. Rather it could be
> inferred from this abstract phrase that everyone hinders the
> satisfaction of everyone else's interest, that instead of a general
> affirmation, the result of this war of all against all is rather a
> general negation. The point is rather that private interest is
> itself already a socially determined interest, which can only be
> achieved within the conditions established by society and
> through the means that society affords, and that it is thus linked
> to the reproduction of these conditions and means. It is
> certainly the interest of private individuals that is at stake; but
> its content as well as the form and the means of its realization,
> is only given by social conditions independent of all these
> individuals.
>
> Karl Marx, *The Grundrisse*

THE *PSYCHOLOGICAL* NOTION OF SELF-INTEREST has been from the start (of
bourgeois ideological dominance) the companion piece to the *economic*

idea of private property. And the *political* concepts of democracy and individual liberty have been the hybrid children of the two. But the child, as is well known, is often not the *synthesis* of the parents. It is, rather, a dialectical unity, filled with conflict and characteristically restrained (self-restrained) in all its efforts to move beyond itself. Such is the paradox of individual liberty. For the *individual* can never be free of the form and content of individuated ideology in an individuated commodified society. We are like laboratory rats trying to escape from a maze that is in fact part of a larger maze (and so on and so on) that conditions us on how to escape. *And yet we do change.* In part, this is explainable by the obvious fact that things happen to us over which we have no control. What seems more important is that some of our changing seems subjectively driven. But how is that possible, given the philosophical conundrum articulated above? Are we deluded in thinking that we change? Some philosophers, from Parmenides and Zeno down to postmodern times, have thought so. They have insisted that change and/or our efforts to explain change are mere illusions. And most certainly, these varied thinkers have insisted, subjectively based change is out of the question. Others (any freshman student of philosophy will tell you), starting with Heraclitus, have insisted that change (or changing) is all there is. But most ordinary people seem happily to accept that things do change, even if it seems philosophically impossible for them to do so. "So much the worse for philosophy" appears to be the commonsensical attitude of the ordinary man or woman.

In Western culture, many would argue that *individuated liberty* and *democracy*, as idea and practice, have solved the ancient riddle of determinism. For the free individual (so the story goes) can participate in political society and cast her or his vote in accordance with her or his self-interest in such a way as to effect change. But as Marx and others have pointed out, the individual's self-interests (wants, desires, etc.) are themselves thoroughly determined by prevailing conditions, and, therefore, acting individualistically in accordance with them will largely leave matters . . . unchanged.

While few these days consider these issues philosophically, many people attend to them in endlessly varied practical forms, political types and psychology types amongst them! Political types and psychology types in contemporary society often appear to treat each other with disdain. But, in my opinion, these two critical human disciplines could learn much from each other if both would properly reject their pompous self-serving claims of being a science and study the activities of each *culturally*. For it is the culture of politics and the culture of psychology that best reveal their "essences" by exposing their respective "essential limitations."

THE CULTURE OF AMERICAN POLITICS

America's[1] earliest social-political engineers (a.k.a. our Founding Fathers)—their views strongly influenced by the Enlightenment and the age of democratic revolution—created a system that was something of a reconciliation between the democratic participation of the mass (though the "mass" was somewhat narrowly defined) and the best person to govern: the expert, the representative—the politician. Over time, electoral democracy became culturally more and more focused on the outcome rather than on the process. It was increasingly less and less about the collective process of decision-making and the self-transformative culture that a civically active and involved society engenders. It was more and more about the decision, pure and simple. The product, not the process; the outcome, less and less revolutionary.

So even as the franchise became fully inclusive, and structural barriers to participation were eliminated, the *culture* of American politics evolved—some might say devolved—into one which is notably nonparticipatory. Among the so-called Western-style democracies of the contemporary world, the U.S. is ranked *fifty-two out of fifty-eight* in terms of voter participation. Over 50 percent of eligible Americans don't vote in national elections. Among the newest voter generation—eighteen to twenty-four year olds—participation in national elections is shockingly below 30%.

There are many political "scientific" accountings of this phenomenon, from claims about the cynicism or apathy of the American voter to recognition of the institutionalized discouragement by the complex system of regulations that protect incumbents and by American two-partyism as it has evolved in the last seventy years. But it seems to me that the problem —for those who take the decline of American democracy to be so—is much deeper and more specific to the current postmodern era. After all, at first glance, democracy's stagnation could, to a large degree, be "fixed" by the introduction of new political reforms that would make participation more possible and desirable. But even structural reforms that lead to an expansion and revitalization of electoral democracy, while desperately needed, do not address in and of themselves what is a more fundamental and far-reaching problem for the American community—indeed, for the international community. That problem is the breakdown of *development*. And ironically, as the developmental capacities of contemporary society have diminished, economic, social, moral, personal, and political democracy has been more and more substituted for development in most so-called advanced societies.

But the mere substitution of democracy for human development, far from resolving the paradoxicality of change, exacerbates it. Hence in American society it should come as no surprise that structural changes of all sorts—which have increased the ability of citizens to participate democratically—have been accompanied by a *de facto* decline in such participation. Apathy is not, in my opinion, the answer, because in point of fact, greater democratic participation without overall development does not effectively produce change. Therefore, it is quite reasonable that many people would not be voting. To put the matter simply, more and more people having greater and greater opportunity to vote for fewer and fewer real choices not only does not yield development, it makes people more and more cynical that there can be such a thing as development.

Consequently, any further efforts to rejuvenate democracy that do not simultaneously and continuously reinitiate development are doomed to reinforce and further institutionalize the nondevelopmental framework, that is, the political culture, of contemporary society. Right now, our choices—the decisions we make—are conditioned by the dominant culture, by what people "want" and "desire" as determined by that culture. Unless the mass can somehow be organized to engage in the process of transforming the culture, our wants and desires will continue to be circumscribed by the culture we are unwilling or unable to change.

Though many (actually most) Americans don't vote, due in no small part to the belief that it doesn't make a difference, there nonetheless remains a curiously steadfast belief in the proposition that the primary way we can change things is through voting. The belief that how people effect change is as liberated individuals, that is, going to the voting booth and individually pulling such and such a lever, prevails. But while individuals—even a substantial collection of them—can change who the governor of Wyoming or Illinois is, individuals—even a large collection of them—do not transform the culture of a society. They cannot because, organized as individuals, they can do nothing but express the dominant culture. Cultural transformation is a group or *mass activity*—an activity of a group or mass, whether of two people or two billion people.

The American nonvoters—their conscious cognitive belief systems aside—have stumbled upon a critical insight. They might be able to change *something* by voting. But they can't change *everything*. And unless you can change everything, that is, the culture, you can't change anything. Why vote, since it only *appears* to effect change, but really doesn't.

This dysfunction of American democracy—which is really a dysfunction of American development—seemingly catalyzed the beginnings of a populist political revolt in the early 1990s. The 1992 independent presidential candidacy of Ross Perot inspired twenty million Americans—considered among the most attitudinally conservative elements of the population—to break with the cultural *sine qua non* of U.S. politics, the two-party system. They declared that they wanted the era of special-interest governance to be over. This phenomenon knocked the socks off just about every political player, pundit, and oddsmaker in the English-speaking world. Naturally, it also caused quite a stir among leftist intellectuals and activists, who were quick to diagnose the rebellion as having "neofascistic tendencies." The American left—perhaps the paradigmatic conservative believers in expertise over popular democracy (with themselves cast as the experts)—had absolutely no idea what was going on. All they knew was that twenty million ordinary Americans were in rebellion and it wasn't coming out of or going into the Democratic Party. That was enough for them to either demonize and/or write off the significance of the movement.

But tactical polemics aside, the Perot phenomenon offered a profound insight into the core American psychic (schizophrenic) conflict between expertise and popular democracy. Perot's message was, on the one hand, a militant populist message: *The special interests have hijacked our government. This country belongs to the American people. We have to take our country back. We have to eliminate corruption, restore accountability, and reshape our political process.* Millions responded to that populist cultural appeal to redistribute political power from the professionals to the people.

At the same time, though, there was another, opposite dimension to Perot's message: *What this country needs is good management. We need to pay attention to the bottom line. Our politicians are managerial nincompoops; they'd never succeed in the private sector. I have. I've built a billion-dollar company. I have the expertise to run this country.* Millions responded to this appeal as well. Arguably, it was the ambiguous mixing of the two that was at the heart of Perot's appeal. For Americans remain deeply conflicted about what we want and about how we see ourselves being governed.

The Jesse Ventura victory in Minnesota in 1998 provoked some related controversies. Some have observed that Ventura, professional wrestler-turned-populist politician, inspired new and nonvoters specifically because they wanted to vote for someone who had no business being governor. That was part (a large part) of the populism. The Ventura vote was an in-your-face defiance of the conventional wisdom that whoever gets elected must be "qualified" according to the prevailing standards of expertise. Perhaps what Minnesotans really "want and need" is not an expert but a leader who can organize the state to fuller levels of participation (Minnesota's turnout in the 1998 election was twenty-four percentage points higher than the national average).

But even that radical view of the significance of the Ventura victory is limited. What if the significance of the Ventura run is simply what took place on Election Day, namely that more than 765,000 people went out to the polls and kicked sand in the face of the establishment? Shouldn't we consider the possibility that its significance was *not* in the fact that Ventura ended up governor, but in the fact that the people of Minnesota engaged in a mass performance which is not best understood or identified as individuals selecting a governor, but as a mass ensemble creating a new political cultural product? What took place in Minnesota was hardly an election. It was a defection. Put positively, it was more a wrestling match than a vote. It did not "seemingly reconcile" a social contradiction by the means of existing institutionalized structures, that is, it was not the workings of the bourgeois democratic state. For while it was not extralegal, in the sense of many of the militant worldwide revolutions of the century, it was more extrainstitutional than even many of those events.

The problem (if there is one) with Jesse Ventura is not that he has no business being governor. Indeed, that is the very essence and the creatively remarkable character of the Minnesota phenomenon. Minnesota has no governor; it has Jesse Ventura (he is the embodiment!) as the ongoing product of a profound mass-cultural transformation. The wrestling match is one of twentieth-century America's paradigmatic ensemble, participatory, cultural performances. Through mass media, millions of ordinary Americans are variously involved in a show that does not for a moment hide the fact that it is a *pretense*. It is, indeed, its pretense that captivates all involved. What is captivating is the opportunity to participate with a mass of human beings to create culturally, that is, to create culture, as only a mass or group activity can. It makes no difference who wins. What makes a difference is the involvement in a creative cultural activity. Jesse Ventura *won* only because Minnesota law required a winner. But the essence of the phenomenon was the mass-cultural activity of violating the politically overdetermined pseudodemocracy of American two-party politics, that is, the performance of revolution.

THE PERFORMANCE OF REVOLUTION

Social therapy (the name we use to describe our Marxian-based, dialectical, group therapy) has, I believe, helped many with their emotional pain. As well, it has been both the breeding ground and the testing ground for numerous transformations of Marxian and post-Marxian conceptions. This "therapeutization" of Marxism is not simply an application of Marx's view (anymore than Einstein's work is merely an application of Newton's); it is, rather, a clinical developmentalist recasting of the classical class-analytic, cognitive view known as dialectical materialism.

Some of the more important Marxian conceptions reshaped by social therapeutics include the conception/practice of power, self, group, meaning, and dialectics itself. My earliest therapeutic/analytic work brought to light the critical distinction between power and authority[2], where power is the creative capacity of the group by the exercise of its emotional labor to generate new environments, and authority is the societally overdetermined predisposition of the individuated members of the group to accept passively class-dominated, patriarchal, emotive environments. In the vortex of the conflict between power and authority, the social therapist is at once the organizer (facilitator) of the group's emotive laborpower and the potential (or even actual) repository of the group members' authoritarian "instincts." Thus, in working out the precise nature of this emerging relationship, the group changes its relationship to power and to authority, that is, it hopefully becomes more powerful and less alienated.

Obviously connected to this work is the group's practical-critical consideration of self. For self and the profoundly overglorified orthodox Western therapeutic principle of "knowing thy self" are, in my opinion, little more than a cover-up for individuated alienation. The Marxian notions of species identity and world historic identity are retooled to do battle against the Freudian (bourgeois) fear of group behavior. As well, Wittgenstein's (1953) critical commentary on private languages (and, of equal importance, his philosophically therapeutic mode of teaching it) serves as a kind of humanistic "shock" therapy to help individuals recognize that they do not (and need not and cannot) know themselves since they are themselves. The social therapist (*qua* organizer or facilitator) works then with the group—not the individuated selves that, reductionistically speaking, comprise the group. To be sure, particular members of the group freely raise and react to whatever they choose and however they choose. Yet any and all remarks that effectively turn the group into a passive body of listeners as opposed to active participants are quickly (though variously) and powerfully responded to. In a word (a Vygotskian word), the group is consistently organized as an emotive "zone of proximal development," or ZPD (Vygotsky, 1978, 1987). The various members, each at a different level of emotional development, are encouraged to create a new unit (the emotional group) with a new level of emotional development, that is, the group's level of emotional development. This ongoing and ever-changing activity is (as Vygotsky shows for more cognitively structured learning groups) profoundly developmental for all—even the most developed individually.

Indeed, this process requires nothing less than totally (qualitatively) changing the focus of the therapy group from the individuated self discovering deeper insights into his or her consciousness to the collective activity of continuously creating a new social unit (the emotional ZPD). "How well is the group performing its activity?" not "How is each individual doing?" becomes the overriding question. This ultrafocus on activity, that is, the conversation, does nothing less than transform meaning itself. Reconsidering Wittgenstein from a purer Marxian (and

Vygotskian) activity-theoretic vantage point, we reject the simplistic equation of meaning and use (so common amongst many followers and students of Wittgenstein, including many postmodernist psychologists) in favor of the dialectical relationship between meaning and activity. The meaning of conversation, we argue, is not to be found in *how* it is used but in *that* it is used (Newman, 1999, pp. 84–85)[3].

The ongoing social-therapeutic group is, like the election of Governor Ventura, a "performance of revolution." Since it meets each week, it is, to jokingly borrow a phrase from Trotsky, a kind of "permanent revolution." Each group is a grouping of human beings doing what our unique (and often disturbed) species does periodically and in varying ways— create culture, that is, self-consciously develop. We are able to do so by virtue of our capacity to perform. Presumably our performatory capacity is inextricably entwined with our vulnerability to being alienated (and, no doubt, individuated). We are able (as childhood proves) to become what we are not. If we were not, we would not develop at all. We are pretenders. We are performers. But we cannot *perform* as individuals. As individuals we can, at best, *act*. The form of individuation (the commodified character of alienation in modern society) is the ultimate inhibitor of performance. We perform only as a group. To change political matters, then, we must perform as a group even as we vote as (legalistic) individuals. To change psychological matters, we must *perform* as (in) a group even as we consume as individuals.

The performance of revolution is not to be confused with the modernist notion of *making* a revolution. Indeed, so far as I know, the origin of this notion of *performing revolution* (revolutionary practice) derives from Marx. Yet (and this has been, in my view, dramatically misunderstood) Marx effectively introduces the concept of revolutionary practice to *distinguish* it from the "making of revolution." The Marxian precursor to the notion of performing revolution appears first (as far as I know) in his famous "Theses on Feuerbach." Thesis one states:

> The chief defect of all hitherto existing materialism (that of Feuerbach included) is that the thing, reality, sensuousness, is conceived only in the form of the *object or of contemplation*, but not as *sensuous human activity, practice*, not subjectively. Hence, in contradistinction to materialism, the active side was developed abstractly by idealism—which, of course, does not know real, sensuous activity as

such. Feuerbach wants sensuous objects, really distinct from the thought objects, but he does not conceive human activity itself as objective activity. Hence, in *Das Wesen des Christenthums*, he regards the theoretical attitude as the only genuinely human attitude, while practice is conceived and fixed only in its dirty-judaical manifestation. Hence he does not grasp the significance of "revolutionary," of "practical-critical," activity. (Marx, 1974, p. 121)

Revolutionary activity, or practical-critical activity, is not, for Marx, a kind of activity. Rather, Marx the methodologist is urging us to consider the need for an *activity revolution*. In the theses, Marx offers schemata for a new kind of understanding—one based on activity (and not the object) as fundamental. Nissen, Axel, and Jensen put the matter well in their comprehensive review of my and Holzman's "trilogy" on the postmodernization of Marx. They say:

Newman and Holzman are among the few who have seen the far-reaching implications of Marx's theses on Feuerbach, not just the famous sixth, which states that we should not seek an abstract essence of humanity in the individual, but also the first, the second, and the eleventh, in which practice, as a sensuous subjective revolutionary activity, is proposed as the foundation of a new kind of theoretical thinking. So far, the arguments for Newman and Holzman seem consistent, even if they build up considerable expectations to be fulfilled. The problem, it seems, lies in the argument that one needs to engage in revolutionary practice to understand. We would tend to agree, if revolution means change of relevant conditions; but we would also point out that the argument begs some answer to the question of how we know (or, if one prefers, how we understand) which practice is revolutionary and when. (Nissen, Axel, and Jensen, 1999, p. 423)

Yet (as is apparent from their final sentences) even these astute reviewers shift back to an *objectified* meaning of revolution (revolutionary activity) in asking "which practice is revolutionary and when." It is not certain practices that are revolutionary. It is the shift from an epistemic conception of objectification to a new mode of understanding (practical-critical, revolutionary, performatory) of activity that is revolutionary.

In "One Dogma of Dialectical Materialism" I make an almost identical point in terms of Marx's understanding (and many Marxists' misunderstanding) of dialectics.

The well-suitedness of dialectics as a method of study is fully dependent on a new understanding of the proper object of study. It is not the object or the thing (large or small) which can be studied; it is activity, practice, subjectivity. Dialectical materialism does not, for Marx, mean the dialectical study of the material organized as things. This is the error of all prior forms of materialism. For not only is the physical object a cultural posit (in Quine's sense); so is object itself. Indeed, it is not the physicality of the object that is most insidiously mythical and, thereby, potentially metaphysical; it is its formal organization (its shape) as a discrete object of study or discernment. (Newman, 1999, p. 93)

The social therapeutic environment attempts to be at once *democratic* and *developmental*. The ongoing group in its ongoing ensemble performance creates its own culture. In this developmental work, *everyone* is not equal because there is no every *one*. The group creates the revolutionary performance, meaning that the group appeals to nothing other than the group activity itself in determining what is happening and/or the understanding of what is happening. To be sure, things of all kinds are brought into the group and, to varying degrees, influence (determine) what the group does. How could it be otherwise? Endless factors having nothing to do with the production process *per se* influence what the finished Lincoln Center production of "Hamlet" will look like. But the performance has an integrity of comprehension because it is not merely a determined product of the process; it is the self-conscious activity of the ensemble creating the play that (even more than the script) gives us a "new kind of theoretical thinking."

Yet the new kind of theoretical thinking is not theoretical at all, that is, it is, in traditional terms, aesthetic and in Marx's terms, practical-critical, that is, revolutionary. It is the practical-critical participation in the nonobjectified (what I often call "pointless") activity that *is* (or better still, *is becoming*) revolutionary. A performance of revolution changes *nothing*. It changes *everything*. Within this environment, each individuated group member is "free" to contribute as often and as openly as she or he chooses. But the hegemonic component of the dialectical process is development. For in its absence, democracy (in therapy or elsewhere) means little. If we cannot creatively transform the culture and thereby the choices themselves, then our capacity to select one *other* determined choice over another is, at best, a Zeno-like illusion.

The dialectical relationship between *democracy* and *development* is precisely what history (Fukuyama notwithstanding) will reveal to us in the new century. Revolution (along with everything else) will come to have a new meaning. And *performance*, in my opinion, will more and more become the practical-critical shape of *activity* even as *dialectics* replaces *objectification* as our mode of understanding. The postmodernist Marxian revolution has yet to come. Of this I feel almost as certain as I do that the modernist Marxian revolution has completely failed.

NOTES

1. Special thanks to Jacqueline Salit for her valuable assistance in the discussion of American politics. While I am aware that all of the Western hemisphere is America, throughout this essay I use "America" and "American" as a shorthand term to refer to citizens, residents, and characteristics of people living in the United States.

2. See Newman, 1974, for early articulations of this distinction.

3. This characterization of social therapy in this and the preceding three paragraphs first appeared in "One Dogma of Dialectical Materialism," an essay on the postmodernization of Marxism that appeared in *Annual Review of Critical Psychology*, 1999. It is reprinted here with permission from Ian Parker, the journal editor.

REFERENCES

Marx, K. (1974). Theses on Feuerbach. In K. Marx and F. Engels, *The German ideology*. New York. International Publishers.

Marx, K. (1993). *Grundrisse: Foundations of the critique of political economy*. New York: Penguin USA.

Newman, F. (1974). *Power and authority: The inside view of class struggle*. New York: Centers for Change, Inc.

Newman, F. (1999). One dogma of dialectical materialism. *Annual Review of Critical Psychology*, *1(1)* , 83–99.

Nissen, M., Axel, E., and Jensen, T. B. (1999). The abstract zone of proximal development. *Theory & Psychology*, *9 (3)*, 417–426.

Vygotsky, L. S. (1978). *Mind in society*. Cambridge, MA: Harvard University Press.

Vygotsky, L. S. (1987). *The collected works of L. S. Vygotsky*. Vol. 1. New York: Plenum.

Wittgenstein, L. (1953). *Philosophical investigations*. New York: Macmillan.

III

EXTENDING

THE

DIALOGUE

We invited four colleagues to comment on the essays of this volume. Drawing others who were not presenters at the 1997 conference into the dialogue would, we hoped, reconstruct the conversation and extend it into unpredictable directions. The result was more than we hoped for: not only do Sheila McNamee, Robert Neimeyer, Harlene Anderson and Vesna Ognjenović share their own views, they have done so in such a way that the previous authors can be heard more clearly.

Most importantly perhaps for our present purposes, the contributions of the commentators enable the appropriation by the wider community of what was produced by the authors. "Appropriation" is an apt term since it conveys a range of styles and attitudes, from reverence (not represented here!) through strategic appreciation to cautious scrutiny to sympathetic debunking—just like psychology's reactions to postmodernism itself. There is, as Vesna Ognjenović would hope, no consensus but much creation, here (pp. 211–212). Like a multiple pendulum, governed by chaos theory if anything, psychology's conversation on postmodernism swirls and thrashes around, juggling small issues for a while and then unexpectedly switching back to big ones, looping around in familiar tracks and then swooping down on a new patch of space.

Dichotomies, Discourses, and Transformative Practices

Sheila McNamee

I HAVE BEEN ASKED to write a commentary on this volume of provocative pieces concerning postmodern psychology and societal practice. What follows is my feeble attempt to *perform* my commentary, rather than *present* it as based on what I know, think, or have learned about the topic. In the end, I am sure my effort will be incomplete and open to criticism. And along with those performances I hope that there might be invitations into some unknown conversations about postmodern psychology.

I understand this text as having two major purposes. First, it is an attempt to provide a "retrospective" accounting of a decade's efforts to move from a "positivist and pragmatically driven mainstream psychology" to a postmodern psychology. Over the past decade, major proponents of postmodernism (many of whose voices are present in the current volume) have generated a wide array of arguments for a postmodern psychology as well as particular ways of talking about such a psychology. The orienting feature of all these discourses on/about postmodern psychology is the emphasis on language as opposed to inner, private aspects of individuals as the focus of psychology. Since much has been said about these issues within this volume, I will not reiterate those arguments here.

There is, however, a second (and to me more central) purpose for the present volume. Holzman and Morss, as volume editors, have invited each contributor into a conversation about *practice*. The emphasis on practice is, as I see it, a direct challenge to refrain from debating the competing ways of talking about postmodern psychology and demanding, instead, a *doing* of postmodern psychology. What, in other words, would each author's attempts to refigure psychology from individual properties of persons to engaged language practices *look like*? Rather than place our effort on elaborating abstract principles *about* postmodern psychology, the editors challenge the contributors to engage in self-reflexive inquiry concerning "whether any of this matters to how ordinary people the world over live their lives" (Holzman and Morss, this volume, p. 11).

My own view is that this is a vitally important evolution for postmodern psychology. It is crucial precisely because metatheoretical discussions, while generative, are the hallmark of modernist psychology. The more we remain locked in conversation about *what* postmodern psychology *should* look like and why, the more we remain within the discourse of modernism itself—implying and assuming that we could *know* the answer to this question if only we worked hard enough on the problem.

Now, I must quickly point out that I am not implying that postmodernism is "good" and modernism is "bad." Unfortunately, these interpretations are rampant in any discussion of postmodernism. Why? Because the discursive traditions within which we participate offer us limited resources for interpreting issues such as these in terms other than "good/bad." And yet, this is precisely the challenge of the present volume: Can we act in ways that encourage new resources for action—even in our "talk" (i.e., activity) about apparently abstract positions such as postmodern psychology? The editors' point seems to be that postmodern psychology is *not* about abstraction. It is about actions of persons in relation. It is challenging (if not nearly impossible) for us to entertain a "new" argument without assuming that "new" is "better" or "more correct."

This conundrum locks us into an unending process of hearing the "new" within the frame of the "old," and consequently leaves us within the "either/or" logic of modernism (one is right and the other wrong)[1]. There is an infinite regress in forms of argument (i.e., ways of talking) that do not provide the resources for new forms of understanding and thus new forms of "going on together." The more arguments for a "postmodern psychology" are made, the more they are heard as arguments that claim the superiority of postmodern psychology. The more arguments are understood as arguments claiming superiority, the more others are "invited" into a conversation of critique, challenge and protection of the already popular mode of interpretation (modernism). There is little way out of such a regressive cycle. In fact, in this very volume we see the boundaries clearly drawn between one's "version" of postmodern psychology and another's.

This is why it is vitally important to appreciate the apparently subtle shift in focus that is at stake here: a shift from an emphasis on essential features of "things in themselves" (including persons and their "positions" on issues) to an emphasis on language (ways of talking *about* things and, more important, ways of coordinating our activities with others). Within the former, we are drawn into the either/or binary which encourages us to compare and contrast for the purpose of discovering the truth (or the better, or the good, etc.). Within the latter, we are invited to approach *both* modernism and postmodernism as *discursive options*. We can talk about them *both* as different ways of *being in relation* with others. And, consequently, we are now able to consider the ways in which *both* discursive options are generative as forms of societal practice.

The terms of the discussion shift with the introduction of language as performance. We can now ask: "What sort of world are we inviting each other into when we act as if language represents the world?" and "What sort of world are we inviting each other into when we act as if language engages us in some joint activity of construction?" Yes, the terms of the discussion shift when we emphasize language practices. We are now consuming the discourse of modernism *within* the discourse of postmodernism. Many critics point to this as the major inconsistency of postmodernism: if there are multiple discourses available and many local realities, then isn't postmodernism discounting itself by arguing for a postmodernist way of talking about modernism (e.g., as a discursive option)? Well, the answer is yes and no. Of course the move is to subsume modernism within the umbrella of postmodernism (another language game). But, at the same time, this is understood as generative of a *form of practice*. That is, the attempt is not to simply "say things differently" and thereby declare "the way it is." Rather, the attempt is to engage others (theorists, practitioners, researchers, as well as all social actors) in activities that broaden our resources for social life.

This emphasis, then, is precisely what Newman and Holzman (1997) argue for in their book *The End of Knowing*, and what Holzman, in particular, argues in this volume. Briefly, rather than assume that people in relation need to "learn" or "know" how to make sense out of daily events, we are encouraged to engage in activities that invite us into the construction of new resources for coordinating with others. In postmodernism, the attempt is not to have others learn or know what postmodernism "is" but rather, through the very *practice* of proposing that modernism and postmodernism are discursive options, we *perform*—literally put into action and thus make *available*—new resources for engaging with others. To this end, postmodernism in general and postmodern psychology specifically are not about "right or wrong" but about shifting the discourse completely.

Now, to the issues at hand in the present volume as they relate to this more general background. There are several issues raised throughout, yet the most intriguing aspect of these issues is *how* they are presented. In light of my discussion above, it is interesting to note that each issue is raised in dichotomous form (a practice I admit to relying on in this commentary as well). This feature is intriguing, because it is the allure of dichotomies that seduces us into the modernist discourse. Let us consider some of the central issues raised in this volume. We see lengthy discussions of performance/activity, but these terms cannot be discussed without pitting them against theory/epistemology. We see arguments in favor of a politicized postmodern psychology that are made against the oppositional "rampant relativism" of the social-constructionist version of postmodern psychology. And there are significant arguments for revolutionary (or anarchistic) activities rather than "reactionary" activities. These are just a few of the more dominant themes that are reiterated throughout the volume. In the space that remains I would like to consider ways to avoid the dichotomies that emerge within this particular way of phrasing the issues at stake. My own concern is with whether or not there are ways of *doing* these arguments outside the realm of our discursive tradition (modernism) and thus *performing* our professional discussions about this very topic.

THEORY AS PRACTICE

There are such rich offerings in this volume's essays that elaborate what I would like to refer to as "practical theory" (Shotter, 1984) or "generative theory" (Gergen, 1994). Many of the authors discard the duality of "theory versus practice" by simply offering "theory *as* practice." Just a sampling will serve as illustrative of this move. Lois Holzman, in her description of social therapy, demonstrates how gathering interested people together to discuss interesting (and sometimes controversial) topics expands the conversational resources for all involved. It is not important in the context of social therapy to "teach" or to make sure those who attend "know" various philosophical and political traditions. What is important is that, through participation in the conversations (through both listening and talking), participants generate new forms of practice, new ways to invite others into relationship. This subtle activity has, as Lois notes, significant transformative potential. Participants have been invited into a very different sort of conversation. Similar to the Public Conversation Project of Laura Chasin and colleagues (1994, 1993) that Ken Gergen describes in his essay (p. 146), social therapy is a community-focused effort that, within a set of "unusual" parameters (e.g., this is not a lecture, anyone can attend, everyone is invited to listen and/or talk, etc.), expands the resources for action available to all.

Similar to Lois's illustration is that of her colleague Lenora Fulani. Lenora's emphasis on the political implications of "research as practice" (a variation on the "theory as practice" argument) is clearly described in her discussion of the All Stars Talent Show Network and the Development School for Youth. She presents both as "cultural-performatory environments in which 'identity play' and 'performing ahead of oneself' can take place."

Erica Burman's essay also serves as a useful illustration of "practical theory." Using three research projects as her cases, she illustrates the multiple ways in which the *process* of research simultaneously deconstructs and reconstructs what our notion of research itself is, when it is framed within an understanding of identity and positions as "fragmentary, relationally constructed and negotiated." Rather than fall into the "quantitative versus qualitative" dichotomy to argue a case for what research is, Burman illuminates the *process* of research as a relational *activity*. The political implications of research as a coordinated (relational) activity are enormously important.

These serve as rich illustrations and are provocative to the extent that they all indicate how forms of practice that have emerged within the general rubric of "postmodern psychologies" *do* make a difference in "how ordinary people the world over live their lives."

TALKING AND WRITING THEORY AS PRACTICE

There are clearly differences in the preferred descriptions, terms, and explanations used to articulate what is meant by postmodern psychology, as well as those terms used to evaluate whether it is worth pursuing. As I see it, the dilemma is not focused on which author "says it best" or which position is credible. Rather, the issue is one of doing precisely what the three illustrations above suggest. Can we avoid the use of dichotomies to *talk about* postmodern psychology and instead employ the relational, situated, and historical significance of a variety of ways of being in *the activity of* postmodern psychology? Specifically, can we learn from Ken Gergen's essay that identity politics is not "wrong" or the "evil other" but that it serves as an impressive illustration of the continual re-creation of social life that is so much a part of postmodernism?

Ken's story about identity politics locates this cultural move within the constructionist/postmodernist effort and simultaneously proposes a replacement of identity politics with relational politics. This is not a reaffirmation of another "good/bad" dichotomy. Rather, Ken is clear to talk about the evolution or transformation to which the discourse of identity politics itself has given rise. This speaks directly to the continual flux and uncertainty that a postmodern emphasis on language addresses. We replace the comfort of saying we now understand and can explain identity politics as a social phenomenon that emerges within an overall understanding that there are multiple, situated realities. We do not stop there. We recognize that it is precisely this "understanding" (i.e., this way of explaining the situation) that allows us to provide the resources for "problematizing" the same situation *and* understanding it. We strive to accept that we do not have an answer "now and forever," but that each new understanding gives birth to yet newer constraints which, in turn, provide the soil for further resources and elaborations, and so on.

When each of us speaks, we draw on the resources available to us. Because I do not have all the same resources as you, I may appear to be critical, demeaning or oppressive to you. What does postmodern psychology *do* to invite us into conversations differently? Mary Gergen provides one creative illustration. She breaks the "conventions" of "academic" discourse by literally performing (making a spectacle) her *continual* crossing back and forth across the border between the world where things in themselves are real, to the world where we can do "otherwise." Mary raises what I see as a very important question: Must we use the format of spectacle to develop (make available) a variety of conversational resources—resources that allow us to remain in a somewhat constant state of transformation rather than in the world of fixedness? What other ways (beyond literal stage performance) might incite us to generate the format of "spectacle?" Are we limited to the creative and difficult-to-achieve writing styles of Calvino, Tyler, and others? If so, we cut off many possibilities, since writing styles that "break the conventions" can quickly become "technique" associated with postmodern psychology rather than the performance of it. Do we have other options?

One might be found in Lois Shawver's term "generous listening" (Shawver, 1999). If we expand this term to include "generous reading" I think we encourage a form of self-reflexive critique wherein we *engage* in the potential multiplicity of a given moment. Instead of being quick to interpret a situation, a conversation, a written manuscript as being "one thing," we pause to inquire about our own possible other voices of interpretation and, eventually, of response. If our activities with others are coordinated with their activities, and meaning is jointly constructed in the lived activity, then when we respond with only one of our possible voices, we temporarily dislodge the other possibilities from emerging. Can we talk about self-reflexive inquiry (e.g., how else might I make sense of what she or he is saying or doing? How else might I respond to this activity?) as "generous listening/reading"? Can either of these terms allow us to see the illustrations provided by Holzman, Burman, and Fulani as *resources* for our own activities with others, rather than *the way it should be*? Such an effort, I believe, requires *both* author and reader to consider the rhetoric they recruit in their own attempts to have a voice. Are there more expansive ways to enter into conversation than the tried and true rhetoric of right and wrong? Generating this way of writing (and of talking) is what it means to perform postmodern psychology and it is, from my vantage point, precisely where we want to be.

Lois Shawver, again (*PMTH News*, 1999), plays with the idea of "paralogue," where many voices participate *in response to each other* yet orienting themselves with what I would call different *conversational resources*. In such a process, Lynn Hoffman has suggested, new ideas emerge. Lyotard (1984), from whom Hoffman borrows the term, argues that paralogy is a form of discourse where instabilities emerge, rather than consensus or agreement. Isn't this the *practice* of postmodern psychology? To the extent that our activities are directed toward gaining agreement or consensus, we are not practicing the very arguments we are making.

I am sympathetic with both our desire for and our inability to move beyond the academic practice of providing description and explanation and afterwards letting practices emerge from these. Yet the difference that can make the difference (to draw on Bateson's famous quote, 1972) is to raise the questions about dichotomies such as "theory/practice," "identity as given/identity as accomplished," "politicized psychology/rampant relativism," and "reactionary/revolutionary" in a voice that, in Lyotard's terms, does not attempt to reach agreement but attempts, instead, to open possibilities. Is there a way to be in conversation, in relation, in engaged activity with others that generates a sense of coherence and the possibility for going on together without imposing one and only one coherence on the wide-ranging set of activities at play? Can a performance like Mary Gergen's or an illustration like Fulani's or Burman's provide us with resources for turning back onto what we consider "traditional" modes of interpretation and seeing them as options for different social performances (and thus identities)? Can the questions Morss raises concerning what happens to responsibility when we argue in favor of possibilities rather than critique be extended beyond the either/or binary into the range of multiple possibilities?[2]

Rather than "policing language" by setting out the "bad" terms (e.g., modernist) and the "good" terms (e.g., postmodernist), can we create conversational arenas that use paralogy as an orienting device rather than debate? I believe the essays in this volume (although I have not mentioned each and every one independently) boldly begin this attempt but do not entirely enact it. Until we are willing to recognize the discourse of dichotomies as a *discursive option* and not a necessary form of argument, we will have a difficult time *practicing* postmodern psychology.

Let me close by suggesting three forms of practice that I find useful in simultaneously allowing me to "see" the dichotomous arguments that sustain academic (and all professional) life and deconstruct the vision of dichotomy. But we should not stop there. The process of reconstructing the dichotomy as the commingling voices of possibility is significant to engage in the *doing* of relational life. The three forms of practice I suggest below, while sounding abstract, have significant utility in practice. My own affinity is toward forms of practice that take multiple shapes, thereby avoiding the concrete establishment of techniques or strategies. Thus what appears abstract I would hope to be rich with possibilities.

First is an attempt to avoid speaking from abstract positions. We see this tendency throughout the academic world, but it is far from absent in other domains. When we speak from abstract positions (e.g., policy, rules, laws, etc.), we disregard the situated activities of persons in relation. It is these very local engagements that give life and meaning to the worlds within which we live. To ignore those communities of construction and instead constantly refer to a set of abstractions about "how the world should be" severely limits our potentials for transformation. Thus one form of practice is to speak from our situated activities, telling the stories or narratives that emerge in our day-to-day living with others.

Another resource for action that I find useful is to avoid blame. After all, blame, like any other descriptor, is a move in an ongoing dance or performance with another. Thus, if I blame you for your "modernist" proclivity, I am likely to have a predictable, academic argument rather than if I enter into conversation with you in a way that invites you to tell me within what relational communities your modernist performance gains credit. Blame, as we perform it, is a relational dance that hinges on the notion of individual responsibility. But what if responsibility is refigured relationally (McNamee and Gergen, 1998)? Might there be other voices—voices of alterior relationships—that bring coherence to my apparently "wrong" activities?

Finally, as discussed earlier, self-reflexive critique, or "generous listening," invites us to employ our less dominant voices—those that we carry by virtue of being simultaneously immersed in multiple relationships (many of which are incommensurate with others)—in any particular situation. We allow ourselves to entertain uncertainty about our own position on an issue. One of the most difficult activities to engage in is interested inquiry, where we bracket our own clarity about something and engage instead in forms of practice that invite others to articulate their own stories—also suspending or bracketing their certainty. How can we do this? Briefly, we might entertain "doubt" about our own well-formed "positions." They are, after all, forms of practice that enable the creation of some realities and not others. To the extent that I never doubt my own activities, I severely limit not only the responses of others but my own as well. Of course, this argument is complicated by our traditional ways of talking which privilege certainty over doubt. Can we play with both certainty and doubt? Can we call upon conversational resources that are *already* available to us by virtue of our relatedness (our living in community with others), thereby opening possibilities for new performances, new ways of "doing" any specific activity like "academic debate" or "creating an intimate relationship?"

The task of postmodern psychology is not to claim its truth value over modernist psychology. Rather, the task we confront is that of expanding our resources for relation beyond those that we have constructed as rational, real, and "scientific." While I think each of the essays in this book opens this possibility, it is also quite possible to *read* each author as providing the "best take" on postmodern psychology and what that *should* mean. But if we take seriously the comments I have offered here, we recognize that reading is an activity as well. Rather than ask how these authors can write outside the modernist mode that entails dichotomies, I ask: How can we, as readers, engage with this book in a way that expands our possibilities for action—even our possibilities for how we *use* this volume in *practicing* postmodern psychology? Perhaps we should suspend our desire to teach or learn about postmodern psychology and ask questions about what new options emerge from this conversation.

NOTES

1. Yet what else do we have but the options provided by our dominant discursive tradition? In my concluding comments I attempt to expand upon our notion of a "dominant discursive tradition."

2. A modest attempt at creating both a relational refiguring of responsibility and the parologue form that Lynn Hoffman suggests is illustrated in McNamee and Gergen (1998).

REFERENCES

Bateson, G. (1972). *Steps to an ecology of mind*. New York: Bantam Books.

Gergen, K. J. (1994). *Toward the transformation in social knowledge.* (2nd ed.) *London: Sage.*

Lyotard, J. F. (1984). *The postmodern condition: A report on knowledge*. G. Bennington and B. Massumi. (Trans.). Minneapolis, MN: University of Minnesota Press.

McNamee, S., and Gergen, K. J. (1998). *Relational resonsibility: Resources for sustainable dialogue.* Thousand Oaks, CA: Sage.

Newman, F., and Holzman, L. (1997). *The end of knowing.* New York: Routledge.

Shawver, L. (October 22, 1999). PMTH Conversation with Richard Rorty and Book Review of McNamee and Gergen's book. *PMTH News* (http://www.california.com/~rathbone/pmth.htm).

Shotter, J. (1984). *Social accountability and selfhood.* Oxford, UK: Basil Blackwell.

Performing Psychotherapy: Reflections on Postmodern Practice

Robert A. Neimeyer

ESCHER'S NIGHTMARE[1]

We are the teller and the story
The writer and the written
The artist and the drawn.

As one hand sketches us into being
The other erases,
Obliterating the certain boundaries of knowing
That configure a self.

Unheld pencil
Animated only by the drawing
Graphite substantiality
Seeking form.

Drawn eraser
Deconstructing its point of origin
Rubbery resistance
Blurring lines.

For whom is the work (de)composed?
Not the pencil,
Tracing an ephemeral itinerary
From then to now.

Not the eraser,
Opening space for that which
Might yet be.

The shifting image takes form only for
The viewer of the work
The reader of the text
The audience of the story,
For whom the performance of the process
Is appropriated into its own.

When Lois Holzman and John Morss invited me to write a brief commentary on these collected critiques and elaborations of postmodern psychology, I accepted spontaneously—and in retrospect, perhaps somewhat naïvely. What intrigued me was the irreverence, freshness, and vitality of a critical, performative, postrationalist approach to central concerns about the way we typically "do" psychology, whether in the classroom, the conference hall, or clinic. The preceding essays easily fulfilled this anticipation of novelty and challenge. What I was less prepared for was the level of thinly-veiled tension among the different essays, some of which strongly defended a no-holds-barred social constructionism (Morss), while others cautioned that unconstrained deconstruction vitiated critique (Parker). Likewise, some celebrated the transformative potential of (at least some forms of) therapy (Holzman and Newman), while others held "the therapeutic" in deeper suspicion (Parker and, to some extent, Burman).

Although initially disorienting, the occasional contradictions among the contributors also carried a fringe benefit, in effect releasing me from any expectation that I could draft a single "grand narrative" that would encompass, integrate, or critique them all. Instead, with Morss, I decided to engage the "diffuse stimulus" of these postmodern contributions in an effort "to identify what aspects of [their] mood or style [I] want to keep, and which let slip." The following commentary, then, can be read as the reflections of a self-identified constructivist psychotherapist on the implications of postmodernism for practice. As such, these remarks are positioned not only within the discourse of the foregoing contributors to this volume, but also within the context of my own developing approach to psychotherapy, of which I will provide passing illustrations.

A word of caution is in order before I begin. Inevitably, I find myself responding to the various dialogues threaded through this book as a kind of "inside outsider"—indeed, I suspect that the editors might have invited my responses for just this reason. On the one hand, as someone animated by many of the same concerns and shaped by some of the same intellectual traditions as the other contributors to this project, I reside sufficiently "inside" a postmodern discourse to make dialogue possible. On the other hand, as someone who is ultimately concerned more with what Ken Gergen terms the "generative" rather than "critical" moments of the constructionist dialectic, I am sufficiently "outside" the frame of molar social criticism to make such dialogue meaningful. Thus, my chief goal in the pages that follow is to draw upon selected arguments of each author in an effort to "unpack" the implications of postmodernism for the practicing therapist and, where possible, suggest ways that therapeutic practices are already being transformed by just such a dialogue. To scaffold my remarks I will organize them broadly under four headings, concerned with (1) deindividualizing the self, (2) reorienting in dialogue, (3) "performing" psychotherapy, and (4) practicing resistance.

DEINDIVIDUALIZING THE SELF

One of the most deep-going challenges to the foundations of modernist psychology to be mounted by proponents of postmodern perspectives is the assault on the essentialized self (Kvale, 1992). Taking issue with traditional conceptions of the self as atomic, autonomous, and agentic, social constructionists argue that the self is constituted in *language*, understood as a situated and shifting symbolic order that structures our relationship to "reality," as well as ourselves . Because the very terms in which we construe ourselves are cultural artifacts, our selves are deeply penetrated by the vocabularies of our place and time, expressing dominant modes of discourse as much as any unique personality. Indeed, "like a fetus floating in an amnion of culturally available signs, symbols, practices and conversations, the 'self' symbiotically depends for its existence upon a living system that precedes and supports it" (Neimeyer, 1998a, p. 140). In more radical forms, this view of the "saturated self" as populated by the contradictory discourses in which one is immersed threatens the very conception of the individual as a coherent entity with identifiable boundaries and properties . From this more thoroughly social viewpoint, the pursuit of "self actualization," "self efficacy," "self-control," and the like in the medium of psychotherapy is at best a romantic delusion, and at worst a "cover-up for individualized alienation" (Newman, this volume).

Although a more profoundly socialized conception of self no doubt lends support to the communally-based, politically aware practices advocated by Holzman, Newman, and Burman, I find myself questioning whether this vision is antithetical to the conduct of individual (gasp!) psychotherapy. In particular, I find myself drawn to precisely the image of selves as "multiple partials," in Ken Gergen's apt phrase, constituted by a shifting and provisional coalition of "voices" echoing the sometimes dominant, sometimes nurturant, and often contradictory discourses in which we are enmeshed. Far from vitiating psychotherapy, such an image can vitalize it, fostering the exploration and enactment of several relevant internal voices that might otherwise be subordinated to the demands for a falsely "unified" conception of self.[2]

An illustration of this was provided in my single session with Susan, a forty-two-year-old woman "haunted" by her "powerlessness" in the face of her mother's lingering death by cancer some three years before . Acknowledging in experientially vivid language both the "ludicrous" part of Susan that battled against her mother's inevitable death and the new "take charge" persona that emerged in her in the crucible of the caretaking, I suggested that she "reopen the conversation" with her mother about what still might need to be discussed with her. With encouragement, Susan not only symbolically sought her mother's understanding of her limitations in caregiving, but also "lent her mother her own voice" and enacted the litany of concrete complaints and demands that Susan had failed to meet. What evolved, as Susan moved back and forth between her own chair and her "mother's,"[3] was a more complex, ambivalent, but also more emotionally resonant and touching dialogue than had been possible as her mother lay dying.

Equally important, Susan came to realize with some astonishment that her own newfound strength as a person was partly an *appropriation of her mother's voice into her*, which we formulated as a way of "honoring their connection, not merely with [Susan's] words, but also with [her] life."

Significantly, we also "historicized" these valuable new developments in Susan's sense of self in the previously unfulfilled "expectations" of her held by not only Susan's mother but also her "strong and independent" daughters, and further anchored her shift in the reactions of others to her "new garment" of authority. In summary, therapy became a stage on which an old drama could be (literally) reenacted, in a way that permitted new themes to be consolidated and new character development to occur. Deindividuating Susan's identity in this way made possible the realignment not only of the relations among her "internal" cast of characters but also of her contemporary relations with the living others who populated her ongoing life.

REORIENTING IN DIALOGUE

Accompanying this deindividuated image of self is a postmodern affirmation of relationship as "the matrix from which meaning is derived. It is in the generation of coordinations—of actions, words, objects—that human meaning is born" (K. Gergen, this volume). Drawing especially on Bahktin, Shotter in this volume argues eloquently that: "we continuously and spontaneously shape, build, or construct our performance in our daily affairs as we 'act into' opportunities offered us." Meaning, in this view, is what we achieve together in the course of coactivity that is dialogically-structured—even in its internalized form.

This "participative" approach to meaning construction is highly congenial to the practice of a "responsive"psychotherapy, one that seeks, in Shotter's words, to develop a "well-oriented grasp" of the therapy relationship as well as the "grammar" or "style" of the client's way of relating to others. An example of this arose in my work with Kaylin, a thirty-eight-year-old woman torn between her commitment to her husband, Kent, and her love for Thomas (Mascolo, Craig-Bray, and Neimeyer, 1997). In one therapeutic moment, Kaylin summarized her impasse in terms of a frozen metaphor, describing herself as "stuck in between," not feeling fully connected to either man. I spontaneously elaborated her description in more deeply-etched metaphoric terms, drawing upon a rock-climbing image that had been part of her experience with her "outdoorsman" husband. Like a climber facing a "wall" too high to negotiate in a single, unbroken climb, I suggested, Kaylin hung suspended in a hammock attached by petons to the sheer rock face. Tired and uncertain as darkness fell, she was unable for a time either to continue her climb toward the summit, where she hoped that Thomas awaited her, or to descend to the familiar ground that was once her marriage.

Kaylin fell silent for a long moment, and then elaborated poignantly on her emotional dilemma: to let go of the marriage, which paralyzed her with fear, or to relinquish the relationship with Thomas, which felt like "giving up being alive." Significantly, she found herself returning repeatedly to the image of "dangling from the rock" in the ensuing week, and opened the next session with a discussion of the "precariousness" of her position and her sense of new stirring, though she was as yet uncertain in which direction it would take her. The joint elaboration of such therapeutic metaphors illustrates Shotter's recognition of the "impossibility of being able to trace the overall outcome of any exchange back to the intentions of the individuals involved in it." Meaning, in this case, arises in the intricate dialogical braiding of perspectives in our prereflective engagement with others, not in the solitary consciousness of client or therapist alone.[4]

PERFORMING PSYCHOTHERAPY

The ironic but liberating insight that the basic "reality" of human beings is that they are "pretenders" lies at the heart of Newman's and Holzman's performative approach to social therapy. As Holzman notes, the "capacity to be who we are and who we are not at the very same time is central to our practice." This nonessentializing stance undermines the totalizing identification of self with any given role, and gives impetus to activity-based initiatives that prompt communities of persons to transcend the limiting scripts they are offered by dominant social institutions. In Fulani's words: "despite how rare and undervalued performance is in our culture, we human beings can, fortunately, reinitiate our performatory capacities with surprising ease. It is the social identities that lock us into acting certain ways because 'that's how we are' that stand in the way."

But not all performances need to be as communal as the All Star Network, or as audacious as Mary Gergen's "Woman as Spectacle" to be liberating. Indeed, I would argue that a perspective on 'identity' as improvisational rather than impositional can inform individual, couple, family, and group therapy as well as more public performances. An example of the power of performance was provided by my therapy with Bill, a divorced and remarried man seemingly unable to maintain anything beyond distant contact with his teenage daughter, Cassie, who lived in another state (Neimeyer, 2000b). Over the three years of his new marriage, Bill had reacted to Cassie's reluctance to be in the presence of his new wife, Delanie, by carrying on a somewhat superficial but furtive correspondence with his daughter, though he found himself strangely "panicked" by the prospect of actually visiting her. This panic had intensified as Delanie had become increasingly insistent that Bill "put his foot down" and include her in his "secret relationship" with his daughter by mentioning her in letters, permitting her to add a note, or even arranging a "whole family" get-together.

As Delanie's demands reached the level of a desperate ultimatum, Bill still found himself "unable to move," even at the risk of "destroying" his marriage. Therapeutic movement was only made on this issue when I asked Bill to close his eyes and visualize Cassie and Delanie together, engaged in some routine activity in the home. After sitting quietly for a moment, Bill visibly winced, then opened his eyes and said, "I wanted to say it was wonderful, but I immediately imagined a fight between two stubborn people." Rather than discussing this intellectually, I further guided Bill to reenter the scene and notice if anything else came up. Eventually, he reported an unbidden memory of Cassie at the age of nine, snuggling with him as he lamented her coming adolescence, when she would no longer want to sit on his lap and have him tell stories to her. In Bill's memory, Cassie hugged him around the neck and reassured him that "whatever happens, I'll still be your little girl." Tears accompanied this recollection for both of us, as we sat quietly with this new connection.

Speaking slowly, I then attempted to capture the "emotional truth" of Bill's current impasse in a sentence, which I wrote out on an index card and asked him to modify until it "rang true" for him. Accepting my formulation without amendment, Bill then visualized Cassie's nine-year-old face as she sat on his lap, and with my prompting, slowly repeated the scripted sentence to her: "As painful as this present standoff is, I would rather suffer this terrible distance from Cassie than to have her walk away, and never feel her arms around my neck, never hear her say, 'I'm still your little girl.'" Choking on the word "arms," Bill stammered out the sentence, and drying his tears, quietly noted that inhabiting this position consciously "made me understand the things I've been doing in a whole different light."

The first steps toward mending the relational ties in his compartmentalized family spontaneously followed.[5] Of course, a performative approach to constructivist therapy can also characterize group work, as exemplified by Sewell's "multiple self awareness groups," in which members enact various roles scripted to reflect their internal "community of selves" with other members (Sewell, Baldwin, and Moes, 1998). As in Newman's social therapy, the therapist in this case functions neither as a psychoeducational trainer of the members in preferred skills nor as a passive interpreter of the group process, but as an active "organizer or facilitator of the group's emotive labor." The result is commonly a developmental process that, while not wholly predictable in advance, prompts new possibilities for relating to self and others.

Practicing Resistance

If there is a spirit that animates all of the contributors to this volume, it is one of resistance against the oppressive institutions that constitute "modern" psychology. Parker is particularly vitriolic in his denunciation of the "psy-complex . . . that dense network of theories and practices inside and outside the academy and clinic . . . [which constitutes] a dangerous and pernicious regulative apparatus." Burman adds to this critical thrust with her analysis of the methodological "fetishes" by which psychologists aggrandize power at the expense of their clients and subjects, and convert their political resistance to dominant discourses into individual psychopathology.

Not surprisingly, this critique is accompanied by an endorsement of social therapy as revolutionary activity (as in the work of Holzman, Newman, and Fulani), but also by a deep suspicion of individual psychotherapy as a purported aid to those in distress. Parker again states the case most baldly in his caveat that: "therapy operates as a domain in which critical reflection all too often turns into decontextualized 'reflexivity.' Reflexivity proceeds from within the interior of the self . . . [whereas] critical reflection traces subjective investments to networks of institutional power." From this perspective, the only ethically appropriate stance for the psychotherapist would be to resign her or his practice and take on the role of community organizer.

Upon (critical) reflection, I see no reason that this should be the case. Indeed, I am struck by the marginalization of fertile possibilities implied in Parker's binary distinction between "interior reflexivity" on the one hand, and "institutional critique" on the other. Altogether missed in this rhetorical dichotomy is precisely that relational field so capably cultivated by Kenneth Gergen and Shotter: the reflexive engagement in dialogical activity with concrete others. Surely, if a postmodern rebelliousness has wide relevance, it should be capable of inspiriting such dialogical encounters, even in the medium of psychotherapy.

An illustration of this arose in the course of my therapeutic conversation with Alan, a young counselor who had felt a "stab" of malaise when he said to a recent client at the end of a session: "It's been good visiting with you." Noticing a slight trembling in his jaw when he repeated this expression, I asked him to close his eyes and attend to any "felt sense" in his body associated with this experience, and to describe it in an appropriate image. Alan offered a depiction of an "anxious, tight ball" in his chest, which when I invited him to loosen it, brought a tearful recognition of the "guilt" contained in its tangled mass. Further processing this tacit meaning, Alan placed it in a larger narrative whose central theme was his lack of "genuineness" in relationships, and the way this was painfully accentuated by his initial attempts to conduct psychotherapy.

As we "tacked" from this self-narrative to the social dynamics that sustained it, Alan linked his sense of insufficient genuineness to stern injunctions delivered during his early graduate training to maintain professional distance, which in turn replicated broader disciplinary and cultural discourses of psychotherapy as a scientific procedure delivered with a minimum of personal involvement. With our own emotionally intimate encounter as a salient counterexample, I then joined Alan in critiquing the dominant narrative of psychotherapy as an impersonal technical intervention and in exploring the hopeful possibility that his experience as a counselor might actually become a setting in which he could deepen, rather than constrain, his engagement with others.

Thus Alan's initially vague awareness of an anxious discrepancy between who he was and who he wanted to be had functioned as a "unique outcome," representing the first emergence of resistance against a dominant script of self-monitoring and restraint (Monk,

Winslade, Crocket, and Epston, 1996). Alan's case therefore serves as a reminder that a critical, emancipatory attitude can find expression in individual therapy as well as broad scale social action. It also underscores Shotter's warning about "the danger of focusing too narrowly on speech communication alone to the exclusion of the larger context of our involved bodily activity," where the first murmuring of protest might be "heard." Other practices of resistance in the context of psychotherapy can include such boundary-blurring acts as sharing respectful, change-affirming progress notes with clients, or directly challenging the pathologizing forms of diagnosis that reinforce professional authority while disempowering clients .

CONCLUSION

Like the meditation on Escher's *Drawing Hands* with which this essay opened, social-constructionist accounts have begun to deconstruct the image of the self as autonomous and self-created, achieving ever greater substantiality and depth as it inscribes its own identity in apparent isolation from the social world. In the place of this modernist dream, critical voices, drawing on a myriad of literary, philosophic, political, and feminist sources, have offered an image of deindividuated selves buffeted by the crosscurrents of the multiple discourses in which they are embedded. But as the more "affirmative" contributors to this volume have noted, these embattled subjectivities are also sustained by the relational engagements through which they find meaning, direction, and the prospect of mutual development. I hope that this same postmodern vision, and the spirit of performance and resistance to which it gives rise, continue to infect and inform the practice of psychotherapy.

NOTES

1. This meditation was inspired by M. C. Escher's familiar work entitled *Drawing Hands*, in which two hands achieve three-dimensionality as each sketches the other. The "nightmare" materializes as one hand takes up an eraser in place of the pencil. A visual exploration of the same theme has been provided by the graphic artist J. D. Hillberry.

2. This deconstructive moment in the dialectic of self-development is artfully captured in the lyrics of "Segnali di vita" [Signs of life] by the Italian singer, Franco Battiato: "Il tempo cambia molte cose nella vita/Il senso, le amicizie, le

opinioni/Che voglia di cambiare che c'e in me/ Si sente il bisogno di una propria evoluzione/ Sganciata dalle regole comuni/ Da questa falsa personalita." [Time changes many things in life/ One's direction, friendships, opinions/ That want to change that which is within me/ It senses the need for its own evolution/ Unchained from the communal laws/ Of this false personality.]

3. For a constructivist discussion of "chair work" in therapy, see Greenberg, Watson, & Lietaer .

4. Shotter is one of a small group of constructivists and social constructionists (Butt, 1998; Mair, 1989; Neimeyer, 1996) developing what might be referred to as a "relational phenomenology," drawing on the work of Merleau-Ponty and Polanyi, as well as more familiar postmodern scholars.

5. This sort of visualization and enactment of the "pro-symptom position" is artfully developed in depth-oriented brief therapy, a constructivist approach that utilizes various forms of experientially-oriented "radical questioning" (Ecker & Hulley, 1996).

REFERENCES

Butt, T. (1998). Sociality, role, and embodiment. *Journal of Constructivist Psychology, 11,* 105–116.

Ecker, B., and Hulley, L. (1996). *Depth-oriented brief therapy.* San Francisco: Jossey-Bass.

Gergen, K. J. (1991). *The saturated self.* New York: Basic.

Gergen, K. J. (1994). *Realities and relationships.* Cambridge, MA: Harvard University Press.

Greenberg, L. S., Watson, J. C., and Lietaer, G. (Eds.). (1998) *Handbook of experiential psychotherapy.* New York: Guilford.

Kvale, S. (1992) *Psychology and postmodernism.* Newbury Park, CA: Sage.

Mair, M. (1989). *Between psychology and psychotherapy.* London: Routledge.

Mascolo, M. F., Craig-Bray, L., and Neimeyer, R. A. (1997). The construction of meaning and action in development and psychotherapy: An epigenetic systems approach. In G. J. Neimeyer and R. A. Neimeyer (Eds.), *Advances in personal construct psychology* (Vol. 4, pp. 3–38). Greenwich, CT: JAI Press.

Monk, G., Winslade, J., Crocket, K., and Epston, D. (1996). *Narrative therapy in practice.* San Francisco: Jossy-Bass.

Neimeyer, R. A. (1993). Constructivist psychotherapy. In K. T. Kuehlwein and H. Rosen (Eds.). *Cognitive therapies in action: Evolving innovative practice* (pp. 268–300). San Francisco: Jossey-Bass.

Neimeyer, R. A. (1996). Process interventions for the constructivist psychotherapist. In H. Rosen and K. T. Kuehlwein (Eds.), *Constructing realities.* San Francisco: Jossey-Bass.

Neimeyer, R. A. (1998a). Social constructionism in the counselling context. *Counselling Psycholoty Quarterly, 11,* 135–149.

Neimeyer, R. A. (1998b). Cognitive therapy and the narrative trend: A bridge too far? *Journal of Cognitive Psychotherapy, 12,* 57–66.

Neimeyer, R. A. (2000a). The language of loss. in R. A. Neimeyer (Ed). *Meaning reconstruction and the experience of loss.* Washington, DC: American Psychological Association.

Neimeyer, R. A. (2000b). Narrative disruptions in the construction of self. In R. A. Neimeyer and J. Raskin (Eds.). *Constructions of disorder: Meaning making frameworks for psychotherapy.* Washington, DC: American Psychological Association.

Neimeyer, R. A., and J. Raskin (Eds.). (2000). *Constructions of disorder: Meaning making frameworks for psychotherapy.* Washington, DC: American Psychological Association.

Sewell, K. W., Baldwin, C. L., and Moes, A. J. (1998). The multiple self awareness group. *Journal of Constructivist Psychology, 11,* 59–78.

Reflections on

and the Appeals

and Challenges of

Postmodern Psychologies,

Societal Practice,

and Political Life

Harlene Anderson

THIS PROVOCATIVE VOLUME is packed with appeals and challenges, and, in my experience, actualizes the editors' aim to bring readers into a conversation with postmodern psychology, into conversation with the authors and with themselves. The editors' aim is in keeping with postmodernism's attempt to promote dialogue, value difference, entertain uncertainty, and self-critique—widening our possibilities—rather than to promote monologue, sameness, and certainty—narrowing our possibilities.

As this volume suggests, postmodern is a family of concepts with diversity in heritage and form. An identifiable family trait within this diversity is the distinction that language and knowledge are relational and generative. That is, reality—the *meanings* that we give to the events, experiences, people, and things in our lives—is communally constructed and inherently susceptible to transformation. This distinction about the nature of reality and particularly realities created within and by the culture of psychotherapy is the tension point where postmodern psychologies and other psychologies meet in ongoing debate. These tensions include the implications that the distinction has for how psychologists think about the people they work with and their problems, and how psychologists position themselves *vis-à-vis* these (and as John Shotter says in this volume, "what we think of as our problems in psychology.") Many debates follow the academic traditions of our institutional communities; for instance, discussing a theory, declaring why it is wrong, and offering the correct one. The academic summons is to abandon the incorrect view and adopt the correct one. Converts and polarizations result.

One appeal of this book is how the editors attempt to present a different way of conceptualizing and performing academic talk. What could be a more dramatic example than Mary Gergen's performative piece. Another appeal is the volume's diversity, the multiple perspectives of postmodern psychologies and societal practices[1] that it posits, including both the possibilities and the risks of postmodern.

Postmodern psychologies are not in search of true psychological knowledge or psychological knowledge as definitive reality, but, rather, invite the multiple interpretations of any psychological phenomenon. This position on multiplicity moves knowledge from something that is fixed to something that is alive, and in and through the interchanges of the multiple viewpoints, something new and novel emerges specific to the participants and their local situations and circumstances. Thus the certainty and predictability of psychological knowledge goes by the wayside.

A postmodern view of knowledge and language as generative and relational supports, as does this volume, an invitation to inquiry as a mutual process. In my own practices, this view informs what I call my philosophical stance (Anderson 1997): the way I prefer to think about the people I work with, the way I prefer to be in relationship with them, and the way I prefer to act and talk with them. This view has influenced me to think about my practices as involving dialogical conversations and collaborative relationships. In these definitions, I emphasize "with"— conversations and relationships that have an active, fluid, in-there-together, back-and-forth, give-and-take, two-way process quality. I think of myself as being in *conversational partnerships* in which understanding comes from within and in which we construct knowledge together through *collaborative inquiry*. When involved in this kind of collaborative or shared inquiry, the inquiry is shaped and reshaped as we go along with each other; and likewise, we are shaped and reshaped as we go along with each other. Thus these kinds of conversations and relationships entail uncertainly and ambiguity.

Shotter introduces Bachelard's notion of intimacy. In my experience, whether we call them performative, think of them as developmental, or declare them revolutionary, the kinds of relationships and conversations that people have with each other in this kind of inquiry—whether we call it therapy, research, education, or consultation—become intimate. In participative approaches, and when a professional takes what Shotter calls a "participatory stance," all participants feel they belong.

RESEARCH AND SHARED INQUIRY

The contributors to this volume challenge the foundations on which psychological research as a method of inquiry is based and advocate alternative methods of inquiry. One way of thinking about these alternative methods is as collaborative or shared inquiry.

The research becomes an inquiry from within by the participants involved, where the researcher is an insider in a side-by-side relationship in contrast to the researcher as an outsider in a top-down relationship with the research object (e.g., therapy clients or agency professionals). Clients participate with the professional(s), similar to James Kelly's (1990) collaborative community research, in determining what is to be researched and how. Participants (e.g., therapist and client) speak for themselves. What is created—method and outcome—is co-constructed from within and is not predetermined. The outcome or the knowledge is constructed during the process and is not already there waiting to be discovered. This process of creating knowledge is similar to Lois Holzman's "practicing method", where the core-searchers are "fully engaged as an integral part of the activity being studied/performed" and are full participants in "creating something relative to the particular people involved in a specific revolutionary task".

The process of this kind of research, as Erica Burman suggests, is itself transformative—in the here-and-now. The method of research can change as the research goes along. As well, the knowledge that is created can be used along the way (e.g., further to inform the research methodology and to inform our practices). And there is acknowledgment of the mutual influence of the researcher on the research and the research on the researcher. The focus, therefore, is as much or more on the process of the research as on the outcome. This is very pragmatic, although it may not quite fit with or it might be a different way of thinking about Fred Newman's bias that pragmatics focuses on the outcome rather than the process.

The knowledge created is local knowledge, fluid, and viable, not decontextualized generalizations or, as Burman says, "dead descriptions." Burman's take is that participatory qualitative research methods can, rather than compete with quantitative methods, act to allow us to look behind the research and see the person(s), hear their voices and "elaborate the meanings behind the numbers." While still leaving in place a questioning of the methods and the ethics of qualitative research in psychology, Burman partly frees us from adversarial either-or positions.

Swelling in the postmodern movement, and including the client (e.g., "patient," student, community agency colleague) as a coresearcher, is the notion of research as part of everyday practice. Clinical scholar Tom Andersen, a Norwegian psychiatrist, has been like a Pied Piper traveling throughout Scandinavia and other parts of the world, encouraging clinicians to think of research as part of everyday practice (Andersen, 1997). Andersen encourages therapists to be collaborative researchers—coresearchers with their clients rather than hierarchical ones.[2]

Postmodernism challenges the dominant psychological theories and the hierarchical and dualistic structures inherent in them—not only in terms of therapist-client, researcher-subject, or teacher-student, but also in terms of theory-practice. Fitting with this challenge, this volume continues the editors' previous challenges to the notion of epistemology and their suggestions for practice based methods, including how we think about identity, culture, therapy, research, knowledge, and education.

What is refreshing and ambitious about this volume is the focus on the notion of performance.

POSTMODERN, CRITIQUE, AND NOT-KNOWING

There seem to be two dominant views of postmodernism and critique: one is that postmodernism is a metacritique and the other is that self-critique is inherent. The risk of the former, as John Morss and Ian Parker suggest, is that postmodernism becomes another ideology, another realism, another grand narrative. It develops a liability, losing its ability to be self-reflective, whether reflection is thought of as critique, analysis, or deconstruction as used in this volume. In the latter view, postmodernism invites not only self-critique but also a continuous examination of the form of critique itself. When self-reflection is viewed as important and inherent, what one knows, what one thinks one might know, and how one goes about knowing are always held as tentative and open to question by others and by oneself. In my bias, if it does not embody self-critique, it is not postmodern. Morss advocates postmodernism as a dialogical process, whether we name it critique or analysis, that does not slip into a "modernist approach to truth-finding" or equating "truth with consensus". We have learned from history that truth or knowledge changes.

Through dialogue, or as Shotter talks about, through the relational process of the "dialogically structured activity occurring between us", professional and client engage in a mutual process in which they coexplore the familiar and codevelop the new. In such a process they create knowledge and expertise that become specific to their local situation and circumstances. This view of knowledge does not imply that professionals do not know anything or should pretend ignorance. Rather, it means that knowledge is dynamic and always evolving; it means that the professional is always a learner, and that the professional's voice should not have any more room than any other. The clinician, the researcher, the educator, and the consultant become not-knowers (Anderson, 1997; Anderson and Goolishian, 1990, 1992). This is to say that what we know or think we might know is always held as tentative and open to question. Predetermined knowledge is not brought into the therapy, consultation, class, or boardroom as expert knowledge but simply as food for thought and dialogue, and it is kept open to question by self and others, keeping it in the realm of dialogue whether with self or with others. Newman and Holzman (1997) provocatively call for an end to knowing, giving up modernist knowing, giving up epistemology altogether.

I read the authors of this volume as advocating for a focus on societal practices rather than units of persons (e.g., individuals, couples, and families). What is refreshing and ambitious about it is the focus that some authors place on the notion of performance and the notion of reconceptualizing method. Holzman emphasizes, however, that the alternative conception of method does not attempt to replace talk therapy but offers a different way of conceptualizing and performing talk.

LEARNING, DEVELOPING, AND IDENTITY

The most provocative aspect of this book is its underlying challenge, or call for a revolution, and implications for the way that we think about and perform our educational practices. It reminds me of Donald Schon's (1983) inspiring challenge to academic knowledge as we know it and invitation to participatory knowledge.

The focus on development is appealing. Think of the possibilities when one adopts the notion that learning is a lifelong endeavor in which the creation of knowledge is a communal and dialogical process. Think of the possibilities when a teacher's stance is not to impart knowledge but to create and facilitate environments, relationships, and processes where learners direct and create their own learning. Think of the possibilities, as so beautifully illustrated by Lenora Fulani's examples, when the process of creating knowledge is more important than the content of knowing or than the rightness or wrongness of it. Think of the possibilities when we believe that we cannot teach another person to be a therapist, but that we can create a space and foster generative conversations and relationships in which he or she can learn to be (Anderson, 1997; Anderson and Goolishian, 1990).

I am often asked in reference to therapy: "What is beyond postmodern?" as if, as Morss notes, postmodern is a chronological period or theoretical stage. Such questions miss the infancy of postmodernism in psychology. Most important at this point in time is to take the opportunity, as the authors of this volume do, to look further into the depths of postmodernism (whether the version is postmodern social constructionism, performative psychology, collaborative research, or narrative therapy) and to explore its risks and how we can widen its yet-to-come possibilities. As Kenneth Gergen suggests of social constructionism, postmodernism offers a range of dialogues that serve as a "means of bracketing or suspending" what we believe to be real and an "orientation toward creating new futures, an impetus to societal transformation."

This volume provides us one opportunity to question and reimagine our theoretical and institutional traditions and the associated practices. And it is a welcomed path on this long journey ahead.

NOTES

1. In this reflection I use practice(s) to refer to all realms of professional activity including therapy, research, education, and consultation; and I use client to refer to the variety of people whom we work with in these realms, including therapy clients, students, research "subjects," and consultees.

2. To see how others promote the notion of research as part of everyday practice, the reader is referred to Levin, London, and Tarragona, 1998.

REFERENCES

Andersen, T. (1997). Research client-therapist relationships: A collaborative study for informing therapy. *Journal of Systemic Therapies*, *16(2)*,125–133.

Anderson, H. (1997). *Conversation, language and possibilities: A postmodern approach to therapy*. New York: Basic Books.

Anderson, H., and Goolishian, H. (1990). Supervision as collaborative conversation: Questions and reflections. In H. Brandau (Ed.), *Von der supervision zur systemischen vision*. Salzburg, Austria: Otto Muller Verlag.

Anderson, H., and Goolishian, H. (1992). The client is the expert: A not-knowing approach to therapy. In S. McNamee and K. J. Gergen (Eds.). *Therapy as social construction*. Newbury Park, CA: Sage Publications.

Kelly, J. G. (1990). Changing context and the field of community psychology. *American Journal of Community Psychology, 18(6)*, 769–792.

Levin, S., London, S., and Tarragona, M. (1998). Hearing more voices: Beyond traditions in writing, research, and therapy. *Journal of Systemic Therapies, 17(4)*, 1–87.

Newman, F., and Holzman, L. (1997). *The end of knowing. A new developmental way of learning*. London: Routledge.

Pakman, M. (1998). Education and therapy in cultural borderlands: A call for critical social practices in human services. *Journal of Systemic Therapies. 17(1)*, 18–30.

Schon, D. (1983). *The reflective practitioner: How professionals think in action*. New York: Basic Books.

Life

Is

Where

We

Are

Vesna Ognjenović

INTRODUCTION

I live in the Federal Republic of Yugoslavia, in Serbia, a small country
where one dogma was destroyed by another that proclaimed the eth-
nic/national interest as the prevailing human right. Enormous human
suffering has pervaded all of the former Yugoslavia, which for forty-five
years had been common space inhabited by people of different ethnic
and religious backgrounds. In March 1999 the creators of global international policy decided to change the local government in Serbia by
laser-guided bombs. This lasted seventy-eight days and nights.

Under the heading "Critique and Beyond," Morss argues: "But in
many ways critique is too good a weapon, too sharp for our wit. It is like
the laser-guided bombs of modern smart warfare and like the official
statements that go with such high-technology destruction. 'We have hit
him hard. . . .' Critique is designed to hit the enemy hard *and then move
on* to the next target."

I will articulate an alternative way related to the same topic. There are
at least two reasons why I have separated this statement from its context.
First, for we who live here, the critique by laser-guided bombs is not
metaphoric. This was and still is a matter of life and death for us. Second, the fact remains that people live all over this earth. There are parts
that are highly exposed to the laser-guided-bomb critique, and other
parts that are highly protected from it. The divisions are due to an

oppressive international power that uses killing technology for gamelike activity. There are millions of people experiencing this kind of game right now, and there are millions who are highly protected from it at the very same moment.

We are in the unprotected zone, and after the intrusion of wars, internal resources were the only ones available. When the war began in 1992, the Vygotskian cultural developmental approach was the only one that could help us create meaningful and proper activity for the sake of preserving and building aliveness. Social interaction was the powerful source of life, almost the only one left. Our main investment was in developing interactive activities involving as many participants as possible. Turning points in developing our activities emerged within the activities themselves. The participation of ordinary people of different backgrounds, especially the participation of children, was the main source of creating new guidelines and keeping the process going. "Undiscovered Treasure" and "Human Beings" are the titles given by two young refugee boys, Sasa and Dusan, to our interactive activities involving many participants of different ages and backgrounds. This was more than encouraging for what we were doing. We recognized the many meanings that could be built into the joint activity of adults and children.

HUMAN BEING AND *HOMO HUMANUM*

The first significant turning point not based on internal resources was the "Vygotsky in Practice" presentation by Lois Holzman at the Second Conference for Socio-Cultural Research held in Geneva in 1996. Among the varying theorizing and practicing of Vygotsky that were presented at the conference, I recognized the uniqueness and asymmetry in Holzman's presentation. This was the only approach that kept intrinsically alive the relationship between the work of Marx and Vygotsky. The significant experience I gained can be briefly summarized: *Homo humanum* is resistant to extermination, and a real chance for "becoming" still exists. This has a special meaning for the group of us living here because the fall of socialism brought a strong and violent wave of anticommunism and a total denial of Marxism. This is much more than a matter of personal and sentimental experience. This is a matter of deadening the substance of meaning in human life.

Undiscovered Treasure and a New Sense of Possibilities

My attendance at the conference "Unscientific Psychology: Conversations with Other Voices" in New York in 1997 was the next relevant step. I went there guided by the desire to meet psychologists joined in an endeavor to make the world a better place to live in. This is a very simple, even trivial, articulation, but one that grows out of my experience that not many psychologists are challenged by world pain. The voices in New York cared.

In this commentary, the papers of Lois Holzman and John Morss will be linked for the purpose of sharing how we are further building new activities. Being a participant in building developmental activities for years, I found this to be a good way for me to comment on this volume. My thoughts will take the form of concise statements.

Constructing Common Joint Activities

This term may sound confusing because of the use of the words "joint" and "common," which carry the same meaning. By making such a construction I wanted to integrate *inclusiveness/accessibility* of activities and their participatory nature.

1. There are no tools for results. There are tools and results.

    This is the only way to keep the totality of the life process going.

2. There are no target groups of enemies, privileged or beneficiaries.

    The common joint activities are open enough permanently to extend and involve more and more participants. There are no special exclusions or inclusions. The activities are not designed for special groups since the real life context is fully contaminated by social exclusions/inclusions. The severely traumatized—children and adults—do not exclude non-severely traumatized, and vice versa. Refugees—children, adults, the elderly—do not exclude nonrefugees, and vice versa. Talented children do not exclude non-talented, and vice versa.

3. There is no critique by hitting.

4. There is no consensus and there are no differences that are mutually exclusive.

Since consensus is replication rather than creation, it has no relevance for joint common activity. Mutually exclusive differences are fighting opposites rather than differences. The small fine differences, which are not easily heard or seen, have decisive value for building common joint activity.

5. There are no I/self and I/you dyads.

Common joint activity does not serve the growth of I/self multitude nor I/you dyads. It goes beyond the coaction of different selves or their balanced expansion. The activity of self is transformed into joint activity, creating a new social entity that is flexible and alive. At the moment it is difficult to articulate this more clearly.

6. There are no centers or margins.

Common joint activity is a collective activity of giving and getting, listening and hearing. It is flexible enough to make the center/margin positions fluid and unpredictable. This keeps the source for joint creation open. The undiscovered treasure can be reached and transformed into real social treasure.

7. There are no knowers and nonknowers.

The participatory relevance of experts and ordinary people is relative. This makes the common joint activity transformative. The knowledge and practice of experts in the different fields of art and science are demystified. The move has been made from subculture toward the culture without any propositions. This means that "live and perform/create culture" will be extensively accessible.

8. There are no limits of ages and stages.

This statement is related to two different meaning patterns. The first one is easily recognizable, and I am not going to elaborate on it. The second aspect is more challenging since it involves time/space issues in the broader sense. Through common joint activity, the past-present relation is unchained. The cultural/historical move through ages/centuries for the sake of the present is liberated. So Hamlet, Don Quixote, or Ostap Bender could be involved in the creative/performatory construction of new meanings.

Forced to live under "to be or not to be" pressure, our response is spelled out through *the discovery of the ways of how to be*. Life is not somewhere else; life is where we are. There is no end.

Index